FAST/FORWARD

FAST/FORWARD

Make Your Company Fit for the Future

Julian Birkinshaw and Jonas Ridderstråle

STANFORD BUSINESS BOOKS

An Imprint of Stanford University Press • Stanford, California

Stanford University Press
Stanford, California

Special discounts for bulk quantities of Stanford Business Books are available to corporations, professional associations, and other organizations. For details and discount information, contact the special sales department of Stanford University Press. Tel: (650) 725-0820, Fax: (650) 725-3457

Printed in the United States of America on acid-free, archival-quality paper

Library of Congress Cataloging-in-Publication Data

Names: Birkinshaw, Julian M., author. | Ridderstråle, Jonas, author.
Title: Fast/forward : make your company fit for the future / Julian Birkinshaw and Jonas Ridderstråle.
Description: Stanford, California : Stanford Business Books, an imprint of Stanford University Press, 2017. | Includes bibliographical references and index.
Identifiers: LCCN 2016039745 | ISBN 9780804799539 (cloth : alk. paper) | ISBN 9781503602311 (ebook)
Subjects: LCSH: Strategic planning. | Decision making. | Success in business.| Industrial management.
Classification: LCC HD30.28 .B575 2017 | DDC 658.4/012—dc23
LC record available at https://lccn.loc.gov/2016039745

In memory of Gunnar Hedlund

CONTENTS

PREFACE

IN TODAY'S HIGHLY COMPETITIVE business world, every company is looking for an edge, a source of differentiation over their rivals, and every leader is seeking to make his or her organization the best it can be. An industry of consultants, academics, and journalists has grown around this set of aspirations, and the diversity of insights and advice on offer is huge.

One common theme, found among the most influential books in this field, is the notion that there are enduring sources of advantage, eternal truths if you like, that the most successful companies and the best leaders have figured out. By understanding and applying these "secrets of success," the argument goes, your organization can also become excellent; it can make the transition from good to great.

In this book, we take a different view on corporate success. We argue that the formulae for success that worked in prior decades offer only very limited insights into what might work in the future. This is because the business context keeps changing: not in the banal sense that we face increasing levels of technological change and higher levels of competition, but rather in the more fundamental sense that every source of competitive advantage carries with it the seeds of its own destruction. This is a version of the famous "Icarus Paradox": the attribute or capability that makes companies successful in one era makes them susceptible to failure in the next era.

This alternative view puts a heavy burden on corporate leaders. It demands that they make sense of how the world is changing and figure out what the consequences of those changes might be in the years ahead; it then requires them to make changes in how they work that take them into unknown territory, without proven "best practice" models to follow.

The companies that succeed in doing this have the potential to gain an *evolutionary advantage.* The conservatism and inertia inside your typical large organizations means that the rate of change outside is usually much greater than the rate of change inside. Corporate generals continue to fight the last war, using structures and methods that were designed for the previous era, and endorsing plans that are linear extrapolations of what worked before.

What we need instead is for companies to figure out how to make the rate of change inside at least as rapid as the rate of change outside. This, ultimately, is what the book is about. *Fast/forward* companies have an evolutionary advantage; they are fit for the future. *Fast* needs no further explanation—it simply refers to the need for decisiveness and a strong action orientation across the organization. *Forward* has two meanings—it is about a direction of travel that looks to the future rather than the past, but it also hints at the need for leaders to make a stronger emotional connection to those around them, rather than allowing sterile, big data-driven decision making to dominate their actions, reactions, and responses. Fast/forward companies, in a nutshell, are those that exhibit decisive action coupled with emotional conviction.

Origins of the Book

We started work on this book almost three years ago, and in keeping with our notion of evolutionary advantage, it changed shape significantly over this period of time. The core themes in the pages that follow emerged from two separate strands of thinking.

The first is a deep interest in paradoxical thinking. A paradox is a seemingly contradictory statement that reveals a profound insight. Jonas had developed a fresh perspective on the way the business world is changing around the four "paradoxes of progress," featured in Chapter 2 of the book. For example, the exponential growth in knowledge at a societal level means that each of us is becoming, relatively speaking, more ignorant at an individual level. This has important consequences for how we harness knowledge; —we can no longer rely on the lone genius inventors. We need instead to become much better at knowledge pooling and collaboration. Separately, Julian had also developed a point of view on a paradox, in terms of the difficulties companies face in exploiting their existing sources of advantage while also exploring new opportunities, as we discuss in Chapter 8.

This paradoxical point of view was instrumental in sharpening our understanding of the big challenges companies face today. Much of the current discourse is about business analytics and big data, and more generally about the value of higher-quality information as a source of advantage. But it seemed clear to us, as we reflected on this debate, that the information revolution was already carrying the seeds of its own destruction, with information no longer being the scarce resource it used to be and with search costs close to zero. The more companies invest in information, we propose, the less valuable (as a source of differentiation) that information becomes, and the more other attributes, such as flexibility, decisiveness, and commitment, come to the fore.

The other strand of thinking on which we lean is one that we had first started work on in the late 1990s when we were colleagues at the Stockholm School of Economics, working under the guidance of the late Gunnar Hedlund, to whom the book is dedicated. Our research at that point in time was focused on how large multinational corporations were organized; we were fascinated by the way in which alternatives to the classic hierarchical way of working were starting to emerge. In studying myriad companies, we came to realize that their formal structure was not really their defining quality. Equally important were the systems used for creating and sharing knowledge among people, and also the informal means by which people were inspired to get things done or to take initiative. Already present in our thinking was the distinction we make in Chapter 3 between bureaucracy, meritocracy, and adhocracy as different models that capture the obvious and hidden aspects of organizational design. Understanding and deploying the full menu is a secret weapon for making progress in the face of paradoxes.

In other words, by putting these two lines of thinking together, we had a genuine "aha" moment. They are, in fact, two sides of the same coin: the challenges we face on the one hand and the big strategic tools we need to wage today's and tomorrow's corporate wars on the other.

But *Fast/Forward* does not fit neatly into the usual business categories. It is about "strategy," but also organization, management, and leadership. If you want to create a company that is fit for the future, you need to work across these levels. The lines are blurring, and we're not that interested in maintaining them for the sake of appellation. To put it slightly differently, fast/forward is a state of mind—it is a way of making sense, a lens through which to see more clearly. If you get the basic design right, we would argue, you can tap people across the firm to take responsibility for adaptability and as a collective make your company fit to face your own paradoxes. Are you ready to let go of the wheel or, rather, hold it with all of your workforce? Let's see.

ACKNOWLEDGMENTS

WE ARE INDEBTED TO a large group of people. Our old mentor, Professor Gunnar Hedlund, from the Institute of International Business at the Stockholm School of Economics, was influential in shaping our thinking and introducing many of the concepts that we elaborate on in this book. Our friend and former colleague, Kjell A. Nordström, also provided valuable feedback during the early stages of our endeavor. Stuart Crainer and Des Dearlove offered important input at several stages over the last three years.

Julian would like to thank Simon Caulkin, Nicolai Foss, Martine Haas, Gary Hamel, Sigi Lindenburg, Costas Markides, Sebastian Raisch, Don Sull, Alex Zimmerman, and many other colleagues for contributing ideas and even some paragraphs of text to the book. Julian would also like to thank the Deloitte Institute of Innovation and Entrepreneurship at London Business School, who funded some of the research projects that are referenced here.

Jonas would like to thank his agents Britt-Marie and Karoline at Speakersnet—a truly dynamic duo who always provide fast/forward services to both him and his clients around the world. He would also like to thank Professor David Hawk and Dr. Johan Stein for many interesting discussions over the last few years.

We interviewed and talked with many executives in putting this book together. Undoubtedly we will fail to remember all their names, for which we apologize, but here is a partial list of those that helped: Eric Achtmann, Ravi Arora, Anders Bouvin, Mike Bracken, Tim Brooks, Jordan Cohen, David Craig, Stuart Crainer, Des Dearlove, Lianne Eden, Jesper Ek, Vimi Grewal-Carr, Rick Goings, Thomas Kurian, Monika Lessl, Kemal Malik, Dena McCallum, Steve McGuirk, Vineet Nayar, Kal Patel, Bart Schlatmann, Jim Slater, Ross Smith, Henry Stewart, David Thorpe, Mark Wilson, Ricardo Zacconi.

A big thank you also to the fantastic team at Stanford University Press, Margo Beth Fleming and James Holt, as well as to Anita Mc-Gahan and George Day, who provided thoughtful peer reviews of the full manuscript.

We both love writing, but like all other activities it does compete for scarce resources. Therefore, we owe our final thank you to our families. From now on, you can count on us both taking decisive action, backed up with emotional conviction, to deserve you.

London and Stockholm, November 30, 2016

FAST/FORWARD

Chapter 1

STAYING AHEAD OF THE CURVE

WHAT IS THE BASIS of competitive advantage in today's business land-scape? Many observers say it is the power to harness information. Best-selling authors Erik Brynjolfsson and Andrew McAfee have ar-gued we are entering the "Second Machine Age," with information technology as the engine of human progress. The McKinsey Global Institute has called big data the "next frontier for innovation, competi-tion and productivity." Academic research points to the importance of knowledge sharing, intellectual property, and R&D as the drivers of competitiveness. Firms such as IBM, American Express, and Caesar's Entertainment have emphasized business analytics and big data as key to their success.[1]

In this book, we offer a different perspective. We believe the case for information technology, big data, and advanced analytics is over-stated. These will of course continue to be important resources for staying in the race, but as information becomes ever more ubiquitous and search costs trend to zero, their capacity to provide any modern organization with a leading edge is diminishing.

That's not the only problem. Information overload at the individ-ual level leads to distractedness, confusion, and poor decision mak-ing. At a corporate level, we end up with analysis paralysis, endless debate, and a bias toward rational, scientific evidence at the expense of intuition or gut feel. These pathologies have a deleterious effect on our companies. They lessen the quality and speed of decision making, delay action, and engender a sterile operating environment in which insightful thinking is quashed unless it is quantifiable. As a result, many companies end up standing still, even as the world around them is speeding up.

So what is the alternative to "Slow-Motion Inc."? Smart executives understand both the potential and the pitfalls of information. They recognize that the notion of competitive advantage is more fleeting than it used to be. They adopt what we call a *fast/forward* approach to business: they emphasize decisive action ahead of detailed analysis, and they are comfortable relying on emotional conviction alongside rational judgments.

Consider a few examples.

Amazon's phenomenal growth, from online bookseller to new economy powerhouse, defies all the established rules about firms focusing on their core competencies. Its success is built on deep insight into the needs of its customers, and an assumption that if you create value for customers, growth and profits will follow. Jeff Bezos, the company's cerebral founder, started his career developing mathematical models for a hedge fund and is a great believer in systematic analysis. But at the same time, he is known for his "harrowing leaps of faith." His most important decisions are not based on studies or spreadsheets, they are "nervy gambles on ideas that are just too big to try out reliably in small-scale tests."[2]

Or look at WPP, which has transformed itself over the last decade from a stable of old-school ad agencies, such as JWT and Ogilvy & Mather, to the world's biggest new media communications company, with 40 percent of its revenues coming from its digital businesses, such as Internet and mobile advertising. For an industry built on fresh thinking, creative talent, and client responsiveness, bigger is not always better. So CEO Martin Sorrell allows the operating businesses to retain autonomy and to compete head-on with one another, while also encouraging collaboration when required—what one observer has called the "kiss and punch" model.[3] Sorrell is famous for his attention to detail, his micro-managing style of leadership, yet like Jeff Bezos he is also decisive, with many of his largest acquisitions based more on gut instinct than due diligence. WPP's "weirdly effective mix of order and chaos" has enabled it to steer through the digital revolution more capably than its big rivals, and yet Sorrell feels there is more to do: "We don't believe that our existing businesses can move fast enough."

Or consider Oracle, the world's leading provider of database management software. Back in 2005, CEO Larry Ellison initiated a major project to rework the company's products as software-as-service applications. Back then, the term *cloud computing* hadn't even been invented, and there were many competing views about the future of computing. But Ellison made it a top priority, putting his very best developers onto a project with an uncertain future and a ten-year time horizon. In doing so, he enabled Oracle to develop one of the most comprehensive "cloud" offerings, spanning software, platform, and infrastructure elements. As observed by Thomas Kurian, Oracle president, "the heart of innovation is to decide early—in the middle of the period of ambiguity."[4]

You might think this is a tech-sector phenomenon, but increasingly executives in large, mature industries are also embracing the fast/forward mind-set. For example, Swiss drug giant Roche is seeking to give greater decision-making freedom to its R&D scientists. As CEO Severin Schwan says, "We need a culture where people take risks because if you don't take risks, you won't have breakthrough innovation."[5] Air Liquide, the Paris-based world leader in industrial gases, has undertaken a major shift in strategy toward innovation and retention, driven by what CEO Benoit Potier calls the "expertise, audacity and intuition" of its sixty-eight thousand employees.[6] Air Liquide, like Roche, is achieving impressive levels of growth in an otherwise stagnant industry.

Or look at Lloyds Banking Group in the United Kingdom. It has put digital working at the heart of its new strategy, following its post-financial-crisis turnaround. In the words of CEO António Horta-Osório, the intention is to "get closer to customers and make the decision cycle happen more quickly." A thousand-person digital team now reports in directly at board level, with a mandate to make the whole bank more agile. "This is a strategy adapting to the new world," says Horta-Osório, "We want to create a high-performing organization . . . to be quicker than others to have a competitive advantage."[7]

These brief company examples illustrate some important themes. Success in a fast-changing business world is a subtle blend of art and science. Rather than getting bogged down in analysis and introspection, fast/forward companies are open-minded, and they have operating cultures that promote action and experimentation. Their leaders know when to listen to the data and when to be decisive. As Jeff Bezos says, "There are decisions that can be made by analysis. . . . These are the best kinds of decisions! They're fact-based decisions. Unfortunately, there's this whole other set of decisions that you can't ultimately boil down to a math problem,"[8] namely the big bets on new businesses like the Kindle or Amazon Web Services.

Riding the Waves of Change

Arguably, decisive action and emotional conviction have always been important traits, but there are trends under way in today's business world making them more important than ever. To appreciate that, let's take a historical perspective.

Most casual observers would readily agree that we live in the information age, the period in human history characterized by the shift from traditional industry to an economy based on information computerization. It started with the roll-out of computer technology, and then evolved with subsequent waves of innovation in Internet connectivity and mobile communication.

At an individual level, we know exactly what living in the information age means, from the new ways in which we communicate with others to the transformation of our shopping and entertainment experiences. For better or worse, our teenage children have never bought a newspaper or a CD. Many young people have never visited a library, and really young kids can mistake a magazine for a broken iPad, as they swipe their finger across the cover page to no avail. There is even evidence that the Internet is literally rewiring our brains—increasing our capacity for "visual-spatial" intelligence and for multitasking, while decreasing our skills in concentration and contemplation.[9]

But what does operating in the information age mean for *firms*? Or more precisely, what are the characteristics of information-age firms that make them different from industrial-age firms?

First and foremost are the changes in the underlying source of profitability—the business model. In the industrial age, firms typically made money through economies of scale and scope. General Motors, Standard Oil, and Imperial Chemicals Industries got ahead by producing standardized products more efficiently than anyone else. In the information age, firms succeed because they create a constant flow of new products and services that their customers are prepared to pay a premium for. Such offerings typically stem from the smart use of information—economies of skill, rather than scale or scope. From Apple to Novo Nordisk and SAP to Nintendo, the leading firms of the last thirty years have achieved their success by harnessing information, creating knowledge, and attracting talent.

Second is the new internal way of working—the management model. The classical way of operating that took shape during the industrial age was the bureaucracy. This was a model built on standardized rules and procedures and hierarchical oversight—complicated structures inhabited by simple people. By structuring themselves in this way, firms such as General Motors were able to retain control over a complex set of operations and close to three hundred and fifty thousand employees. As the information age took hold through the 1970s and 1980s, tight control over employees became less feasible (as they had direct access to information) and less necessary (as they had the skills to make their own judgments). Gradually, an alternative management model—the meritocracy—emerged. This one was built on personal accountability and mutual adjustment—a simpler structure for more complicated people. Science-based firms, such as Merck and Intel, and professional services firms, such as McKinsey and Goldman Sachs, exemplify this approach.

Management thinking has also reflected this broad transition from the industrial to the information age. The 1920s saw the invention of scientific management, capital budgeting, and the multidivisional structure. In the postwar years we witnessed the rise of operations research, yield management, management by objectives, and matrix organizations. These managerial innovations were basically methodologies for enhancing efficiency and control. Move forward to the 1980s and beyond, and most of the new ideas were about harnessing information more effectively—intellectual capital, knowledge management, open innovation, design thinking, intellectual property rights, empowerment, and corporate venturing.[10]

The transition from the industrial age to the information age sets up an interesting question: What comes next? If the information age is just another period in human history, then we should not simply assume it lasts forever. The legendary Austrian economist Josef Schumpeter formulated one of the most pervasive principles of economic progress. He called it the cycle of creative destruction—there is always something new coming along that will succeed at the expense of the old. And this logic applies to historical eras as much as to industries or technologies. In fact, it applies to anything from high jumping to coffee bars. So how will historians in a hundred years interpret the period we are living through right now? Are we in the early stages of the information age, or in its twilight years? And what would a potential *next* age look like?

One influential view says, in essence, that we ain't seen nothing yet. The changes brought about by the information revolution are still in their infancy. They will continue for many years, and indeed they will accelerate. Ray Kurzweil, the renowned futurist, inventor, and part-time director of engineering at Google, is the high priest of this movement. Born in 1948, Kurzweil has been a leading figure in artificial intelligence for forty-plus years. In his book *The Age of Spiritual Machines* he put forward the law of accelerating returns—the notion that technological changes are compounding over time, so that computer intelligence will actually overtake human intelligence within our lifetimes. A subsequent book, *The Singularity Is Near*, took this argument further and provided a specific date, 2045, for the singularity—the point at which progress is so rapid it outstrips humans' ability to comprehend it. Several recent best-selling books, including Brynjolfsson and McAfee's *Second Machine Age* and Martin Ford's *Rise of Robots*, have expanded on this argument with bold predictions about how the world of business is being transformed.

For technophiles like Kurzweil, the basis of firm-level competitive advantage for the years ahead is simple: more data, more information, more knowledge. In other words, the competitive edge will come from finding new and better ways of harnessing information. And there are plenty of real cases illustrating this. For example, IBM has pledged its future on a "smarter planet" theme, and on investing hundreds of millions of dollars in its artificial intelligence division, Watson. Indeed, many of the corporate growth stories of the last decade involve companies (Google, Amazon, Facebook) that have been built on superior analytical techniques—figuring out the best algorithm for searching the Web, clever ways of predicting purchasing behavior, and so on.

But where these folks see a world of accelerating change, we see the seed of creative destruction taking hold. To be clear, technological innovation is a big part of our future, and harnessing information will continue to be an important part of every firm's strategy. But we believe the costs and side effects of the information revolution have not been sufficiently understood. Following are a few quick observations:

- *Information is ubiquitous.* We can access an obscure piece of information in a matter of seconds while sitting on a train to Paddington station or a beach in Thailand, or during a walking holiday in the Alps.

- *Search costs have plummeted.* A day's worth of research in the library or microfiche department in the 1980s might take half an hour today. It takes us longer to find an academic paper in our filing cabinet than to retrieve it online.

- *Nothing is secret anymore.* Even copyright-protected documents are often freely available. Open-access journals are on the rise. Even state secrets find their way into the public domain, thanks to the likes of whistleblowers such as Edward Snowden and Julian Assange.

- *The veracity of online information is increasingly uncertain.* For example, one study estimated that only 44 percent of website recommendations relating to infant sleeping were consistent with official guidelines.[11] The old saying "Don't believe everything you read" has taken on a new meaning in the era of information overload. In fact, there are many cases in which even the experts don't agree on the implications of the facts. Just consider the dispute over global warming or which diet to follow.

Put these points together, and it is clear that information is no longer a "scarce resource" in any sense of the term. Nowadays, information technology is electronic plumbing—available to everyone. Of course, it is still possible for firms to create proprietary insights out of public information, but also this is becoming harder and harder. The idea that firms might generate sustainable competitive advantages through their privileged access to information is surely obsolete. Today, no one has a monopoly on information access—no country, no parent, no business, no teacher, no guru.

Attention!

So then what *is* the scarce resource in this world? What is the difficult thing to access and control that firms will base their future competitive advantage on? Actually, the answer to this question isn't that tricky to find. In fact, Nobel Laureate Herbert Simon wrote about it forty years ago: it is our *attention*, our capacity to focus on and respond in an effective way to the stimuli we receive, that we need to worry about:

> [I]n an information-rich world, the wealth of information means a dearth of something else: a scarcity of whatever it is that information consumes. What information consumes is rather obvious: it consumes the attention of its recipients. Hence a wealth of information creates a poverty of attention.[12]

This insight is even more relevant today than it was back in 1971. The more we obsess over the power of information, the more we believe that the answer is in the data, the more blinkered we become. We lose the capacity to move fast, or the capacity to bring an intuitive point of view forward. We become victims of paralysis by analysis.

The negative consequences of having too much information—and too much faith in information—can be exemplified in a single number: 42. If you remember Douglas Adams's *Hitchhiker's Guide to the Galaxy*, this was the answer to the great question of life, the universe, and everything. Unfortunately, this answer had a few weaknesses: it took seven-and-a-half million years to compute (a severe case of analysis paralysis); it was expressed in a sterile, quantitative way with absolutely no context to help the user make sense of it; and as Douglas Adams himself pointed out, the question to which 42 was the answer wasn't even clear. To figure that out, the computer concluded, they needed to build a bigger computer.

The problem of too much information is played out at multiple levels.

Individuals. We often claim we don't have enough time in the workday. Actually, our biggest problem is a lack of focus and attention. We can't make more time, but we can use the time we have in a more structured and productive way. Many people have their e-mail, their Facebook account, or their Twitter feed open all the time, resulting in an intermittent stream of distractions over the course of a working day. Studies have shown that if you are focusing on a difficult task— writing a report or thinking through a complex issue—a single distraction such as an e-mail takes up to twenty minutes to recover from.[13]

Easy access to information also creates an opposite problem, in that some people lose themselves in the data-collection process. As academics, we live in a "publish or perish" world—we become successful by making sense of what others have done and then building on that by creating our own unique contributions to a field of study. Over the years we have had several colleagues who never figured out when to stop reading and start writing. They became extremely knowledgeable, but they perished because they didn't put their ideas down on paper. The same thing happens in a corporate context and with similar personal ramifications in a business world inhabited by "the quick and the dead."

Teams. Have you ever experienced a meeting in which the absence of agreement on a tricky issue was resolved with a decision to collect more information? The answer is obvious—we all have. And did these additional data-gathering efforts resolve things? Again, the reply is self-evident. Difficult decisions by their nature require us to go beyond the data—to make a judgment call on fundamentally uncertain issues—to rely on intuition and gut. These are the kind of situations in which you are choosing between two bad alternatives or two good ones. Managers who crave the security of hard data just end up slowing everything down. You could probably not fit all the studies of decision making that have been done over the years into the Chrysler Building, but they all point us in the same direction. It is clear that lack of information is rarely the problem—when mistakes are made, it is much more likely to be a function of blinkered thinking, lack of character, or poor internal team dynamics, not an absence of data.

Firms. Most companies have a *stage/gate* process for bringing new products to market, and as time goes by such processes typically become lengthier and more sophisticated. To avoid making costly mistakes, the people running these processes ask for more and more information, and they insist on careful market testing. The result is typically an over-engineered, slow-to-market product. Examples include *Lego Universe*, an online game that lost out to *Minecraft*; IBM's wasted investment in the OS/2 operating system in the 1990s; and the Volkswagen *Phaeton*, a masterpiece of engineering that never took off. Many big firms have fallen into the same trap over the years, putting their money into the products that "survived" the stage/gate process, only to find themselves beaten to market by nimbler or more market-savvy competitors.

Industries. Every now and then, entire industries are led astray by a fixation on the power of information. Look at the pharmaceutical industry. During the 1990s, the techniques of combinatorial chemistry and high-throughput screening were set to revolutionize the drug discovery process. They allowed researchers to create and test thousands of new organic compounds every year. It was a brute-force approach. The new way of doing things encouraged scientists to try all the possible compounds that might address a disease target. But the results were underwhelming. Big pharma R&D productivity declined through the 2000s. Increasingly, it was the biotech companies, working with "large molecule" biologic drugs rather than "small molecule" compounds, that were bringing the exciting new drugs to market.

Over the last decade, the pendulum has swung back toward a more traditional, hypothesis-driven approach to drug discovery. Under the rubric "rational drug discovery," this approach seeks to get the best of both worlds. It does so by combining modern analytical techniques with creativity and insight, and it is facilitating some important medical breakthroughs. The lesson is clear—too much faith in the power of computer-based analysis is dangerous.

There are many such instances of firms and industries getting wrapped up in the value of information as an end in itself, rather than as a means to achieving their real objective.

There are other manifestations of this syndrome as well. Consider the old saying "A little learning is a dangerous thing." As individuals, we are quick to access information that helps us. But we often lack the ability to make sense of it, or to use it appropriately. One of us has a brother who is a medical doctor. He encounters this problem on a daily basis (and we might add, he is not too happy about it). Patients show up with (often incorrect) self-diagnoses derived from spending a couple of hours on the Internet. It is the same in business: senior executives second-guess their subordinates because their corporate IT system gives them line-of-sight down to detailed plant-level data. At a societal level, people believe they have the right to information that is in the public interest (think Wikileaks), but they are rarely capable of interpreting and using it in a sensible way.

We can also think about the consequences of ubiquitous information for customers. Most of us now use sites such as booking.com or expedia.com to book flights and hotels on line, and we are keen to utilize comparison sites like pricerunner.com before making major purchases. Search costs have dropped precipitously. Switching costs are not far behind. In many industries, from air travel and holidays to banking and insurance, customer ignorance and loyalty-by-tradition were the biggest sources of profitability, but this is no longer the case. The transparency created by the Internet has empowered and educated us.

In sum, our argument is straightforward: information is no longer a scarce resource so it cannot be considered a source of competitive advantage for firms.

This is not an argument everyone wants to hear, as it goes against the prevailing wisdom of the last couple of decades. So when confronted with it, many observers say, "Yes, fair enough, information is a commodity. But our goal is to create firm-specific *knowledge*. This is distinctive and proprietary. Therefore, it serves as the basis of our competitive advantage." Again, there is some truth to this argument. Think about a patent. It is a piece of codified intellectual property. Many firms also have genuinely distinctive "best practices" that others struggle to replicate. But even here, the story isn't so simple.

First, knowledge is increasingly shared. Scientific knowledge is created more and more in research teams rather than by lone geniuses. Analysis of academic papers shows the average number of authors rising from 2.5 in 1981 to 5.1 in 2012.[14] In physics, the discovery of the so-called Higgs-Boson particle was described in a 2015 paper with 5,154 authors.[15] And the more knowledge is shared in the creation process, the harder it is for any one firm to gain proprietary advantage over it.

Second, the generation of new knowledge can end up being an end in itself. Truth be told, at most universities, creating knowledge for its own sake is the norm. Being called the smartest person in the room is a compliment. And that seems fair enough—it is in fact why universities were created in the first place.

But there are plenty of scientists and professionals working in firms today with a similar worldview. There is even a body of management thinking, the "resource-based view of the firm," that encourages executives to look inside at their own distinctive resources and attributes as a way of justifying their existence.[16] Needless to say, this is a dangerous habit to get into—we can all identify things that make us special; the much more important question is whether customers value those things enough to knock on our doors.

Third, knowledge is often defined too narrowly in business circles. The world-famous psychologist Howard Gardner has argued that there are nine types of human intelligence.[17] Each one of these therefore has its own associated body of knowledge. But, as you may know, when it comes time to make tricky business decisions, only one of these really counts—the so-called "logical-mathematical" intelligence. This is the one we typically associate with engineers or accountants. It comes in the form of a well-structured business case, with lengthy spreadsheets, sensitivity analyses, and a Net Present Value calculation at the end—the stuff that you typically learn at a business school. A second type, "linguistic intelligence," is also useful, as it helps us to convey our logical-mathematical evidence in a compelling way.

But what about emotional intelligence? And how do creativity, intuition, and personal feelings find their way into the discussion? Many famous leaders, including GEs Jack Welch, ABB's Percy Barnevik, and Apple's Steve Jobs, prided themselves on following their gut instinct, but this is not the norm. Instead, many firms do their best to squeeze out any sort of contribution that cannot be rationalized or quantified. Our view is that this approach is all very well, but it leads to sterile decision making—devoid of any sort of emotional resonance, either with the employees who have to implement it or the customers who have to live with it. And then there is of course the question of how an emotionally impotent leader can engage others—talent, customers, or other stakeholders.

So once again, the secret of corporate success is often the seed of its own downfall. All paradigms come with a best-before date. A single-minded emphasis on logical-mathematical-type knowledge helps firms to create clever and unique offerings, but with a risk that beauty, joy, surprise, spontaneity, and individuality are driven out. In every industry, there is a battle between the more "technical" brands (think Samsung or Toyota) and the "emotional" brands (think Apple or BMW), and while both can be successful, it is the latter group that captures the imagination and typically gets the higher margins as well. In fact, Kevin Roberts, former CEO of Saatchi & Saatchi, calls these *lovemarks*, rather than brands, because of the emotional resonance they create with their customers and employees.[18]

The Core Argument

In this book, we are proposing a new way of looking at the drivers of firm success in the information age. In many established firms, there is such an emphasis on information and knowledge for their own sake that people get distracted. Decisions are delayed, and attention becomes fragmented. But there are also some firms in which executives understand both the power and the limits of information. The leaders of these organizations know there are times when getting the "right answer" is imperative. But there are other times when being decisive and intuitive, acting swiftly and experimenting, works better.

Recall our examples of Amazon, WPP, and Oracle at the beginning of this chapter, companies whose leaders have shown how to blend rational and intuitive decision making. Facebook is another example—it's a company famous for its clever analytical tools for monitoring and influencing our social networking behavior, yet it was still able to acquire WhatsApp in 2014 for $19 billion in record time, and largely on the basis of gut reasoning.

The pharmaceutical industry also exemplifies this point—the traditional big pharma players such as Merck, GSK, and Pfizer have the deep expertise and cutting-edge scientists, but they are losing out to nimbler biotechs such as Gilead and Amgen, and private-equity-style outfits such as Actavis Allergan, who understand that high science and commercial acumen can be successfully combined.

So here is the argument in a nutshell.

In today's rapidly changing world, it is rarely the firms with the greatest processing power, the smartest data scientists, or the fastest connectivity that come out ahead. Instead, it is the ones that move forward faster than the others by developing the capacity for *decisive action*—the ability to address opportunities as they emerge, to experiment with new offerings, and to make big bets when called for. But action without direction is a dangerous commodity. To channel it in an effective way, firms also need to develop *emotional conviction*—to listen to their own intuitive reasoning, and to create meaning for their employees and their customers. To be effective, action needs adrenaline—in sports, in ballet, and in business.

The firms that succeed in this evolving information age will be characterized by decisive action allied to emotional conviction. This success formula can be summarized as fast/forward:

- *Fast* means alert, agile, experimental, capable of decisive action.

- *Forward* means proactive and searching, and it also means seeking to create an emotional connection with others.

These twin themes represent the core message in the book, and we will return to them throughout.

However, this is ultimately only one half of the story. It is easy to talk about decisive action and emotional conviction, but it is extremely difficult to enact them in a large, established firm. Traditional ways of working, as noted earlier, guide firms toward reflection and risk-aversion, and people need a very clear alternative model to move away from such habits and norms.

So the other half of our contribution in this book is to outline a new way of working, a new management model, for delivering on this fast/forward imperative.

Consider ING, the Amsterdam-based banking giant with fifty-two thousand employees around the world. ING went through a painful restructuring after the 2008 financial crisis, selling off product lines and rethinking its business model in the face of increasing levels of regulation. But rather than retreat into defensive mode, its executives embarked on an ambitious transformation program—a cleaning up and simplification of its internal processes, and then a strategic push into digital banking using organizing principles more commonly seen in Silicon Valley start-ups than staid European banks.

For the thirty-five hundred HQ employees, the old hierarchical structure was thrown out. In its place, starting in June 2015, people were assigned to autonomous nine-person "squads." Each squad focused on servicing specific user needs (some internal, some external), with freedom to shape their own work-flow and physical space. The squads were then clustered into "tribes" of linked activities and supported by "agile coaches."

We describe ING's story in more detail later in the book. For the moment, the key point is that its new management model, inspired by fast-growing tech companies such as Spotify and Google, is built around addressing customer needs as efficiently as possible: squads are small, their responsibilities are forever changing, team members are empowered, and formal processes are used only when required by law.

This agile way of working requires a very different mind-set—executives have to be prepared to give up their traditional sources of power, and new skills have to be developed throughout the organization. But the benefits in terms of lower costs and higher levels of employee engagement are enormous, as ING has discovered.

The term we use to describe ING's new management model is *adhocracy*. While this word has been around for years, it has typically been used in an informal way to describe the opposite of a bureaucracy. We are using a much more precise definition, one that links directly to the preceding arguments. To be specific,

- The default management model of the industrial age was the *bureaucracy*—in which coordination of activities occurs through standardized rules and procedures, and an individual's formal hierarchical *position* is what matters.

- The now-standard management model of the information age is the *meritocracy*—in which coordination of activities occurs through the mutual adjustment of self-interested parties, and an individual's *knowledge* and expertise is what matters.

- The newly emerging model that we believe is now required is the *adhocracy*—in which coordination of activities occurs around external opportunities, and an individual's *action* is what matters, particularly when this is backed by emotional conviction.

We will have much more to say about these three models, but for now it is important to emphasize two points. First, these three models are about relative emphasis. In any organizational setting, formal position, knowledge, and action all matter, but typically one is privileged over the other two. In a traditional bureaucracy, the senior executive calls the shots because of her formal status (literally, the word *hierarchy* refers to one individual's legitimate authority over another). In a meritocracy, such as a professional partnership, the person with the best argument holds sway over his fellow partners. And in an adhocracy—picture for example a hospital emergency room or a skunk-works project team—taking action is often more important than discussing or defaulting to the boss.

Second, these three models are "pure types," meaning that they are easier to identify in theory than in reality. In real firms, you often see a mix of types. For example, an investment bank might have an analyst team that operates as a meritocracy, a trading floor that operates as an adhocracy, and a risk and compliance team that functions as a bureaucracy.

Given these two points, some people say to us, well surely we can be all three at the same time? Why do we have to choose? Our answer is that each model represents a *default* mode of operating, and for most people the default continues to be the bureaucracy or the meritocracy. When faced with an ambiguous situation, or a crisis, people revert to type, and the old established ways of working take over. So, given everything we have said so far, the challenge firms face today is to figure out—in broad terms—when they need to increase their emphasis on decisive action and emotional conviction, and to explicitly create an adhocracy to support this agenda.

The Fast/Forward Playbook

This book provides you with a blueprint for how to compete in today's fast-changing business environment. We offer some important theoretical ideas, detailed case-study examples, and also some practical guidance to help you implement the ideas in your own firm. Figure 1.1 summarizes the overall structure of the book.

First we make the case that the world is changing in some surprising ways (Chapter 2). It is customary to point to the increasing levels of knowledge in society and the greater connectivity between individuals and firms. We acknowledge these points, but we also identify some second-order effects that are often ignored and indeed throw up

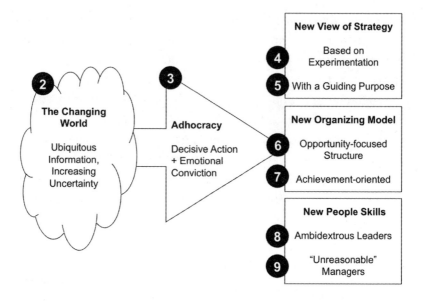

FIGURE 1.1 The Structure of the Book

some interesting paradoxes. For example, while each of us individually knows more every year, the rate of growth of knowledge in society is so much greater that actually we are becoming more ignorant, on a relative basis, over time. Similarly, the increasing level of connectivity between individuals, organizations, and economies results in a complex system with nonlinear features, which actually makes the future *less* predictable. We also do a deep dive into the surprising role of emotional belief in shaping behavior. One might expect advances in science to reduce our attachment to nonrational beliefs, but in fact the opposite seems to be true.

How do these trends affect the business world? We go back to first principles, to the basic *raison d'etre* of the business firm, in order to explain how and why they work (Chapter 3). By revisiting these fundamental concepts, we identify three idealized management models, bureaucracy, meritocracy, and adhocracy. As briefly noted earlier, each of these models has a different emphasis, and each works better under certain conditions. And each one brings a different set of choices in terms of how decisions are made, how work gets coordination, how people are motivated, and how leaders do their work.

The second part of the book looks at each of these elements in turn.

A distinctive approach to strategy (Chapters 4 and 5). The classic approach to strategy was to think of a cascade of decisions: What do we want to achieve, Where will we play, How will we win? This logic was reasonably effective in a stable environment, but in a complex, fast-changing world it is too slow and too formulaic. So we need to turn this approach on its head. We develop a reverse-cascade model, in which insights based on interactions with customers drive the reflection-and-sense-making process, which ultimately informs the big-picture strategy. Chapter 4 describes this model in detail, and in particular the iterative nature of the strategy-making process between front-line employees and senior managers. Chapter 5 connects the day-to-day action in the firm with the overall sense of purpose that the firm has vis-à-vis its broader set of stakeholders.

A distinctive approach to organizing (Chapters 6 and 7). We home in on the adhocracy as the structure that enables decisive action and emotional conviction. In the adhocracy, action is privileged over formal position and individual knowledge. To operationalize this approach, firms need to build the appropriate set of structures, processes, and incentive systems. Using a whole range of contemporary examples, we show how this can be done. Chapter 6 focuses mostly on coordination issues, and how it is possible to organize the firm around its opportunities rather than its internal processes. In Chapter 7 we emphasize issues of individual motivation and engagement, and look more closely at the thorny challenge of encouraging well-intentioned failure.

A distinctive approach to leading (Chapters 8 and 9). Leaders who generate strong emotional conviction with their employees and customers are rare, perhaps not surprisingly when most of them are MBAs or engineers. But there are some exceptions to this rule, and in this chapter we describe their guiding principles, in particular the notion of ambidexterity, being able to do two very different things equally well. We also play up the aspects of leaders that are specific to the adhocracy: for example, they have a much greater emphasis on getting things done, learning from trial-and-error, and making a connection with customers than the type of leader who works best in a bureaucracy or meritocracy.

Finally, in Chapter 9, we discuss what fast/forward means for the individual employee working in the middle of a large organization. If you are such an individual, you have an unprecedented opportunity, in today's business world, to take initiative and to make a difference. We invite you to become a bit more "unreasonable" in how you address and respond to opportunities on a day-to-day basis. Such an approach brings challenges, of course, but it beats taking a passive, fatalistic approach to your career and your working life.

Many of the concepts we are proposing will be familiar to you, but don't be fooled into thinking they are easy to implement. Our hope is that by pulling these strands of thinking together—across the worlds of strategy, organization, and leadership—it will become easier for you to develop the language and methodologies of a fast/forward approach to business.

Chapter 2

THE PARADOXES OF PROGRESS

MANSA MUSA, OF WHOM you have likely never heard, is the richest person to have ever walked the face of our planet. It is estimated that his assets were worth about $400 billion, far surpassing the $80 or so billion that is the net worth of Bill Gates today.

From 1312 to 1337, Mansa Musa, aka the Emir of Melle and the Lord of the Mines of Wangara, ruled the Malian Empire—stretching from present day Mali to the African west coast. He controlled important trade routes and was the purveyor of commodities such as salt and gold.[1] Toward the end of his life, Mansa Musa embarked on a final series of major building projects, raising the mosques in Timbuktu and Gao. He sponsored advanced research in fields such as mathematics, astronomy, literature, and arts. This initiated an economic and intellectual expansion that continued into the later Middle Ages. In the process, Mansa Musa managed to establish Mali as an economic superpower and one of the intellectual capitals of the world. He was a game changer. Then, the game changed.

Fast forward to today and you will find that the Republic of Mali, one of the twenty poorest countries in the world, is plagued by civil war. In the United Nations Development Programme human development index, it ranks as number six—from the bottom.

The narrative of economic history is packed with stories of waxing and waning influence. Mali was one of the wealthiest countries in the world, and today it's one of the poorest. Look at a list of the biggest and most influential cities in the world in the year 1000; it included Cordoba, Kaifeng, and Baghdad. These are not exactly the kind of places that today's power brokers and billionaires choose to make their homes.

Mali, like Rome and ancient Greece, became a victim of one of the paradoxes of progress—the one that implies that when you are number one you look forward to change as much as a turkey to Thanksgiving. In this chapter we will take an in-depth look at four paradoxes that shape the modern business landscape so that you and your company can avoid becoming the next casualty of progress.

The First Paradox of Progress: Creative Destruction

The same phenomenon that we see in our history books gets played out in the corporate world, but on a much shorter cycle. Of the companies that made up the original Dow Jones industrial average a century ago, only one (GE) is still on the list.[2] Glimpse the top thirty firms in the United Kingdom in 1935; only five still exist as independent firms today.[3] The average life span of a listed corporation is now about forty years. It used to be that organizations outlived the people working for them. Today, the opposite seems to be true. While we live longer and more prosperous lives, most corporations pass away before ever reaching their mid-life crisis.

We see the same thing in the music industry. Look at the Billboard 200, the weekly ranking of the two hundred best-selling albums in the United States. The list of artists with the most top-ten albums is topped by acts such as The Rolling Stones, Frank Sinatra, Barbra Streisand, The Beatles, and Elvis. These are artists that all peaked in the 1960s and 1970s. In fact, the list of most weeks as number one features only two albums from the 1990s or later—*The Bodyguard Soundtrack* with Whitney Houston, and the absolutely unforgettable *Please Hammer, Don't Hurt 'Em* by MC Hammer from 1990.

Now, think about Kodak. The company was founded in 1888. It was the Google of its day—a cool, innovative company that completely dominated the early days of photography. No one had brighter minds, better research facilities, higher salaries, or better access to advanced technologies. Yet Kodak was unable to respond to the digital revolution, and it declared bankruptcy in 2012. A cruel irony, when you consider that we live in an era when more people than ever, using more gadgets than ever, take more pictures than ever. How many selfies did you or your kids take last week?

Kodak placed its bets on a strategy focused on individual printing rather than virtual sharing. The guys running the company weren't stupid. They could see that digitization was on its way. Indeed, Kodak invested more money in digital imaging technology through the 1980s and 1990s than any other company. But they weren't able to convert that investment into products, services, and experiences for which people were willing to pay a premium, or buy at all. They simply couldn't get their heads around the fact that they needed to cannibalize their cash cow (film and processing) with unproven new technologies in order to cheat death. A few months after Kodak's bankruptcy, Facebook acquired Instagram, the popular photo-sharing app launched in 2010, for a billion dollars. At the time of the purchase, Instagram had a mere thirteen employees.

These examples are important reminders that economic development does not happen in a straight line. Obliteration begets innovation, and innovation begets obliteration. It's yin and yang. By definition, every act of creation is also one of destruction. It is no coincidence, we think, that the Hindu god Shiva is both creator and destroyer. As noted in the opening chapter, progress occurs through a cyclical process called *creative destruction*. In a well-functioning market economy, we find entrepreneurship, change, and turmoil; we see winners and losers. Examples of creative destruction can be observed in all walks of life, and at many different levels of analysis.

When Albert Einstein published his theory of relativity, he shattered hundreds of years of research in the field of physics. All the other professors' books and lecture notes were relegated to historical archives thanks to one idea. The rise of creative cities like London, Geneva, and Boston spurred the decline of industrial giants like Manchester, Marseilles, and Detroit. American high jumper Dick Fosbury tried leaping over the bar backward, and while his new jumping style was ridiculed and called a "flop" at first, he eventually prevailed by introducing a new technique that would later put straddle jumpers out of business.

The process of creative destruction is occurring right before our eyes. Netflix and Amazon are changing the way we consume video content; Spotify is transforming how we access and enjoy music; Tesla is challenging the hundred-year dominance of the internal combustion engine; and the Khan Academy and Udacity are promising to revolutionize education. These are, indeed, disruptive days.

Three Steps to Creative Destruction

Creative destruction is a paradox: *the more we create, the more we destroy.* Behind this simple maxim lie three essential steps:

An innovator launches a heretical idea. Those who disrupt make their mark by deliberately pushing against the conventional wisdom of the time. In business, think of the likes of Apple, Southwest Airlines, FedEx, or IKEA; consider Newton, Darwin, or Curie in science; Picasso or Mozart in art; Lady Gaga or Eminem in contemporary music.

Of course, these are the success stories, and for every heretical idea that works out, there are many that did not. But that is the beauty of a market-based system; it encourages people to try. Failure doesn't reap rewards, but it isn't penalized either.

The established order is slow to respond. When the iPhone was launched on June 29, 2007, the reaction was dismissive. Microsoft CEO Steve Ballmer said, "There's no chance that the iPhone is going to get any significant market share, no chance."[4] Anssi Vanjoki, Nokia's chief strategist, said Apple "[has] remained a niche manufacturer. That will be in mobile phones as well."[5] This story played out in a highly predictable way, with denial and disbelief leading to anger and negotiation, and finally acceptance.

In a completely different arena and a completely different era, you can observe the same phenomenon. Consider the exhibition held at 35 Boulevard de Capucines, Paris, from April 15 to May 15, 1874. It was the first showing of impressionist paintings, featuring 165 works by artists such as Degas, Renoir, Monet, and Cézanne. The press slaughtered them. Inspired by Monet's painting *Impression: Sunrise*, the renowned critic Louis Leroy called his satirical review "The Exhibition of Impressionists." In his attempt to discredit their work, however, he also gave a radical movement its name. And, gradually, these artists came to be accepted by the establishment. On April 10, 2011, the Royal Family of Qatar bought *The Card Players* by Paul Cézanne for approximately $260 million, then making it the most expensive painting ever.

The innovator becomes part of the establishment. By the end of George Orwell's *Animal Farm*, the victorious pigs were almost indistinguishable from the humans they had sought to overthrow. And so it goes in real life—Live Aid's Bob Geldof, Paul Weller of the Jam, Bruce Springsteen, and Madonna were all game-changers in their time; now they are music business royalty. Microsoft was the revolutionary in the 1980s, and now it is the big beast, doing everything it can to protect its turf in the world of computing.

Despite this predictable sequence of steps, it is remarkable that creative destruction continues to catch established players off guard. Perhaps this is because the waves of creative destruction are hitting the shore more frequently than ever before. (Remember what we said about the life span of a business). Or perhaps we are still stuck in an old way of thinking about competitive advantage. Today, any advantage a firm has over its competitors comes with an extremely limited shelf life, one that has a lot more in common with ice cubes than diamonds. Diamonds are the hardest naturally occurring material; ice cubes are unstable and prone to melt away. Firms that seek to protect their advantage in today's competitive world are metaphorically trying to stop their ice cubes from melting in the desert—a fruitless task that will ultimately leave them with nothing but wet sand.

In a world in which creative destruction happens more frequently, there is an important shift that we need to make in our mind-sets. Competitiveness is no longer a question of defending our current assets or market position. It is about agility, the capacity to stay abreast of the changes in the environment around us. Winning boils down to moving forward faster and in a different direction than the others. The message is clear: evolve or dissolve.

The Industrial Age, the Information Age, and What Lies Beyond

Let us now apply this way of thinking to the big transition introduced in Chapter 1, namely the emergence of the information age and the decline of the industrial age. As we'll see, the changing sources of competitive advantage, brought about by the information revolution, allowed new firms to succeed at the expense of old, established players. It spurred on creative destruction.

The automotive industry provides the clearest evidence of this transition. In the postwar years, it was the most important industry in the world. It once accounted for as many as one in six private-sector jobs. General Motors was the undisputed leader. Ford was number two. Their success was built on unbeatable economies of scale and scope, and on a management model that sought a return on the scarce resources of the age—capital and labor.

But the onset of the information age created an opening for a new approach to automobile production. This new approach, pioneered by Toyota and subsequently adopted by Honda, Hyundai, and others, turned the traditional orthodoxy of squeezing capital and labor upside down. Toyota developed new methods for analyzing and minimizing defects. It took a longer-term perspective on market needs, and the company invested in the problem-solving skills of its front-line workers. In short, it sought to capitalize on the availability of better information and on the human capital—the brainpower—of its employees.

GM and Ford were slow to respond. For many years they simply didn't believe the productivity and quality numbers claimed by Toyota. It was only when Toyota started manufacturing at the same levels in their U.S. factories, using U.S. workers, that once-leading firms recognized the truth: they were competing on industrial-age principles with competitors who had moved into the information age.

A similar story could be told in many other industries, from steel to consumer electronics to telecommunications. While the specifics in each case are different, the underlying argument is consistent. Success in the industrial age was about making efficient use of capital and labor. But by focusing on narrow metrics (return on capital or labor productivity), many firms became blinkered. In a famous 1980 article, "Managing Our Way to Economic Decline," Harvard professors Robert Hayes and William Abernathy wrote, "By their preference for servicing existing markets rather than creating new ones and by their devotion to short-term returns and 'management by the numbers,' many of them [American executives] have effectively forsworn long-term technological superiority as a competitive weapon."[6]

Of course, this was a simplistic and hyperbolic argument, but it caught the mood of the time. In retrospect it was emblematic of the transition from the industrial age to the information age under way, which Figure 2.1 illustrates.

Let us now turn the spotlight on the information age. Seeing that creative destruction is a cycle, we'd be foolish to rest on our laurels and assume that the current model will be with us forever. What does the future hold? And how can the logic of creative destruction help us make sense of it? It would be easy enough to surmise that the information age is on the decline, and will soon give way to a new "post-information age." Indeed, a number of other writers have gotten here already.[7]

However, this argument isn't quite right. For starters, even if you only partially accept Erik Brynjolfsson and Andrew McAfee's *Second Machine Age* thesis of techno-optimism,[8] you will probably agree that there is still going to be a decent return on investing in information technology for many years to come. So even if firms compete on new terms—we'd argue for decisive action and with emotional conviction—they will do this while also investing heavily in information and knowledge (recall our examples of Amazon and Facebook from Chapter 1). These are complementary, not competing, approaches—just as some of the industrial age principles still proved relevant during the information age. Fast/forward firms don't succeed by discrediting the information-based model of their competitors; instead, they recognize both the power and limits of information.

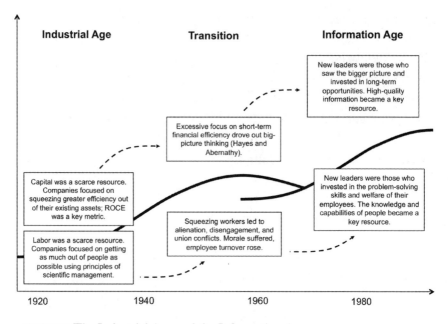

FIGURE 2.1 The Industrial Age and the Information Age

In short, we are not proposing the imminent arrival of a new age beyond the information age. That will surely come, but it is a ways off. Instead, what we have is an interesting set of dynamics within a maturing information age. These dynamics can be framed as a set of paradoxes that sit alongside the first paradox of progress: the logic of creative destruction (Figure 2.2).

The Second Paradox of Progress: Knowledge and Ignorance

Think of Aristotle. Some have described him as a mere advisor to Alexander the Great; others have caught him in the shadow of his own master, Plato. Most people, however, regard him as the greatest philosopher to have ever lived. Plenty of books have been written about his many accomplishments in physics, ethics, linguistics, and politics, but his importance to our story rests with the fact that he is often regarded as the last human being on our planet to have known everything that

Paradox 1: The more we create, the more we destroy

Paradox 2: The more we know, the less I understand

Paradox 3: The more we connect, the less I can predict

Paradox 4: The more we know, the more I have to believe

FIGURE 2.2 The Paradoxes of Progress

was worth knowing. Aristotle was the ultimate polymath, the very picture of knowledge.

More than two millennia later, *The Simpsons* hit the airwaves in the United States. Since its debut in 1989, this parody of middle-class American life has gone through twenty-six seasons, and at the time of writing it has 592 episodes under its belt. The patriarch of the family, Homer Jay Simpson, is sometimes described as the greatest comic creation of all time. In 2001, his famous catchphrase, "D'oh," was included in the *Oxford English Dictionary*. Some of his most famous quotes include, "Operator! Give me the number for 911!" and "'To start, press any key.' Where's the ANY key?" While Homer excels at some things, like loafing, donut eating, and beer drinking, he certainly doesn't have it all in hand. Far from it.

Without a doubt, we all want to be Aristotle, rather than Homer. The problem is that today, we can't be. Even the most brilliant scientist can master only a tiny fraction of the knowledge that exists. While the human race is becoming collectively more knowledgeable every year, each of us (as individuals) is becoming relatively more ignorant. Thus the second paradox of progress: *the more we know, the less I understand*. Every morning, when we wake up, we are in relative terms a little bit more stupid than the day before.

Linear People in an Exponential Reality

To understand why we are fated to become more ignorant, picture the simple graphic in Figure 2.3. The lower line is a case of linear growth, while the upper one illustrates exponential growth.

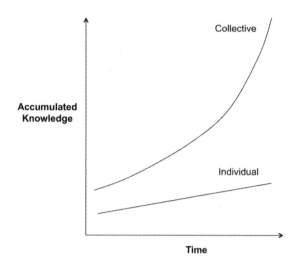

FIGURE 2.3 Individual and Collective Intelligence

The linear growth curve represents how individual intelligence evolves over time. It suggests that most of us are a little bit brainier than our parents. Another implication is that, in all likelihood, your kids will become, or perhaps even already are, a little bit smarter than you. It may not seem like that right now, but just be patient! Academics call this *The Flynn Effect*—after New Zealand Professor of Political Studies James Flynn.[9] The effect refers to the sustained linear increases in IQ-test scores over time that researchers have observed. It turns out that, in general, each successive generation is a little bit smarter than the previous one, with about three additional IQ points over every ten-year period. Explanations for this phenomenon range from better nutrition and smaller families to better education and something called *heterosis* (the occurrence of genetically superior offspring from mixing the genes of its parents—possibly an effect of urbanization). That is the good news.

The upper curve is the challenge. It's the bad news. It's there to illustrate all the knowledge out there—all the books, all the gurus, all the stuff on the Internet, the lot. As you can see it is not growing at a linear rate, but exponentially. Unlike in the age of Aristotle, no one can keep up.

There are many reasons behind this development: population growth, globalization of education, new technology enabling the big data movement and the increasing proliferation of research domains. Put it all together, and you end up with the phenomenon of *accelerating change* that we mentioned in the opening chapter. Kevin Kelly, founder of *Wired* magazine, and Google chief economist Hal Varian have calculated that for many decades worldwide information has been growing at an annual rate of 66 percent.[10] Derek de Solla Price has shown that the number of PhDs awarded worldwide has been doubling every fifteen years, and that 90 percent of all the scientists that ever lived are alive today.[11] In fields such as nanotechnology, stem cell research, and the area of global warming prevention, the number of patents granted doubles every two to three years.

As a result of the divergence between the two curves, advances in knowledge increasingly occur through collaboration. Where breakthrough ideas used to be associated with individuals (Heisenberg's Uncertainty Principle, Keynesian Economics), they are increasingly linked to teams, such as the 5,154 scientists at CERN who demonstrated the existence of the Higgs Boson. Nobel prizes were traditionally given to individuals (Niels Bohr in physics, Linus Pauling in chemistry, Max Theiler in medicine), but this has also changed—in 2015 the physics, chemistry, and medicine prizes were each shared among multiple scientists.

For us as individuals this paradox implies that we need to develop both the depth *and* the breadth of our competence. In a competitive world, we need our special area of expertise to help us stand out from the pack. But we also need the ability to work collaboratively, so that our fragments of knowledge can be combined effectively with the knowledge of others. In large part this is about having a broad knowledge base—a "T-shaped" skill profile that combines depth in one field with a reasonable level of understanding of multiple fields of study.[12] And when success is a matter of getting people with the right "know-how" to collaborate, "know-who" also becomes a critical factor to consider. The smart thing to do, even for the smartest of people, is to hone your social skills so that others want to team up with you and complement your strengths with theirs. Today, more than ever, Lone Ranger needs Tonto.

The other part of the story, for individuals, is the increasing importance of soft skills, the emotional intelligence that helps us connect with and figure out others. Consider poker. Once, success in this game boiled down to your ability to count cards and do the math, plus a little intuition. Now, computers can help any online poker player with the math, so the importance of psychology increases dramatically. The best poker players are increasingly the ones with soft skills—that is how you differentiate yourself.

And it's the same in the world of business. With the rise of big data, managers can monitor their employees and analyze their activities more accurately than was ever possible before. This puts a greater premium on their soft skills—their ability to motivate and support the people who work for them, and to make carefully balanced judgments based on a combination of hard data and emotional conviction.

Firms in an Exponential Reality

For corporations, this knowledge gap has two important consequences. First, your capacity to cooperate becomes an important differentiator. Firms operate primarily through division not multiplication—they are good at breaking activities down into their constituent parts, but they are poor at reassembling them in novel ways. So there is a lot of room for progress here—in terms of collective production (combining disparate knowledge in creative ways), collective decision making (tapping into the so called "wisdom of crowds"), and collective action (mobilizing people to work in a focused and aligned way).

These forms of collaboration increasingly go beyond the firm's traditional boundaries. The term *open innovation* is often used to refer to the capability to tap into external networks of customers, suppliers, and other partners in the pursuit of new and better offerings. In industry after industry, we see old, closed business models battling it out with new and open ones—iOS versus Android, or NASA versus Elon Musk's SpaceX. User-generated content began to go mainstream in the early 2000s and has gained in importance ever since. Even large, successful companies are forced to rethink the ways in which they operate. IBM embraced openness with its free open-source Eclipse software platform. In a similar vein, Procter and Gamble launched Connect + Develop, a platform for tapping into expertise and ideas from around the world.

Now, if knowledge is increasingly shared across firms and other stakeholders, and "closed information" (for example, in the form of patents) is obsolescing more quickly than before, the winners will be those organizations that move more quickly in order to gain a piece of the collective pie instead of hoarding their own small slices. However, moving quickly requires both new capabilities and a very different mind-set. For example, IBM orchestrated a series of "innovation jams" a few years ago, opening up some of their ideas to thousands of people inside *and* outside of the firm's boundaries. We asked Mike Wing, vice president of strategic communications at the time, if this was a risky approach. His answer: "It is a bet that there is enough diversity and expertise in IBM that we can apply these insights for commercial ends ahead of our competitors. The fact is, no one gets to be the Roman Empire anymore."[13]

Also inside the firm, the knowledge gap forces us to abandon old ways of working. In the industrial age, a key principle of management was to reduce deviance and turn people into interchangeable parts in a big machine. This principle served us well as long as the game was about perfecting the known—squeezing out a little more efficiency. Today, that principle has been turned on its head. When asked why he had as many as fifty people reporting to him, former Google CEO and now chairman Eric Schmidt responded, "If you get enough direct reports, then you can't manage them. That was the goal."[14] Eric had realized that he was not smart enough to have all the answers or to formulate all the questions that would determine the fate of Google. He therefore created a reporting structure under which even the slightest effort to run the company in a traditional way would make him go nuts. This doesn't mean that Eric Schmidt could not play an important role as a leader at Google. On the contrary, he played a pivotal part, but also a very different one. Fast/forward leaders have to draw upon all the deviance and diversity that exists within the organization, create a discussion, and make sure that it is a debate with a deadline.

The bottom line, then, is that a team of diverse Homers who know they are no Aristotle is better than a man—or company—akin to the world's greatest philosophy standing alone in today's landscape.

The Third Paradox of Progress: Connectivity and Unpredictability

In 1555, the French apothecary Nostradamus published his now famous book *Les Propheties*. It was a compiled volume with a collection of major long-term predictions about the future. He has been credited, in retrospect of course, with foreseeing major world events such as the Great Fire of London, the rise of Napoleon Bonaparte and Adolf Hitler, and the 9/11 tragedy. Five hundred years later, on a fairly regular basis, management teams around the world bring out their own horoscopes, tarot cards, tea leaves, and crystal balls to try do the same. In the world of business, Nostradamus's craft goes by the name of strategic planning.

Do all these efforts to foretell the future really make sense? Of course not—but that doesn't mean we should give up and simply hope for the best. Instead, we need to understand where the volatility and uncertainty in today's business world comes from, so that we can help our firm develop appropriate ways of coping. So understanding the third paradox of progress is key to forecasting responsibly and well: *the more we connect, the less I can predict.* Let's take a look at each of these elements in turn.

Connectivity

During the last thirty years, the global market economy has incorporated some four billion new members. With the exception of North Korea, Cuba, and a few other bastions of communism, capitalism now rules the world and the seven seas.

During much of the nineteenth and twentieth centuries, the world economy had only one economic powerhouse at a time—Europe and then the United States (with a brief Japanese interlude). Today the global economy no longer follows a traditional core-periphery model. Travel around the world and you'll see many new economic engines: brawn-based ones like Shenzhen in China, brain-based ones such as Bangalore in India, and those based on beans like Dubai in the Middle East.

On top of that, these economic hubs are increasingly interdependent. And more and more so, it is the emerging nations that are calling the shots. In 2015, the U.S. trade deficit with China was approximately $365 billion.[15] The Global Fortune 500 list from 2015 had 132 companies headquartered in emerging markets, a dramatic increase from the 21 such firms in 2000. The biggest Sovereign Wealth Funds in the world, with the exception of oil-rich Norway, were all from non-OECD countries: Saudi Arabia, UAE, Kuwait, and China.

Also, the growing diversity of the evolving economic space drives complexity. At a societal level, most of us speak Capitalism, but as with English we speak Capitalism with different accents. The U.S. accent is economically liberal, highly individualistic, and shareholder led; the European accent is more socially liberal, with support for regulation and for the needs of multiple stakeholders; the Indian model puts a lot of emphasis on long-term thinking, community development, and employee concerns; and China runs its own version of State Capitalism with a socialist market economy.

In terms of political models, plurality is the order of the day. In the post–Reagan and Thatcher world, after the Wall came down, it seemed obvious that liberal democracy would win. But not so—Russia and many middle-eastern countries have reverted to more autocratic models, nationalism is on the rise in parts of Europe, and China shows few signs of abandoning its autocratic political model.

As for the people factor, the diversity of the workforce is changing before our eyes. Working in the business school environment gives us an interesting window on this dynamic: when we teach a program for senior executives, the ones who have made it to the top, they are still predominantly white males in their forties and fifties; but when it is a high-potential program, for the next generation of leaders, the white males are suddenly a minority.

This is not just a matter of ethnic diversity. Women throughout the world are often better educated than men. In the majority of OECD countries, and increasingly elsewhere, most university graduates are now female.[16] Women now hold more wealth than ever in history, and work for pay in unparalleled numbers.

Finally, these trends are amplified by increasing mobility. We don't just mean the ease of moving digital products, or on-the-move communication technology. There is also increasing migration. The UN estimates that, fueled by the recent conflict in Syria and beyond, in 2015 there are approximately 244 million international migrants around the world.[17] Also, international travel is rising. Despite the availability of better and cheaper videoconferencing, business travel expenditure keeps going up at about 6 percent per year.[18] The number of Americans with passports has risen from about 25 million in 1995 to more than 125 million today.[19]

Put all this together, and we have what academics call a complex system—one with so many economical, political, technological, and physical linkages and feedback loops that it sometimes leads to entirely unpredictable consequences. No one knows when a deadly virus might hit us on a global scale, or when the next geopolitical or financial crises will erupt.

It is well known that the weather is a complex system. The so-called Butterfly Effect says that small variations in initial conditions (for example, the butterfly flapping its wings in Brazil) can produce large variations in long-term behavior (such as a tornado in Texas). Despite their best efforts and the power of modern computers, meteorologists still cannot predict the weather accurately more than a couple of days into the future. It turns out that the global economy is similar, which leads us to the next piece of our puzzle.

Unpredictability

It's sometimes said that it's difficult to make predictions—especially about the future. Today, this statement is truer than ever. Lebanese American thinker Nassim Nicholas Taleb popularized the term *Black Swan* a few years back to shed light on the seemingly random events that shape our lives.[20] Black Swans, according to Taleb, are events like the credit crisis that could not be predicted on the basis of rational analysis of past trends. In retrospect, Black Swans can be readily explained as the consequence of various trends coming together, but at the time they happen they take everyone by surprise.

The reality of our times is that things have progressed beyond the point of being merely complicated. In complicated matters, such as sending a man to the moon, interactions follow specific patterns and you can make accurate predictions. You can rely on expertise, top-down planning, and a finely tuned machine-like organization for implementation. (Of course, from time to time, screw-ups still happen. We can all recall the news of the Chernobyl disaster, the live pictures of the Challenger space shuttle catastrophe, and the BP oil spill in 2010. Like it or not, in complicated matters, there is no escape from the human factor.)

But complex procedures, like getting your kids to succeed in school or dealing with the so-called Islamic State, are different. Complex procedures are characterized by unforeseeable events, unintended consequences, and feedback loops. There are patterns, but they constantly change—like in a kaleidoscope.

Connectivity, complexity, and unpredictability therefore create challenges of a different nature than those that we had to deal with in the past. And this forces us to change our way of thinking about strategy, planning, forecasting, and organizing. Look at how the U.S. military was designed to deal with a geographically structured world, in which the enemy was called the Soviet Union, rather than a biographically structured world in which a global tribe organized into largely independent cells, like Al-Qaeda, can pose a threat anywhere, at anytime, without any notice.

Can we use big data to help us deal with this paradox? Yes, up to a point. By incorporating more factors into our algorithms, and by harnessing the recent advances in artificial intelligence, we are able to make more precise and defensible decisions. We can lean back in our ergonomically perfect chairs and let the computers tell us how to run our companies. Yet, in addition to the ever-present GIGO issue—garbage in, garbage out—there are at least three additional problems with this solution to the challenges caused by cluelessness.

One is that efficiency and effectiveness are not the same thing. A former top executive of German IT giant SAP once pointed out to us that "intelligence is the ability to improve efficiency, while wisdom is the ability to improve effectiveness." Competitiveness and peak performance are about being different, not being an improved version of someone else. The lure of big-data-based strategies is that they tempt you to keep on refining the answers to the old questions instead of asking new ones. In a fast/forward world of change and surprise, there is a risk that the combination of new technology and old questions means that you end up with answers that are *exactly* wrong, rather than roughly right.

A second problem is that while the growth in computational power helps us to solve more complex problems by making them merely complicated, the very same growth in computational power also makes the world increasingly complex. Remember when you only had a stereo and TV? Then you got a PC and a digital camera and a PDA. Eventually, the biggest problem was not to figure out how the individual products worked, but how to get all these gadgets to work together. It is the same in business. The more analyses you have available, the harder it is to figure out how they interact and what it all means. The challenge of the meta-analysis is that each new answer triggers two new questions, ad infinitum. Simplicity breeds complexity.

Third, competing on computational power is a race to the bottom. If you invest in sophisticated technologies as a way of keeping up with your competitors, and they do the same, it is pretty clear that the only real winners here are the providers of the technology. Computational power becomes necessary but not sufficient.

Act Now

Like it or not, we live in a world of butterflies and black swans, and it goes without saying that this increasing unpredictability has enormous consequences for business. Hit by new technologies and the competitive forces that globalization unleashes, firms have to redefine their businesses and look for a sustainable way forward. Here is the dilemma: the more unpredictable things become, the more plans we would like to make. And planning is alluring because we have more access to data than ever before. But, gradually, firms are figuring out that this "arms race," in which an ever-more-complex world is matched with an ever-more-complex plan, simply is not the way to go.

If you cannot make any decent predictions about the future, you cannot really make any plans. And if you cannot formulate a strategy (a fancy term for plan), you cannot have a budget, since a budget is simply a plan in numbers.

The trouble is, the new tools aren't well developed, and we still have those old tools to play around with. So we keep fine-tuning, even after our tools have lost their relevance. To begin to pave the road to better options, here are a couple of principles to bear in mind.

First, when you cannot predict the future, you have to assume responsibility for creating it. This calls for a focus on action—experimentation and learning. Consider the approach used by the military under conditions of extreme ambiguity. When you can't get access to the right intelligence and focus your attack on what you know is the weakest link in the chain of your enemy, you have to re-deploy your forces and attack randomly along a broad front line and then focus efforts once you've learned where the weak spots are. And in business, experimentation is by no means restricted to technology. Fast/forward companies experiment with anything from how you put together teams to incentives and recruitment procedures.

Herb Kelleher, the co-founder and former CEO of Southwest Airlines, the original low-cost carrier, famously once said, "Strategy is overrated, simply doing stuff is underrated. We have a *strategic plan*. It's called doing things."[21] As pointed out by former Nokia executive Mikko Kosonen and Professor Yves Doz in their book *Fast Strategy*, "in the face of high-uncertainty, trying is better than guessing."[22]

Second, access and make use of real-time information. Think about teenagers. These days, before they go out, Friday or Saturday evening, how much do they plan? Short answer: they don't—at least not like our generation did. You'll see them tapping their smartphones—texting or snapchatting—and then they are off. Young people know that planning makes little sense when change is a constant. They also realize that under such circumstances, real-time information is a strong substitute for forecasting and planning. While we cannot predict the future, we often do know enough about how the world is changing to be able to play out a range of possible futures or scenarios. By increasing our awareness of these future scenarios, we are likely to respond more effectively when they transpire.

Third, we need to reduce the level of central control and give those on the front line, where the action goes on and where change can be felt first, the power to adapt in real time to unfolding events. In the language of military doctrine this is called mission command—a style that promotes freedom and speed of action, but within certain constraints. In the world of business, it is often labeled strategy as simple rules—the notion that an overall sense of direction, and some basic guidelines for what to do in a given situation, is all front-line managers really need.[23]

Fourth, in unpredictable times, leaders must ask people around them to take a leap of faith. In effect, it is vital to be courageous and inspire courage. If the knowledge-ignorance paradox calls for competence through collaboration (complementing know-how with know-who), the complexity paradox implies a greater emphasis on a can-do attitude (readiness to act in the face of uncertainty). Trying to develop the perfect strategic plan in advance is just futile. This naturally leads us to the question of how to deal with the combined impact of expanding environmental complexity and accelerated change.

The Fourth Paradox of Progress: Knowing and Believing

The Tohoku earthquake in northern Japan measured 9 on the Richter scale; it was the biggest quake on record. It started at 2:46 p.m. on March 11, 2011; fifty minutes later the tsunami that it created hit the Fukushima Nuclear Power Plant, located about 150 miles north of Tokyo on the coast. The plant's emergency procedures were already in operation, with the three live reactors undergoing automatic shutdown. But the fifteen-meter wave knocked out the emergency diesel power supply, the cooling system shut down, and some materials were discharged, including small amounts of radioactivity, to reduce the pressure in the containment structure.

More than three hundred thousand people were evacuated from within a twenty-kilometer radius. Emergency procedures inside the plant were put into operation, and after two weeks, the three reactors were stable. As an effect, the Japanese government suspended its entire nuclear power program. Other countries also reacted: Germany announced it would permanently shut down eight of its seventeen reactors and pledged to close the rest by the end of 2022; Switzerland and Spain banned the construction of new reactors; Taiwan's president called for a dramatic reduction in the country's reliance on nuclear power.

The subsequent inquiry into what went wrong revealed that it was the combination of multiple factors that mattered—the biggest tsunami on record, an old plant short on safety features, the failure of both the mains electricity and the diesel backups, lack of decisiveness in the early hours of the accident, and insufficient crisis training. Fukushima "cannot be regarded as a natural disaster," wrote Tokyo University professor emeritus Kiyoshi Kurokawa in the inquiry report. "It was a profoundly man-made disaster—that could and should have been foreseen and prevented. And its effects could have been mitigated by a more effective human response."[24]

Even today, more than five years later, Fukushima is largely deserted. Teams of engineers are in the process of shutting down the damaged plants. Many evacuees have still not been allowed home. The threat of radiation poisoning remains, but to date there have been no fatalities directly linked to the accident (whereas almost sixteen thousand perished from the earthquake and tsunami).[25]

So much for the facts. The bigger question, for most people, is what the Fukushima accident means for the future of nuclear energy. For the governments of Germany, Switzerland, and Spain, the incident was sufficiently scary for them to cut back their nuclear programs. The Greenpeace view is also clear: "The Fukushima nuclear disaster showed us once again that nuclear reactors are fundamentally dangerous. Not only do they cause significant damage to the environment, the health of populations, and to national economies, the heavy financial cost of a meltdown is inevitably borne by the public. . . . The lives of hundreds of thousands of people continue to be affected by the Fukushima nuclear disaster, especially the 160,000 who fled their homes because of radioactive contamination."[26]

But many others have offered a different view, saying in essence that the lesson from Fukushima is that nuclear is safe. Here is British journalist and author George Monbiot, well-known for his environmental and political activism, writing in the *Guardian*: "A crappy old plant with inadequate safety features was hit by a monster earthquake and a vast tsunami. The electricity supply failed, knocking out the cooling system. The reactors began to explode and melt down. The disaster exposed a familiar legacy of poor design and corner-cutting. Yet, as far as we know, no one has yet received a lethal dose of radiation."[27]

Does Fukushima illustrate the perils of nuclear energy? Or does it show that nuclear is actually pretty safe? Where do we come out on this question? To be honest, we don't know. This is not the cop-out it sounds like. What we mean is that we lack the knowledge to come to a clear view. We are not nuclear experts. And, in all likelihood, neither are you.

So to come to a judgment, we either get to grips with the evidence ourselves, or we rely on others to help make sense of this complex case. Unfortunately, even the supposed experts don't entirely agree. So what do we do in this situation? We typically gravitate toward whichever expert opinion seems to ring true, that is, the one that is consistent with our intuitive belief, our experience, our gut feel.

Moving beyond nuclear energy, there are many things on which we are expected to form an opinion, from scientific matters (global warming, genetically modified crops) to economic and political matters (Brexit, U.S. policy in the Middle East) to social matters (gun control, abortion, gay marriage). These are all matters for which personal beliefs come into play. They involve people forming judgments that are based to some degree on feelings and sensibilities. Even issues that can supposedly be resolved purely through science, such as global warming, end up being laden with emotion.

Where do these beliefs come from? In theory, we might gather all the evidence, apply logical reasoning, and end up with a clear judgment. But in practice, this rarely seems to happen. The more likely sequence, as New York University sociologist Jon Haidt and others have argued, is that we come to an intuitive view first, which helps us to reach a judgment, and then we seek evidence that supports that position.[28]

Now, combine this line of thinking with some of the other trends in this chapter. Recall, we have argued that the amount of knowledge in society is growing much faster than knowledge at an individual level, and we have argued that increasing levels of connectedness make the world a more unpredictable place.

Obviously, these trends make Haidt's argument even stronger. The process of "reasoned judgment" is increasingly rare. Instead, as our ability to keep track of all the advances and changes in society goes down and complexity moves up, we fall back more and more on belief—on an intuitively grounded point of view that we then seek to reaffirm by talking to like-minded people and by reading the right news stories.

Herein lies our fourth and final paradox: *the more we know, the more I have to believe.* Despite advances in knowledge, the importance of nonscientific belief systems is more important than ever. Awash in information, our opinions are being shaped less by hard evidence than by appeals to our emotions, our intuitive beliefs, and our hidden values.

As we complete this book, in the Fall of 2016, the United Kingdom has voted to leave the European Union and the US has chosen Donald Trump as its next President. Every pollster predicted that these events would not come to pass, and the vast majority of respected economists and media organizations argued that these would be bad choices. For example, a leading figure in the Brexit campaign dismissed all the mainstream views, saying "people in this country have had enough of experts."[29] And so it proved—voters in both countries ignored all this expertise and rational argument, and instead voted with their gut.

Thinking Machines and Belief Engines

Why is the human mind so "belief prone"? Several arguments have been put forward. First, we are constantly looking for meaningful patterns—even in meaningless noise. We crave patterns and are perfectly willing to fill in the blanks. Not only that, we're also looking for intention and agency, the one in charge. American author and professional skeptic Michael Shermer has argued that the human brain is a "belief engine" as much as a thinking machine.[30] Theoretically speaking, this phenomenon is called *apophenia*[31]—the identification of meaningful connections in meaningless data. In statistics, it's also referred to as the Type I error—the identification of false patterns in data. A simple exercise illustrates the idea. Take a piece of paper and draw an image like the one in Figure 2.4.

Then, ask a friend or colleague to describe what he or she sees. In all likelihood, the response will be a face, or something along those lines. Then, ask if the person knows anyone who looks like this. Of course, your friend won't. Instead of responding by seeing three circles and a straight line, which is really what we are looking at, we go for the pattern.

Second, as pointed out by renowned biologist Lewis Wolpert, humans have the ability to understand anything from simple to really complicated cause-effect relationships, but it comes with a side effect.[32] Because we value logical reasoning, we want to understand all causal relationships, even the most complex ones—such as why we got ill or what happens when we die. Indeed, we frame anything and everything with a cause-effect mind-set. We are hardwired for belief.

Third, evolutionary biologist Lionel Tiger describes religiosity, also known as belief, as a secretion of serotonin from the brain.[33] This neurotransmitter is linked to feelings of well-being when it floods our central nervous system. Therefore, beliefs in something or someone and

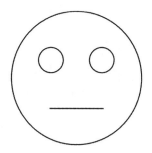

FIGURE 2.4 What Are You Looking At?

antidepressants like Prozac are clearly substitutes. Numerous medical studies also show that faithful people suffer from less stress and anxiety than the nonbelievers.

Some would object and say that the antidote to all this nonscientific belief is more information, more education. We're not so sure. In fact, an argument could be made for the direct opposite. Through talent and training, smart people are better equipped to defend beliefs, even though those beliefs were often developed for less smart reasons. You will often find the most ardent believers in the dustiest corridors of our universities and the darkest boardrooms of our corporations. Smart people stick to one diet that they believe in for life. Your average Joe Schmoe tries a new one every month.

Some years ago, famous British biologist Richard Dawkins published a book called *The God Delusion*. He made the argument that there is strong scientific evidence suggesting that a supernatural creator does not exist. A more daring hypothesis is the one put forth by his fellow Brit and biologist Rupert Sheldrake in the book *The Science Delusion*. He takes the limitations and hubris of contemporary science to court, claiming that scientific dogma itself has become a gospel protected by the high priests of science.[34]

But is he not right? Even when there is only one truth out there, rather than a set of contesting and confusing theories, in many cases we still just believe. Five hundred years ago, mankind believed that the earth was flat. For hundreds of years, the medical science believed that bloodletting cured many diseases. The truth, it seems, comes with a "best before" date. When faced with complex issues, we never know, we guess. We don't select—we elect.

Belief in Practice

So what are the implications of this paradox?

For us as individuals, the key is to better understand the way our own minds work. Many of us like to think of ourselves as rational and logical, capable of reasoned judgment on the basis of the evidence presented. But we also have strong intuitive views based on triggers and influences of which we often aren't even conscious. It is useful to surface these views—and those of our colleagues—when faced with difficult decisions, so that we know why people are taking certain positions. We should also respect that our intuitions may, indeed, be right. Just because we cannot fully rationalize a point of view doesn't mean it is invalid. We need to find smarter ways of bringing a full range of perspectives into our decision-making processes.

A related point is that there are many times we don't want or need to understand the details. You don't need to be an expert on global warming, and you don't need to understand every last nuance of your firms' financial accounts; you just want a trusted and legitimate expert to summarize the evidence for you. The notion of transparency (that is, full sharing of information) is popular in today's business world, but it turns out there are limits to transparency, as well as its benefits.

That brings us back to firms, for which the implications of our fourth paradox are enormous. By harnessing the emotional beliefs of individuals, it is possible to achieve extraordinary outcomes ranging from fantastic to horrific, as faith-based organizations from the Jesuits to Alcoholics Anonymous to Al-Qaeda have shown over the years. In the world of business, emotional beliefs are often suppressed, especially so in certain cultures. But harnessing beliefs can be an opportunity—a way of standing out from the crowd.

Steve Jobs, for example, brought a curious mix of engineering, design, and spirituality to Apple. The supply and logistics side of Apple was a smoothly running machine, built on rational business calculations, while the product development and brand positioning side was all about emotion.

Many leading companies, from Harley Davidson to Burberry and BMW, have emphasized the emotional connection with their customers as a defining characteristic. And others, including Tupperware, Zappos, John Lewis, Lego, and Disney, succeed in large part through the emotional attachment of their employees to the firm.

The bottom line: where complexity and ignorance intersect, it is often our emotional beliefs that guide our behavior. And knowing that, working with it as a fact, can make all the difference. In a society in which collective knowledge is growing at an exponential rate, there is still enormous scope for people to be swayed by arguments based on intuition and emotion. Do it right, and what you add in the emotional dimension will have a positive impact on the transactional one.

The New Agenda

We have covered a lot of ground in this chapter, and we have opened up many issues that will be resolved in the chapters ahead. We hope our paradoxes help you to see how profoundly the business environment is changing, so that it becomes obvious why and how the approach to competitive advantage must also change. The information age has brought enormous benefits in terms of processing power, connectivity, and increased mobility. But there are limits to people's processing capacity, and this makes the ability to focus and act decisively a key differentiator. There are also limits to people's rationality, and this makes the ability to understand and tap into the emotional beliefs of those around more important than ever.

The success formula for the years ahead requires these ingredients, but they themselves are not enough. Instead, they are the seeds of a new agenda, and how it maps onto strategy, organization, and leadership. This mapping is just what we turn to next.

Chapter 3

MODELS OF MANAGEMENT

PICTURE A REALLY FANCY cocktail reception at the Ritz in London. You've probably attended an event similar to this one, in which business people from around the world are present and you don't know many of the attendees. You get to talking to someone you've never met before. Let's call him Stanley. A minute or two into the conversation, he asks you about your line of work. How do you reply?

One approach is to hand Stanley your business card. This is a bit gauche—not what we would recommend, but we have seen it done. And in some ways it is highly efficient. It tells Stanley your name, your job title, and the company you work for, which provides a nice springboard for a conversation. You work for Imperial Corporation: that was an interesting acquisition you made last month, how have people reacted internally to the announcement?

But Stanley also gets to pigeon-hole you on the basis of your title. And, if he is the sort of guy who cares about status, he is going to be a lot more interested in prolonging the conversation if the card says "Executive Vice President" than if it says "Manager" or "Associate."

The second approach is to eschew the exchange of business cards, and to start talking about the body of expertise you have built up as an actuary, a project manager, an editor, or even the subject you studied at university. Frankly, this approach is also socially awkward. Stanley might think you are a bit pushy, perhaps looking for a job. But again, the curriculum-vitae approach provides useful information about you, and perhaps it opens up an interesting line of conversation about your common interests or experiences.

A third option is to tell him an anecdote about something you did at work that day. There was an incident in the factory that you had to fix; there was a big drop in the Euro (again), so your team had to scramble to cover their positions. Stories usually go down well in these settings, especially when they are self-deprecating or humorous. Stanley may well enjoy this anecdote, and he will also learn something about you in the process.

Finally, you can sidestep all the practical stuff about your work, and you can tell Stanley what your job means to you, how you get on with your team, and how you juggle your work and family life—how you feel. You might talk about your nightmare boss, or your worries about what your colleagues think of you. This is probably a bit intense for a first conversation, and Stanley may suddenly realize he needs another drink. But we have seen it done, and chances are you have as well if you have been to enough of these receptions.

So what's the point? Each of these four opening gambits reveals something different about you:

- Your business card represents your formal *position*, who you are at work.

- Your background, expertise, and education represent your *knowledge*, what you know.

- Anecdotes about your working day represent *action*, what you do.

- Information about how you relate to those around you represents *emotion*, what you feel.

These are four different and complementary perspectives on you in the workplace. Depending on the context, one may be more important than the others. But the key point is simply that they are all valid, and if we are to fully understand you and your work, we need all four.

Four-Dimensional Organizations

The four perspectives described in the preceding section don't just apply to each of us as individuals, they also provide a useful way of looking at firms and organizations of all types—from a family to a Fortune 500 company.

Mirroring those perspectives, every organization has four dimensions:

- Position—a formal structure defining who reports to whom.

- Knowledge—an accumulated body of expertise and capabilities.

- Action—what people do on a day-to-day basis, individually and collectively, through projects and processes.

- Emotion—an intangible culture, a way of working that taps into the feelings and values of the people working in the organization.

It turns out these four dimensions are everywhere you look. While not always expressed as such, this four-dimensional model underpins many existing bodies of thinking. For example, Aristotle argued that to inspire followers to pursue a course of action, the leader should appeal to formal authority (ethos), rational argument (logos), and human emotion (pathos). Action was the end goal for Aristotle, and the other dimensions were the means to that goal.[1]

In *Gods of Management,* the Irish management writer Charles Handy argued for four basic forms of managing: the club culture (Zeus), based on formal power and influence; the role culture (Apollo), based on logic and rationality; the task culture (Athena), based on problem solving and getting things done; and the existential culture (Dionysus), that exists to serve the purpose and passions of its members.[2]

Meredith Belbin's well-known workbook *Team Roles at Work* suggests individuals working in a team (a formal positional structure) play one of three roles: thought-oriented (knowledge), action-oriented (action), and people-oriented (emotion).[3]

We could go on, but hopefully you get the point. This four-dimensional framework has certainly withstood the test of time. It provides a highly practical way of understanding the choices firms make about how they are organized.[4] To be specific, each of these perspectives suggests a very different management model. Let us look at each in turn.

Bureaucracy

Who is the most important business person of the last hundred years? When we ask executives or MBA students this question, the usual suspects include Henry Ford, Thomas Edison, Jack Welch, Steve Jobs, and John D. Rockefeller. Depending on their nationality, Europeans might suggest Ingvar Kamprad, Richard Branson, Ferdinand Porsche, Gianni Agnelli, or Amancio Ortega. Japanese students and executives often think of Akio Morita or Eiji Toyoda.

We would like to nominate Alfred P. Sloan. He isn't a household name like Ford or Jobs. There will probably never be a Hollywood blockbuster featuring Leo DiCaprio about his life and accomplishments. But he isn't exactly an unknown either. In fact, *Fast Company* magazine had him sixth on their all-time list, and Forbes ranked him twelfth. The reason he isn't as well-known as other business people is that there is no particular product or brand associated with him. But he actually created something vastly more impressive—a new form of organization. His invention is often called the "Multidivisional Form" ("M-Form" for short), and it was the defining management model of the industrial age.[5]

As president of General Motors from 1923 to 1937, Sloan restructured the firm into five separate brands (Chevrolet, Pontiac, Oldsmobile, Buick, Cadillac), putting a general manager in charge of each one and retaining central financial and strategic control at the headquarters. He emphasized individual accountability, with each general manager being responsible for the profit and loss of his division, and he believed deeply in professional expertise and business education (hence, the Sloan Fellowship program at Stanford, MIT, and London Business School).

While Sloan didn't use the word, his creation was the archetypal *bureaucracy*. The term, of course, goes back to the writings of German sociologist Max Weber,[6] who saw a depersonalized system of work, in which coordination was achieved through standard rules and procedures, as being superior to one based on tradition or personal charisma. Such was the power of this new structure (as documented in Alfred Chandler's landmark book *Strategy and Structure*[7]) that GM became the undisputed leader in the world auto industry from the 1930s through to the 1970s.

And Sloan's influence went much further than the auto industry. The M-Form became the *de facto* standard for structuring any large business firm, and it was gradually rolled out across multiple industries and multiple countries during the pre- and postwar years. Indeed, it is hard to find any large firm today that has *not* got some elements of Sloan's M-Form structure in its DNA.

Let us clarify the definition of bureaucracy a little more, for the purposes of the argument we are building here. The essence of bureaucracy is that it privileges formal position ahead of knowledge, action, or emotion. A key aspect of bureaucracy is hierarchy, which means that one person has authority over another. In other words, your boss can tell you what to do, whether you think it is a good idea or not. As a subordinate, you might want to suggest a course of action, but everyone knows that your boss will ultimately decide. In some ways, bureaucracy is the organizational form that we suspect Kim Jong-un, the "born of heaven," outstanding third supreme leader of North Korea, would favor. Bureaucracy is no democracy.

The point we are making may seem obvious, but that is only because the principles of bureaucracy have become pervasive. Terms such as *command-and-control, line manager, subordinate*, and *reporting relationship* all reinforce the notion that formal position is what matters.

But of course bureaucracy also has limitations, and we would argue these have become more significant over time, as the effects of the paradoxes of progress have become more apparent.

First, it is understood that expertise in a bureaucracy sits mostly at the very top. Back when Max Weber introduced the concept, there was at least some chance that the leader of the organization could be an expert on most things that people inside the firm did. Thomas Edison, for example, was known for having deep expertise in all of GE's technologies. But this notion of the all-knowing leader is no longer valid. Even the best leaders today are experts only in certain limited domains. As knowledge becomes deeper, more fragmented, and geographically dispersed, we will need to rely more on the many than the few. If people are indeed becoming increasingly ignorant, there is no reason to believe that the group of top executives is the only exception to the rule.

Second, bureaucracies are genuinely bad at the kind of radical innovations that drive creative destruction. There are many reasons for this deficiency, but at the core of it all is the fact that division and specialization rarely produce a result greater than the input. Innovation usually requires a horizontal combination of competencies across silos. If you place your bets on vertical subordination, rather than horizontal collaboration, and you favor division over multiplication, don't expect a continuous flow of revolutionary products that will wow the market.

Third, the increasing importance of emotional beliefs and employee engagement runs counter to the rationality implied by bureaucratic principles. In Weber's world, the well-functioning bureaucracy was a depersonalized, almost soulless entity in which formal rules and procedures dictated action. But there is plenty of evidence that emotion cannot be simply switched off in the workplace. For example, the model proposed by American psychologist Paul Ekman, who was once described as "the best human lie detector in the world," classifies our emotions into six such states that we constantly drift between; anger, disgust, fear, happiness, sadness, and surprise.[8] Combine this idea with the strong evidence from neuroscience suggesting that the limbic system, which governs our feelings, always takes precedence over the neocortex, where logic and reason rest.[9] There is but one logical conclusion: you cannot *not* feel anything. Disregarding feelings means that instead of the organizational adrenalin so critical to execution and engagement, the end result is often apathy and disengagement.

In sum, bureaucracy as a management model has clear benefits and costs. It worked beautifully during the industrial age, when corporate success was based on efficient productivity and high-volume sales, but it proved less effective as we moved into the information age, when the environment was less stable, the future less predictable, knowledge increasingly dispersed, and competitive advantages no longer eternal.

Meritocracy

Look a little further down the list of top businesspeople of the twentieth century, and you may find the name Marvin Bower. Ohio born and raised, Bower was the architect of McKinsey and Co., today the premier strategy consulting company in the world. McKinsey embodies the very notion of meritocracy.[10]

Bower became head of McKinsey in 1937 and developed a set of principles that are still recognizable. Professionalism was at the heart of his worldview. This meant a single-minded focus on clients, acting with strong integrity, and deep expertise. He developed a "one firm" policy, so that the entire expertise and knowledge base of the firm could be brought to bear on every client's challenges. And he placed a lot of emphasis on human capital—hiring the best people, promoting from within, and continuing professional development.

The term *meritocracy* is less well defined than *bureaucracy*, but for our purposes it boils down to one key principle: knowledge is privileged over formal position. In Bower's view, and indeed in that of McKinsey's leaders today, what people in the firm know is much more important than where they sit in the organizational structure. To be clear, McKinsey has a hierarchy just like any large firm (director, principal, associate principal, engagement manager, associate, analyst), but there is also a core principle, an obligation to dissent, that encourages lower-level consultants to challenge their senior colleagues if they disagree.

In practice, this means that it is the person with the best argument, not the one with the highest-ranking job title, whose view prevails. Working in the university system, in which meritocracy is common, we have direct experience of how this works. Julian was head of an academic department for five years. On paper, this meant he was "in charge of" the activities of twenty faculty members. In practice, they just did their own thing. If he called a meeting, they decided whether to attend depending on how interesting the agenda sounded. If he proposed a course of action—say, hiring a new professor—they listened to his point of view, then offered their own, and the weight of the argument carried the day. If he pushed his view too hard, they pushed back equally hard.

For anyone used to a more traditional bureaucratic structure, this probably sounds rather dysfunctional or even anarchical. For information-age firms in which creativity, innovation, and empowerment are important, however, meritocracy has become the *de facto* gold standard. And, given the new realities of business, it is a clear improvement over the bureaucratic model that it superseded. But it also has significant shortcomings in dealing with some of the effects of the paradoxes of progress. So it is not the end of the journey.

What then, more exactly, are the benefits and costs of the meritocracy as a management model?

It works best in a business context in which deep knowledge makes a difference. Besides universities, this means professional services firms in law, consulting, accounting, banking, or engineering; high-tech firms in IT, telecoms, or medical science; and creative environments like advertising, TV, or publishing. These are the sectors, of course, that increasingly dominate the business landscape. And they have done so by creating a management model that puts knowledge first. The same logic applies at other levels of analysis. Countries such as Singapore even go as far as to identifying meritocracy as one of the guiding principles for public policy formulation.

The meritocracy has a number of notable failings and challenges, though, and these are becoming more acute as the paradoxes of progress take hold.

The first is that at times knowledge becomes important *for its own sake*. This means that the most sophisticated, smartest, or technically most advanced solutions are those that prevail. Sometimes this is a good thing, but often it means you overshoot. You find yourself with an offering that is over-engineered, and therefore too expensive, for your largest body of customers.[11]

The importance of knowledge for its own sake also creates internal tensions. In meritocratic organizations, the goal of many people is to be the smartest person in the room, and it is not unusual to find that nine out of ten people in that room believe they are (especially if the organization is male-dominated). What constitutes merit is not always objectively clear; in neither a business nor an academic setting do the less acclaimed automatically acknowledge the superiority of the arguments proposed by those apparently smarter. In most meritocratic organizations the words "Of course, you are right" are rarely uttered.

A second failing is that meritocracies move slowly. They agonize over seemingly routine decisions. They build consensus gradually, one person at a time. They put a lot of time into internal reviews and appraisals. The need for discussion and agreement among those at the top means they end up getting as bogged down in internal procedures as bureaucracies, though for slightly different reasons. If bureaucracies suffer from the shortcomings of even a benevolent dictatorship, meritocracies display the same disadvantages as those of a democracy.

A linked point is that pure meritocracies are not well equipped to handle emotional beliefs. Such organizations are often sterile, rational, and analytical, and they tend to suppress arguments that appeal to emotion, intuition, or gut-feeling. A workplace where the closest thing you'll ever get to positive feedback is the absence of negative feedback—silence—does not tend to take rapid action, and when action happens it is rarely backed by high levels of emotional conviction and personal engagement. Meritocracies bear no mark of confidence, optimism, or hope.

A third failing is that meritocracies tend to emphasize the individual ahead of the collective. Many such organizations are akin to an imaginary reality show called "The Battle of the Brains," with their focus on the individual—the nutty professor, nerd, geek, or mad scientist. But, if we are all becoming relatively ignorant, firms need to put a greater emphasis on collaboration rather than confrontation, a culture with a "united minds" rather than a "mind your own business" mentality. Know-how needs to be complemented with know-who and a new attitude.

The journey of organizing is an ongoing evolution, which is never finished, per se. Clearly, despite its current popularity and success, meritocracy is not the end of road. To truly understand how fast/forward organizations work, we must move on to the final model, which fills the gaps left by bureaucracy and meritocracy in how they address the paradoxes of progress.

Adhocracy

The third and final model is the adhocracy. It is particularly suited to firms operating in highly unpredictable business environments. At its core, the adhocracy is a management model that privileges action over position and knowledge. When faced with a difficult decision, for example, some people will defer to their boss, some will reflect and discuss it with colleagues, while some prefer to act—maybe by trying out low-risk experiments to resolve a key uncertainty. Going back to your conversation with Stanley, if you prefer to talk about what you do and why, then you are hinting at an intuitive preference for adhocracy. This doesn't mean knowledge and formal position are ignored in adhocracies; it means that on the margin *doing* something beats reflecting or deferring upward. For those corporations and individuals that aspire to move forward faster than the others, there is no substitute for action. They know that, at times, authority and analysis become organizational speed bumps.

The concept of adhocracy is not entirely new. The term was first coined by the leadership sage Warren Bennis in his 1968 book *The Temporary Society*, picked up and popularized by futurist Alvin Toffler in his best-seller *Future Shock*, and subsequently adopted by strategy guru Henry Mintzberg in *Structure in Fives* and by *In Search of Excellence* author Robert Waterman in *Adhocracy: The Power to Change.*[12] The common theme through these books is that adhocracy is a flexible, informal way of working that is suited to dynamic environments. It often involves creating temporary units for tackling specific opportunities. And it is typically positioned as the opposite of bureaucracy.

While we pick up on many of these ideas, our view of adhocracy is distinctive in two important ways. First, Bennis, Toffler, and Waterman all saw adhocracy as, essentially, the antidote to a slow-moving bureaucracy.[13] They envisioned a simple spectrum, with bureaucracy as the traditional form on the left and adhocracy as the modern, progressive form on the right. But as our discussion makes clear, this is unduly simplistic, because it leaves no room for meritocracy. By framing adhocracy as distinct from both bureaucracy *and* meritocracy, we offer a much more precise definition of the term. We also clarify that each model has its place, even in today's fast-moving world. For leaders, this creates the additional challenge of knowing when and how to switch between these three different models.

Second, we put much more emphasis on the emotional dimension.[14] In our experience, action without conviction rarely produces spectacular results. Emotion is everywhere (even if it is often suppressed), and it is interwoven with the knowledge, the actions, and even the formal roles of people within a firm. In this respect, the emotional dimension of a firm is qualitatively different to the position, knowledge, and action dimensions. It sits in the middle, so to speak, as the organizational adrenaline that fuels action, influences knowledge, and attaches itself to authority.

The fact that the emotional dimension is different should not be taken as a sign of the fact that it is less important or impossible to manage. There are many different practical ways in which leaders effectively influence such things as the confidence, hope, optimism, and resilience of their employees.

Think therefore about adhocracy as a management model that privileges *action infused with emotion*.[15] We have seen how information-age firms become so overwhelmed with information that they suffer analysis paralysis, and their emphasis on logical or rational knowledge makes their decision processes sterile. The best way to counter these problems is the adhocracy. In a bureaucracy and a meritocracy, emotions are seen as negatives or irrational, while an adhocracy thrives on positive and personal engagement.

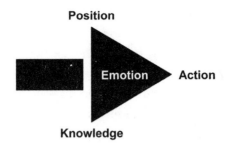

FIGURE 3.1 Adhocracy Action Infused with
Emotion

In graphical terms, Figure 3.1 illustrates how adhocracy looks: a
bias for action, represented by the arrow head, with positional power
and knowledge as contributory components, with emotion as the
spark in the center.

So what does an adhocracy look like in practice? As we have already noted, there are plenty of real-world examples: hospital emergency rooms, trading floors in banks, "skunk-works" project teams,
and so forth. However, what is notable about these examples is that
typically they are fairly small units that sit off to the side of a larger organization that operates using more traditional methods. An interesting question, therefore, which we explore throughout the book, is how
the principles of adhocracy can be scaled up and used on a corporate-
wide basis.

In terms of pros and cons, the most important advantage of adhocracy is simply its external focus. In bureaucracies and meritocracies, the focus of our attention turns inward, and the needs of our
customers or clients become of secondary interest. The adhocracy, in
contrast, is a vehicle for taking action based on external opportunities.
It often involves temporary project-based work, and it typically has a
minimal amount of overhead or corporate infrastructure associated
with it.

The other key benefit is that adhocracy is highly empowering. Because of its emphasis on action and opportunity, employees are typically more inspired, and they bring higher levels of discretionary effort to their work. There is a constant sense of urgency. The additional energy that is brought to bear on important issues is good for the firm. It is also good for the individuals in question: most people reach much higher levels of job satisfaction when they work on interesting, challenging projects.

Obviously, the downside of the adhocracy is that it can appear chaotic. It requires a significant amount of managerial oversight and progressive human resource practices to keep it functioning in an effective way. It also lacks the predictability or comfort that more well-established models provide. In addition, there are few role models out there of up-and-running adhocracies, and many executives prefer to stick with their tried-and-tested ways of working rather than experiment with something new. Luckily, an organization needn't bet the farm (or the firm) on adhocracy in order to see the benefits of this approach.

The Trinity in Reality

Each of the three models has its place in the modern organization, so the question you should be asking is not, "Which model is better?" but "Which model do I need for this particular set of challenges?" Here are a couple of examples of how these models coexist. First, consider a typical investment bank, which includes elements of all three:

- *Adhocracy:* Think of the traders, for whom speed and decisiveness is everything. The trading room, even in today's world of electronic transactions, still has a vibrant, emotion-infused atmosphere. Think also of the team that is pulled together to do a "deal," often working around the clock as a deadline approaches.

- *Meritocracy:* This model applies to the industry analysts and the client relationship managers, for whom deep expertise and knowledge are critical. There are also increasing numbers of "quants" who devise fiendishly clever derivative products to pick up on systematic irregularities in market prices.

- *Bureaucracy:* This is the large numbers of people who work in middle- and back-office functions, settling trades, overseeing risk, and ensuring compliance. Efficiency and avoidance of mistakes are their key success factors.

Or consider the pharmaceutical industry. As a first cut, you might hypothesize that R&D operates as a meritocracy, manufacturing or sales as a bureaucracy, while a few narrow functions such as business development might be an adhocracy. But you can take a more granular approach and see differences even within functions. Take the R&D division of a big pharma company such as GSK or Roche and consider the three main steps in the value chain:

- Basic research is often done in collaboration with universities; it is about the advancement of science first and foremost, and it is best managed as a meritocracy.

- Drug discovery requires creativity and fresh thinking, and in recent years it is the smaller biotech firms that have been setting the pace here. In many cases, adhocracy is the best model.

- Drug development is careful, painstaking work, involving thousands of patients in clinical trials in its latter stages, and with big downside risks if it goes wrong. Bureaucracy is recommended.

We can see here that the three management models have fractal qualities, meaning that they can be seen at multiple levels of analysis. Regardless of your role within your own organization, you can usefully think about when and where each model might work for you and your team. Even if you sit in the midst of a bureaucratic structure, there may still be space for carving out your own distinctive way of working within it, based on more meritocratic or adhocratic principles.

Which Model Should You Use?

We hope this discussion of different management models has got you thinking about your own organization. We use this framework a lot when working with executives, and it is always instructive to ask them to figure out which model they gravitate toward in their own firm, and which one they should be using given the circumstances. So here is your chance to do a bit of simple self-diagnosis. It is in two parts.

Your Current Default Model

Answer the six questions in Survey 1. These questions aren't about the high-level principles or intentions of your senior executives; they are concerned with the day-to-day choices people make. They capture what we might call the revealed preferences of people regarding their preferred way of working. Look at the distribution of your answers, and you will likely see that they cluster around one of the three types. This is your default model.

Survey 1: What Is your Management Model?
Your organization likely exhibits elements of all three models, but it is useful to know which one people have a preference for. For each question, choose the answer that is most typical of your function or business (note that it is typically more informative to answer at this level, rather than for the firm as a whole).

Question 1. Your company is exploring a strategic alliance with an important supplier or customer. Which of the following approaches do people gravitate to?

A. We have a very structured approach, we are cautious about the risks involved, and we pay a lot of attention to the legal contracts.

B. We spend a lot of time getting to know the other party, to see if there are complementarities and to see how well we can work with them.

C. We start very informally, trying out something low risk quite quickly, and building up from there.

Question 2. You are seeking to get various functions or business units to align around a complex project; how do you proceed?

A. We define clear deliverables at the outset, and we make sure everyone knows who is accountable and what their roles are. We monitor progress against these deliverables.

B. We bring key people from the various functions together; we spend time discussing our respective roles and how we can all contribute. We meet periodically, and we adjust depending on how things are going.

C. We work closely with the end user or customer for the project, and we provide frequent updates to them; project meetings are frequent, and often involve significant changes depending on user feedback.

Question 3. A front-line employee is dealing with an unhappy customer, who feels the service the company has provided hasn't been as good as expected. How does she typically respond?

A. She pushes back, explaining that the company acted in accordance with its formal policies. If the customer pushes harder, she escalates the problem to her boss.

B. She seeks to get to the bottom of the problem, so that the system can be improved in the future.

C. She realizes the customer is upset, and takes immediate action to placate him.

Question 4. There is a request from a business unit or team for some additional funds (a further 5 to 10 percent over the allocated amount) to invest in what they say is an important new project. How does their boss respond?

A. He says no. There is a well-established process for requesting funds; wait until next year.

B. He asks the subsidiary for more information: What is the business case? Why does this merit special consideration? Depending on these answers, he may make an exception.

C. He tries to help the subsidiary by providing a small amount of money, so they can test out their idea with limited funding and then ask for more money later if necessary.

Question 5. Where do your senior executives prefer to spend their time?

A. At their desks, chairing reviews and board meetings, seeking input from direct reports.

B. Debating strategic issues with colleagues, reading up on the latest thinking, in the lab or talking to experts about developments in the industry.

C. Out in the field meeting with customers and prospective customers, walking the corridors, talking to front-line employees about their work and their challenges.

Question 6. What is the primary source of motivation and job satisfaction for mid-level employees?

A. Getting well paid for their work, getting a bonus for delivering on goals, getting promoted.

B. Doing a high-quality piece of work, being recognized as an expert in an important area, working with smart colleagues.

C. Making things happen, meeting difficult deadlines, being recognized for delivering creative or surprising results.

If your answers were mostly As, your preferred management model is a bureaucracy.

If your answers were mostly Bs, your preferred management model is a meritocracy.

If your answers were mostly Cs, your preferred management model is an adhocracy.

The Model You Need

The six questions in Survey 2 ask about the external business environment in which you operate. Again, answer the questions as best you can, and add up your answers. The results should indicate the model that is best suited to your current operating environment. As a follow-up to this analysis, many people also think about the model they believe they will need three to five years from now, to see if there are any differences.

Survey 2: Which Model Is Best Suited to Your Operating Environment?
Now consider the external business environment in which you operate. Again, please focus on the specific function or business you work in, rather than the firm as a whole.

Question 1. What is the level of regulation and compliance imposed on your function or business by external actors? (on a scale: very low—low—medium—high—very high)

High to very high—Bureaucracy is favored.

Very low to medium—Meritocracy or adhocracy is favored.

Question 2. What are the downside risks (in terms of safety and cost implications) if something goes wrong?

High to very high—Bureaucracy is favored.

Medium—Meritocracy is favored.

Very low to low—Adhocracy is favored.

Question 3. What is the rate of technological and/or scientific change in your business area?

High to very high—Meritocracy is favored.

Medium to high—Adhocracy is favored.

Very low to low—Bureaucracy is favored.

Question 4. To what extent does your function or business require advanced-level professional training to operate effectively?

High to very high—Meritocracy is favored.

Very low to medium—Adhocracy or bureaucracy is favored.

Question 5. How much volatility is there on the "demand" side, for example in terms of customer needs changing or new segments emerging?

High to very high—Adhocracy is favored.

Very low to medium—Meritocracy or bureaucracy is favored.

Question 6. What is the level of "ambiguity" in your operating environment, meaning a lack of clarity about what course of action is required for you to succeed?

High to very high—Adhocracy is favored.

Medium—Meritocracy is favored.

Very low to low—Bureaucracy is favored.

Add up the number of times each model (bureaucracy, meritocracy, adhocracy) is favored in your answers. It is likely that your answers will not be entirely consistent, so you should choose your desired model according to which is favored more often.

The simple logic behind this second survey is that, in a more knowledge-intensive and unpredictable world, the meritocracy and the adhocracy become more effective than the bureaucracy. To be a bit more specific, Figure 3.2 illustrates how the three different models more formally link back to the paradoxes of progress.

In a predictable, heavily regulated environment, in which the costs of getting things wrong are severe and innovation happens rarely, a traditional bureaucracy works best. Examples would be an oil refinery, a computer assembly line, or an airport.

In a world of accelerating knowledge growth and technological change, in which creativity and judgment are important, we need to

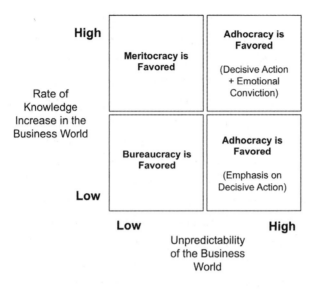

FIGURE 3.2 Choosing the Right Management Model

let those with the deepest knowledge and the greatest experience call the shots. In these settings, knowledge is more important than position, and the meritocracy is the preferred way of working. Examples would be a law firm, a nuclear research facility, or an advertising agency.

In a complex and unpredictable world, it becomes impossible to foresee how things will change, and there is a premium on trying things out in an experimental fashion rather than working up a grand plan. In these settings, taking action is more important than knowledge or formal position, and the adhocracy becomes the favored model. Moreover, when we face a world of rapid technological change *and* unpredictability, our capacity to fully understand what is happening goes down, and our openness to acting on intuition and other less-rational feelings increases. This makes emotional conviction, as part of an effective adhocracy, more important. Examples here include firms and start-ups competing in new industry spaces, such as Fintech, social media, or personalized medicine.

Old Habits Die Hard

Before we complete this chapter, it is worth offering a few final observations on how you get the best out of these three models.

When we have used this framework in workshops, a common response from the executives is that they want all three—at the same time. But we would argue this is escapism; it is not possible to emphasize all three dimensions at once, because one always ends up taking precedence over the others. Balance is therefore the wrong term. Firms that move forward faster than their competitors know when to shift perspective, and why they should. They are in sync. The problem is that most organizations, when faced with challenges and conflicting demands, retreat to their fallback mode.

Let's say you work for a high-tech firm, and you and your team are championing an acquisition—a small firm in an emerging digital space has really fired you up. You know a couple of competitors are also interested in it, so time is of an essence. The total cost is not scary, maybe 5 percent of your net sales. You argue for speed—your team knows the target firm well, and there is a window of opportunity to do a deal now, before the competitors get their acts together. "Slow down" says your CEO, "we need to give this some thought. Please put the case together, and we will discuss it at the next board meeting." The CFO then offers his view: "I just want to do a bit more due diligence here, get the lawyers involved, and make sure the numbers add up."

You get the picture: in most business settings, the desire for rapid action (adhocracy) is tempered by the views of those who like to talk things through (meritocracy) and those who do things by the book (bureaucracy). And the bigger the firm, the more likely it is that those urging caution, debate, and due diligence win out. Meritocracy trumps adhocracy, and bureaucracy trumps meritocracy. And needless to say, after this initial feedback, your level of engagement, as well as that of your team, will begin to wane.

This is, in essence, why our book focuses on adhocracy—and how to infuse it in your work environment when the timing is right. It is easy for senior executives to talk about "a bias for action," but when it comes time to put these principles into practice, in the heat of the moment they usually default back to the behaviors that have served them well in the past. The majority of senior executives have reached their positions by acting cautiously and by not making mistakes, and it is not easy to change those habits.

Interestingly, many of the exceptions to this rule are to be found in tech companies where the founders are still in charge. Think about Facebook's Mark Zuckerberg paying $19 billion for WhatsApp in early 2014; Amazon's Jeff Bezos moving into consumer electronics; or Oracle's Larry Ellison pushing his company into cloud computing. These are executives who didn't get acculturated into traditional big-company ways before going out on their own. They also have unusual levels of power—even though all three of these firms are publicly traded, their CEOs have very high personal ownership stakes (and outright control in Zuckerberg's case) that lets them move more decisively than would be possible in most firms.

To give decisive action a chance, you need to put in place the structures and systems, principles and processes that support it. If people are prone to default back to the operating assumptions of a bureaucracy or meritocracy, you have to be more explicit about the circumstances in which adhocracy is needed, and you have to provide the people operating in these circumstances with the tools to do their job. This doesn't mean abandoning all the checks and balances that have served large firms well for so many years: rather, it means knowing when it is okay to experiment, and how to mitigate the downside risks if things don't go well.

Here is a practical example. We were talking to the CEO of one of the largest mobile gaming companies in the world, and extolling the benefits of adhocracy. "Yes, I buy your argument," he said, "but if my developers think they have a license to take action just for the sake of it, we end up in chaos. They have to learn when to follow the script, and when to experiment." There is, in other words, a world of difference between "good adhocracy," when experimentation is hypothesis-driven and undertaken to resolve important uncertainties, and "bad adhocracy," which involves action for action's sake. In the chapters

TABLE 3.1 Comparing the Three Models of Management

	Bureaucracy (Formal positional authority is privileged)	Meritocracy (Individual knowledge is privileged)	Adhocracy (Action [infused with conviction] is privileged)
Appropriate Conditions	Relatively stable environment	High levels of knowledge intensity	High levels of unpredictability
How Strategic Decisions Are Made	Through the hierarchy in a top-down way	Through argument and discussion; the power of the idea	Through experimentation and trial and error, within a clear guiding frame
How Activities Are Coordinated	Through rules and procedures	Through mutual adjustment, and the free flow of ideas	Around a problem or opportunity
How People Are Motivated	Through extrinsic rewards, such as pay	Through personal mastery, interesting work	Through achievement of a goal and recognition

that follow, we will get deeper into this issue by providing some practical advice for how to operationalize the concept of adhocracy.

Table 3.1 provides a summary of our key arguments so far. In the next chapter we will take a deeper look at what a fast/forward strategy process looks like.

Chapter 4

THE ACTION IMPERATIVE IN STRATEGY

'MINECRAFT' IS THE BEST-SELLING PC game of all time. As of June 2016, it had sold in excess of 106 million copies (including Xbox sales and mobile downloads). The story of its origins is now well known. Swedish computer geek Markus "Notch" Persson—a guy who started programming on a 128 Commodore at the tender age of seven—built it in his spare time, without really thinking of it as a money-making venture. In 2009, he made it available through a gaming website to some of his friends. It was sufficiently well received that in 2011 Notch quit his day job as a programmer, created a company, Mojang, and hired a couple of people to help him commercialize it. *Minecraft* grew like wildfire, becoming the game of choice for preteen kids around the world. In 2014, Mojang was acquired for $2.5 billion by Microsoft, not bad for a company with forty-nine employees that never received venture capital funding.

Notch now lives in Beverly Hills in what the *Washington Post* called an "insane mansion," complete with a candy room, several vodka and tequila bars, and a car showroom. He paid $70 million, allegedly the highest price ever for a house in Beverly Hills, outbidding no less than Beyoncé and Jay Z in the process.

So what's the bigger story here? If you think about it, *Minecraft* is basically an online version of Lego. It is about giving kids the bricks, the tools, and then a giant sandbox in which to construct their own fantasy world. Which makes you wonder, why on earth didn't Lego create *Minecraft*? How did Lego allow Markus Persson to steal this entire market from under their noses?

The strategists at Lego were fully aware of the digital gaming market. They had experimented, years earlier, with digital versions of Lego on CD products, but these were slow and clunky and never took off. More recently, they created *Lego Universe*, a multiplayer online gaming environment that coincidentally became available around the same time that *Minecraft* was launched. *Lego Universe* was an impressive product. One early review said the following:

> Lego Universe is like the very big brother of Minecraft, it has up-to-standard graphics, it has in-game cinematics, it has a storyline, it has over 80,000 different bricks, it has mini-games with highscores, it has a storyline, it has adventure, it has races . . . you can quest with them to achieve better weapons/combat levels, achievements, and so much more.[1]

Despite all this, *Lego Universe* failed to resonate with its target audience. Kids flocked to *Minecraft*, and *Lego Universe* was retired in 2012.

Why did Lego get it wrong? Why did a firm with smart people, deep pockets, and a strong brand lose out to a computer nerd with a bright idea and a scruffy beard? Lego listens to its customers, even allows them to help it create its new products, but these are the super-sophisticated customers who want all the bells and whistles. Lego has a respected brand to defend, and therefore cannot afford to put shoddy products out on the market. The company has a clear view of what sort of business model should be used for online gaming products. Lego has divided its market into clear segments, and knows what each one wants. These are all admirable qualities. But put them together, and it is also obvious that hell would freeze over before a simplistic, cheap-looking product like *Minecraft* would get past the first gate in Lego's product development pipeline. This leaves the door open for start-ups such as Mojang to create a niche product at the low end of the market, and occasionally these products take off, leaving the established players like Lego scrambling to catch up.

In fact, Lego is a classic case of disruption, as made famous by Clayton Christensen in *The Innovator's Dilemma*.[2] Studying once-dominant firms that later fell from the pedestal, he argued that the main reason they failed to remain ahead of the curve was because they were *too good* at managing things—not too bad, not too disorganized or anarchical, but too good at managing things. Since management historically has primarily been concerned with becoming a little bit better at that which one is already pretty good at, these firms became victims of their own success.

In terms of our argument, Lego found themselves on the wrong side of the process of creative destruction that we sketched out in Chapters 1 and 2. Many perspectives have been offered for why established firms struggle to respond effectively. We can summarize them in terms of five Ps:

- *Power*: Those at the top of a hierarchy typically ended up there because they are experts at what was important yesterday. Their implicit priority is to protect their legacy, and that makes them cautious and conservative. Too many corner offices and boardrooms are inhabited by "counter-evolutionaries"—a movement in opposition of any movement.

- *Psychology*: Humans are programmed to avoid uncertainty. Business as usual may be tedious and it may offer diminishing returns, but it feels safer than branching off down an uncharted and potentially dangerous track. Innovation is indeed risky business. Most experiments fail. The problem is that in the world of business we generally hail success and punish failure.

- *Performance*: Success gives rise to rigidities. We are great learners, and the more positive feedback we receive around one course of action, the more we repeat it. We love success. Over time, exploitation of givens therefore crowds out creation of novelty. We continue down Repetition Avenue because we know it so well and excel at what it takes to win—until a disruptor forces us to realize that we were chasing down a dead end.

- *Promises*: Organizations get trapped in a web of commitments to suppliers, customers, employees, and other stakeholders. Think for example of GM and Ford's union and health care obligations. Even when they want to change direction, organizations often struggle to break such promises. For example, the Co-operative Bank in the United Kingdom shied away from modern governance procedures because of loyalty to its historical membership structure, and found itself close to bankruptcy.

- *Permanence*: Breaking up is hard to do. Just like in a marriage, even if the *raison d'etre* of the organization, a particular division or product line, no longer exists, we often shy away from making the right decision. A case in point is Berkshire Hathaway. When its eighty-six-year old CEO and biggest single shareholder, Warren Buffet, finally retires, his smartest move would be to break the company up—it isn't much more than a holding company anyway, and the chances of finding a new CEO with his golden touch seems slim. But chances are he will seek to keep it going—indeed, he has already started to put succession plans in place.[3]

While the new entrants usually beat the incumbents in periods of disruptive change, this is not an iron law. There are some well-known examples of established firms making the transition into new technologies (IBM moving from mainframes to PCs, Thomson moving from newspapers to digital information services, Roche moving from small-molecule to biologic drug development), and for many reasons these are the stories we want to focus on, because they provide insight into the strategy-making process that is required for competing in today's fast/forward world of accelerating change.

The aforementioned legendary investor Warren Buffet is reported to have said, "Only when the tide goes out do you discover who's been swimming naked." He was referring, we believe, to the world of investment, in which anyone can make a good return in a bull market, but when the market turns soft you figure out which investors actually know what they are doing.

This aphorism also applies to the world of strategy making. Every firm believes itself to be agile—capable of adapting to the ever-changing realities of its operating environment. But it's only when there is a real disruption or discontinuity that we figure out which ones are genuinely agile: Fuji survived the shift to digital imaging while Kodak did not; Goldman Sachs and JP Morgan navigated their way through the financial crisis unscathed, while Lehman, Bear Stearns, and UBS did not; Samsung coped with Apple's entry into the smartphone industry in 2007, while Nokia and Blackberry did not. These examples of similar-looking firms taking divergent paths help to shed light on what exactly the capabilities of agile are. It is possible to keep the swimming gear on.

You already know roughly where we come out on the question of what it takes to succeed. The combination of excessive analysis and deep introspection is a good way of getting it wrong. Decisive action and emotional conviction are important parts of the solution. But we can go a lot deeper here, and the purpose of this chapter is to provide a detailed and careful look at how firms develop and implement their strategies in these situations.

Fast/Forward Strategy: How Does It Work in Practice?

How do you define and implement your strategy? It is the oldest question out there, and many academics, consultants, and former captains of industry have offered their views. For example, a highly influential book by A. G. Lafley and Roger Martin, *Playing to Win*, boils it down to a five-step cascade of questions:[4]

What is our winning aspiration?

Where will we play?

How will we win in our chosen markets?

What capabilities must be in place for us to win?

What management systems are required?

You can see why this framework is attractive—it creates great clarity and order, and it helps people at different levels and different departments to figure out their roles. The cascade of questions mirrors the hierarchy of a large firm, and you can almost picture the Gantt chart, the detailed project plan, that flows from it. But you can also see where this framework falls short. It assumes a level of predictability about the markets you are competing in, and the capabilities you need, that often doesn't exist. It also assumes that the people at the top have greater foresight or insight into what is needed than those on the front line—a particularly perilous assumption in a world of increasing environmental complexity and individual ignorance.

So in a world shaped by the paradoxes of progress you need something else, and of course there have been many attempts over the years to frame strategy making in a less linear way—for example with a bottom-up process alongside the top-down one, or as a loop or a set of simple rules, as an emergent process, or even as a garbage can.[5] While these are all valid points of view, we draw inspiration here from an unusual setting, namely how the world of software development has been transformed over the last fifteen years.

Waterfall Development

One of us started his career in computer programming in the late 1980s, and the other is married to a woman who did the same. They both have vivid and not-too-pleasant memories of the experience, working in windowless rooms alongside dozens of other programmers, translating detailed specifications into computer code. Neither of them really knew what the system was for, and they had no idea how the code might subsequently be tested, combined with other modules, or ultimately used. Like Chaplin's Little Tramp in *Modern Times*, they were but two small cogs in really big machines. Both of them soon quit, so tedious was the work.

The 1980s and 1990s were the era when big integrated system

developers such as Accenture, IBM, and Infosys grew in leaps and bounds. They took on immensely complex systems from big commercial and public-sector clients. It was not unusual for a team to have several hundred people all working to a single project plan. These plans followed a "waterfall" logic, with a clear hierarchical flow of activities from the top-level design down to the low-level programming. The big developers competed with one another for rigor. An independent assessment tool, the Capability Maturity Model, emerged, providing bragging rights to those with the most painstakingly detailed methodologies.

But systems development was a hit-and-miss affair, and many large projects failed. For example, the U.K.'s *Independent* newspaper ran a story in 2010 called "Botched Projects: The Cost of IT Failure," listing among others the £9.9 billion write-off of the National Programme for IT for the NHS and the partial failure of the £7.1 billion Defense Information Infrastructure and £5 billion national identity scheme.[6]

By then it had become obvious that the integrated systems development model had some deep structural flaws. One was that the entire set of deliverables was locked down at the start, which works only if (a) the client knows exactly what its needs are, (b) those needs don't change during the development period, and (c) there is no major technology breakthrough along the way. A second problem was the complexity of the system being created—everything was dependent on everything else, so an error in one place had horrible domino effects on other parts of the system. The integrated approach was also disempowering and tedious for those doing the work. This, of course, resulted in high turnover and low engagement, thereby increasing the likelihood of mistakes being made.

The Agile Revolution

But help was on its way. Through the 1990s, software developers had been experimenting with new ways of coding that turned the waterfall model on its head. They had the revolutionary idea of working directly with the user, the actual person who would be interacting with the IT system, and building a series of rough prototypes, iterating fairly quickly, until they had a product that worked. They would then work back, linking together the user-oriented modules and building the underlying functionality to create a complete working system. These innovators came together at a conference in Utah in 2001 and launched the *Agile Manifesto* to help legitimize this new way of working (the full text is reproduced below).

> *The Agile Manifesto*
>
> We are uncovering better ways of developing software by doing it and helping others do it. Through this work we have come to value:
>
> Individuals and interactions over processes and tools
>
> Working software over comprehensive documentation
>
> Customer collaboration over contract negotiation
>
> Responding to change over following a plan
>
> That is, while there is value in the items on the right, we value the items on the left more.
>
> www.agilemanifesto.org

This agile approach to systems development has its own language (for example Scrum and Extreme Programming), and its proponents are as passionate about its merits as the waterfall advocates before them. Of course, agile development has its own challenges as well—it is harder for those in charge to keep on top of things, the documentation tends to be less rigorous, quality assurance is harder to conduct—but our sense is that it has now become the preferred model for large parts of the business world.

So, over the last fifteen years, that is what has been happening in the world of software development. For us, it is a clear analogue to the broader shift in how strategy is developed and implemented in fast/forward firms, from a top-down plan to a bottom-up, iterative, trial-and-error and user-led process. Indeed, there are many other bodies of thought today that echo this new approach—Rita McGrath and Ian McMillan's Discovery-driven planning, the Design Thinking methodologies of Roger Martin and Tim Brown, the Lean Start Up approach to entrepreneurship advocated by Eric Ries and Steve Blank.[7] But the reason we start with agile software development, rather than any of these other frameworks, is simple: it really works. The world of software has been transformed, while the world of strategy making is still largely stuck with a waterfall or cascade mind-set, notwithstanding all the good advice from the world of academia.

In the rest of this chapter, we spell out what a fast/forward approach to strategy making looks like. As you would expect, it involves a greater emphasis on action than on planning and reflecting, and it also requires a greater emphasis on emotional conviction—on acting on intuition, rather than purely rational analysis, and on ensuring employee engagement. Our mind-sets need to be rebooted. We should stop thinking about strategy as a mainly intellectual activity aimed at creating a unique position in an unknown future. Instead, fast/forward strategy making is about doing things—a hands-on, real-time process of enlightened trial and error in which experimentation and engagement reinforce one another and build momentum.

You probably also expect our approach to put more weight on the views of front-line managers than top executives, as they are closer to the action. This is partly true, but as you will see there is still a vital role for managers at all levels. In our experience, the disconnect—the gap that needs filling—is not so much between those at the top and those on the front line; it is between those who prioritize process and reflection and those who prioritize action and emotion.

Priorities and Pitfalls When Riding the S-Curve

Consider the classic S-curve. You run a business in a mature market—a fancier term for a tired industry—and you are enjoying solid profits. Yet there are clouds on the horizon in the form of emerging technologies, changing consumer needs, or new regulations. You have read the stories about Kodak, Nokia, and Blockbuster, and you wonder if the same fate could befall your business. Is there a new S-curve starting that will undermine your market position? How do you figure out what it looks like? And when do you make the transition? Make no mistake; these issues are what strategic leadership is all about. Anyone can lead a firm that is fine-tuning its position on a well-established path. And turning around a crisis-ridden company isn't that challenging from a strategic perspective—there is a clear playbook for the steps you need to take. It is this territory in the middle, where you and your team have to make sense of and respond to an ambiguous set of stimuli, where you justify your salary—and you find out if you are swimming naked.[8]

To provide structure to your analysis, we have divided the job that needs to get done into three stages: sensing, responding, and scaling. This is of course a simplification, because there is some back-and-forth between them in practice. But as a first approximation it works well. Figure 4.1 illustrates these three stages.

Sensing

In every large firm we can think of, there is a team or a department (sometimes several) tasked with looking into the future, picking up trends, and monitoring what is happening in progressive places like Silicon Valley, Curitiba, Hong Kong, or Stockholm. They have names like foresight team or scouting unit, and they use techniques such as trend analysis, scenario planning, and three-horizon planning. These activities yield lots of useful insights about how the business world could change, but many people seem to think that this horizon-raising activity is valuable as an activity in its own right. Let's be absolutely clear on this—it isn't. Such stargazing is only valuable when it leads to action. All too often, the process takes on a life of its own, and visioning ends up as a substitute for acting, or just simply a list of "wish-ons."

Are we being unfair here? Well, consider some of the high-profile failures of recent years, from Blockbuster to Nokia and Kodak. We have read the detailed accounts, and we have talked to people at these

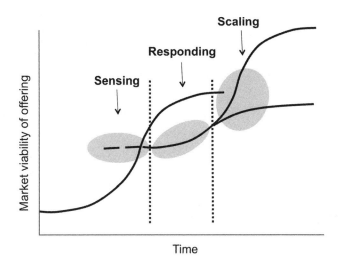

FIGURE 4.1 Three Steps in Managing Disruption

firms. In every case, there was no lack of awareness of the fundamental technological and behavioral shifts under way in their markets.
Nokia, for example, had teams working on touch-screen phones, app
stores, and clamshell designs many years before these offerings took
off. We would go so far as to say that *when established firms fumble the future, they never do so through lack of awareness.* Instead, they do so because
they fail to act on the signals they receive. Or to be more accurate,
they fail to pick up on the important signal among all the noise, or
just go into denial. For all the reasons discussed earlier in this chapter,
Nokia's top executives didn't see the touch-screen as a priority, even
though the engineers who had developed it were calling on them to
commercialize it.

So what does sensing look like when it is done well? Following are
three very different examples.

First, consider Netflix, which offers an example of a single-minded
vision. How did a company that made a living sending DVDs through
the mail as recently as 2006 become the dominant force in video
streaming, ahead of players such as Amazon, Apple, and Google? Arguably, it was the single-minded vision of CEO Reed Hastings, who

saw the future of the movie industry long before the technology existed to make it possible. In a 2003 interview, he said, "Our hope is that we'll eventually be able to download movies. It's why we named the business Netflix and not DVD-by-mail." And much later, during a difficult period in Netflix's recent history, he said, "My greatest fear has been that we wouldn't make the leap from success in DVDs to success in streaming."[9] Sensing, in Reed Hastings' world, isn't about making sense of an uncertain future; it is about shaping the immediate ecosystem to fit his vision.

Thomson Reuters provides an example of rapid sense-making. On September 15, 2008, Lehman Brothers collapsed. Three days later, David Craig, head of strategy at information services provider Thomson Reuters, was scheduled to speak at a board meeting. "We were supposed to be reviewing the group strategy, but we put those discussions to one side and instead we brainstormed what the consequences of Lehman would be," he recalled. And the view was clear: "there would be more regulation, if not overregulation, of financial markets, and aggressive enforcement."[10] And this quickly led to an important conclusion: "Thomson Reuters needs to become the leader in this new space," said one executive. David Craig took the challenge on. Three months later, he came back with a proposal for a new business titled Governance Risk and Compliance (GRC), and it was officially created later in 2009. By the standards of any large firm this was a rapid process, and it gave Thomson Reuters a head start in this booming space, as we will outline further on.

Our third example, finding the signal in the noise, is far messier than the Netflix and Thomson Reuters cases. The *Guardian* newspaper was an early mover into online news. Its technology section had moved online already in 1995, and a full-fledged "*Guardian* Unlimited" offering was in place by 1999. The *Guardian* was the first U.K. newspaper to allow user comments, and it was early in building out its user communities. By 2001 it was the most popular U.K. newspaper website, with a rapidly growing international presence as "the world's leading liberal voice." What was the clever sensing process the *Guard-*

ian used? There wasn't one. But we know, from working with the management team during this period, that they spent a lot of time making sense of the emerging online world—bringing in dotcom entrepreneurs, trialing new offerings, and debating the future of newspapers. A clear vision of the future (it is owned by a trust, which safeguards the newspaper's editorial independence) certainly guided them in the sensing process, and they were thoughtful about making their discussions cross-functional (especially in bringing techies into the debate early on) and multilevel (not just the executive team). But ultimately it was a messy process, out of which emerged a stream of initiatives that helped the *Guardian* to get ahead of the curve as the transition to digital took place.

These three cases represent very different approaches to sensing, and that is perhaps the key point. The specific technique you use is less important than the overarching principle that sensing should be action-oriented. It should also embrace intuitive and emotional reasoning alongside rational analysis. Four specific points are critical to bear in mind.

Seek out dissonant information. We have run many scenario-planning workshops over the years, and a common outcome is for people to latch onto the scenario that confirms their prior assumptions (recall the discussion in Chapter 2 about the myth of reasoned judgment). The trick here is to do the opposite of what comes naturally: it is to embrace those "dissonant" data points that your subconscious is asking you to filter out. For fast/forward companies abnormal is the new normal. A quick example: a team from Roche, the Swiss pharmaceutical company, opened up a competition to graduate students from all over the world, asking for their views about future medical breakthroughs. By examining more than a hundred proposals, they got a very different picture about emerging areas—from health apps to 3D printing—that were not being prioritized in the firm.

Enliven the debate. Countless studies have picked up on the importance of diverse and often conflicting points of view as inputs into effective decision-making processes. Some firms even have words for this—"constructive confrontation" at Intel, "obligation to dissent" at McKinsey. ASSA ABLOY, the world leader in door-opening solutions, used a big chunk of one of their annual management meetings to bring in teams of young people from their trainee program. The much older and more homogeneous group of top executives invited them with the sole purpose of actively questioning the strategic choices made.

To avoid getting stuck in an existing network of relationships, learn from the Internet dating world. Here, two of the most interesting current acronyms are MBA and MBL—Married But Available and Married But Looking! The analogy to the business world should be clear—true champions of disruption take great care of those they are "married" to but also build an informal network of somewhat more promiscuous relationships—the lovers and mistresses that will guarantee a good life in times to come.

Our additional observation is: go beyond the facts. Fast/forward companies put a premium on emotion. Intuition and gut feeling play vital roles, and we shouldn't be afraid of creative or contrarian inputs to the debate. One senior manager that we worked with kept a special file of letters and e-mails labeled "From angry old ladies." Perhaps not politically correct, but in an industry quite obsessed with every whim of young people, to him this was one of the most valuable inputs as a reality check in the product-development process.

Be more opportunity-focused. Most of all, the sensing process needs to avoid being too process driven or too academically sophisticated. Don't look ten years out (there are a few industries for which this may be appropriate, but they are rare). Instead, focus down on the emerging opportunities that you can tackle in the short to medium term. Fast/forward firms know that business happens in real time. In the Thomson Reuters story, David Craig left the board meeting in September 2008 with more than just a bunch of useful ideas—he got a clear and specific mandate to develop a new business case. The output from a future-oriented brainstorming session should typically be a set of actionable hypotheses, not just a better understanding of the future. We often get teams to run management experiments, low-risk probes to test these hypotheses, and this approach provides enough data within a six-month period to push everyone's understanding forward.

Expose your customers' unarticulated needs. A useful complement to foresight is called insight. This requires hands-on sensing. Try walking in the shoes of your customers. If you're running a pitched roof tiling solutions company like French industry giant Monier, spend more time on a roof with installers and roofers, under different weather conditions, or talk to architects, monitor what's happening on the social network platforms that you've provided. Fast/forward capabilities rely not only on real-time processes, but also on getting real.

Consider the automotive industry. Most people buy station wagons because they load a lot of stuff. Many of us have probably been standing behind our station wagon after having done our weekly grocery shopping with two bags in each hand. Before you can start loading the car, you face two challenges; unlock the trunk and open it. To do so you must first put down the bags. Annoying. By observing customer behavior in parking lots, BMW developed insight and a great solution to this problem. As you approach the car, your key automatically opens the trunk. By waving one of your feet underneath the bumper, by magic the trunk opens. There is no longer any need for putting the bags down.

Here's the eye opener: if you want to figure out what customers *could* be doing, a good starting point is to take a really good look at what they are *currently* doing. It is hard work, often involving many weeks of painstaking observation, but it can lead to some really neat insights.

Responding

The stock response when faced with the threat of a new, potentially disruptive technology is to dabble: to set up a small team, often in a research lab or skunk-works, and give them a modest budget to see what they can make of it. This was Kodak's response to digital imaging. By 1989, it had created more than fifty products that involved electronic image capture or conversion, including a scanner, a digital printer, an image enhancer, and an HDTV projection system.[11] Nokia's dabbling took a different form, namely a range of minority investments and start-ups in the so-called "Nokia Ventures Organization." We have even seen this approach in our own backyard. The business education industry is trying to make sense of how important e-learning might be in the future, so London Business School, like many others, has made a tentative foray into online content with three MOOCs (Massive On-line Open-Enrollment Courses).

Don't misunderstand us; this type of dabbling isn't necessarily wrong, and indeed sometimes it is exactly what is needed. But we use the term *dabbling* advisedly, because it reminds us that the people who really call the shots rarely take these activities seriously. They are a nice-to-have, a sop to the contrarians who think the current business model is on its way out. And of course this becomes a big problem if these new technologies start to take off, because their backers lack the political clout and high-level connections to move into the main-stream. The new business incubator becomes an organizational or-phanage for the unwanted and abandoned, and the promising new technologies get forgotten. If you assign responsibility for your big legacy businesses to the Sumo wrestlers of your organization while the emerging businesses are left to the featherweights, don't be surprised that the end result is destruction without creation. As we noted in the first chapter, software company Oracle does this right, by putting their *best people* on the new technologies—that sends a clear message about where the priorities lie.

So what's the right way forward here? How can you make your response more effective? Consider the seemingly lackluster case of the U.K.'s Government Digital Service. It is an unusual and interesting story, and it merits an extended discussion.[12]

The public sector is the last place you would expect to see innova-tive thinking, and yet the U.K.'s Government Digital Service (GDS) over the last five years has transformed the way U.K. citizens access government services. It has achieved savings of £1.7 billion, and its website, www.gov.uk, won a prestigious design award, beating compe-tition from the Shard skyscraper and the Olympic Cauldron. And ac-claim has come from outside the United Kingdom as well. Following the troubled launch of President Obama's healthcare.gov system, the *Washington Post* claimed, "Since its launch in 2010, GDS has emerged as the gold-standard in the global world of digital government."

The U.K. public sector had been experimenting with a succession of digital programs throughout the 1990s and early 2000s, offering things such as tax returns, passport renewals, and small business services on-line. The result had been a mixed success, and every government department was doing things their own way. In 2010, a hard-hitting report from Martha Lane Fox, dotcom entrepreneur and U.K. digital champion, said the United Kingdom had fallen behind in the provision of digital services and called for "revolution not evolution." Cabinet secretary Francis Maude, a member of Prime Minister David Cameron's inner circle, gave the initiative his blessing and hired Mike Bracken, former head of digital at the *Guardian* newspaper to run the new GDS unit.

But how do you achieve radical change across a sprawling and often conservative civil service with half a million employees? "I told Francis Maude I needed three things—a separate building, a team with the right specialist skills, and control over the Internet domain, www.gov.uk." And with these in the bag, Bracken's team set about getting things done, starting with simple projects such as online e-petitions and tax discs for drivers, and working up from there. "Rather than go in and try to win hearts and minds, we just thought the best result is when you do stuff people like," explained Bracken. The team developed a set of principles based on the agile movement: start with needs—user needs not government needs; iterate, then iterate again; make things open. Small groups were sent out to work with different departments, identifying the key services that could go online quickly, and working with them to deliver rapid prototypes.

Behind the scenes, Bracken followed up with some smart political tactics: he built a network of digital leaders across the various departments, and he ensured the necessary budget authority was in place, getting Francis Maude to provide high-level support when resistance was encountered. "But the biggest influencer was the ability to demonstrate the GDS team could quickly develop and launch high-quality digital content. Show, don't tell was our motto."

At the time of writing, all government departments had moved onto the www.gov.uk website, all major transactions (for example, driving license renewal, tax self-assessment) had gone online, and the important final stage of opening up to third-party app developers had begun. In 2016, the GDS budget was £112 million per year, twice what it had been the previous year. The goal of making U.K. government services "digital by default" was on track.[13]

What is the lesson here? Mike Bracken's approach was *the strategy is delivery*. Ponder these four words, because in many ways they sum up our entire argument. He knew he would never succeed by writing white papers and creating steering committees. The only way to make progress was to reverse the usual sequence, by acting first and strategizing later. As his policy director, David Thorpe, observed, "There are 17,000 professionals in Whitehall with policy in their title: they have seen an important part of their job as writing the requirements someone else has to implement. This creates an implementation gap. GDS, with its user-led approach and multi-disciplinary teams can help close the gap." For example, one initiative Mike Bracken pushed was called G-Cloud, "a whole new way of buying digital," which put small and medium-sized businesses on an equal footing with big IT vendors when bidding for government work.

As a staunch advocate of agile software development, it is not surprising that Mike Bracken adopted this act-first approach to strategy making. Indeed, the language used by these IT pioneers has started to take off in boardrooms. In talking to executives at tech firms such as Google, Facebook, and Amazon, and also firms in other sectors such as Lloyds Bank or Lego, we hear terms such as *rapid prototyping* and *beta testing* applied to decision making broadly—not just on IT matters. ING, the Dutch bank, as we saw in Chapter 1, has recently introduced an *agile way of working* across its head office operations. General Mills, the U.S. cereals and snacks business, recently tried a program called Launch to Learn, which was a fast-track way of bringing a product to market on a trial basis.

And sometimes you don't even need the agile language to get to the same conclusion that decisiveness and speed are important. Recall the story of David Craig, the head of strategy at Thomson Reuters, who put together the case for the GRC business during 2009. While the firm already had many services in this area, he argued that they needed to create a comprehensive offering and to move quickly. He proposed an acquisition-driven business (to fill in the gaps in their portfolio of offerings), CEO sponsored (to overcome the resistance from existing lines of business), and with "no rules" (to avoid getting caught up in bureaucracy). He was given the green light in late 2009, and by 2011 the business was a profitable, twelve-hundred-person operation.

In sum, there is an overarching principle at work here, suggesting that in an unpredictable and fast/forward kind of world, it is usually smarter to act quickly and get feedback from the market than to put together a detailed plan. Action, with a side serving of intuition, is a better bet than sophisticated thinking or clever policymaking with a desert of authority. Here are three specific points to bear in mind:

The strategy is delivery. Find out who will use or buy your product or service, and build your prototype around them. This doesn't mean you always have to listen to what they say—sometimes they have entirely unarticulated needs that they don't understand themselves. But the process of testing out your idea, seeking feedback, and going through multiple iterations is a much more promising way of clarifying what you stand for than any amount of desk-based research.

Speed is your strongest ally. An action-oriented approach to strategy making is fast, and this has two enormous benefits. One, of course, is that it helps you get to market ahead of your competitors. The other is that it neutralizes your detractors. At GDS, Mike Bracken's team had often developed a working alpha prototype before the relevant government minister could offer a view. For David Craig at Thomson Reuters, the mandate he had been given to act quickly allowed him to overcome many of the obstacles thrown in his way.

Keep it connected. There is one big risk with the action-oriented approach we describe here, and it is the risk of isolation. We have seen many cases of skunk-works teams doing groundbreaking work on their own, but by failing to create the connective tissue with the rest of the firm their innovations were not implemented. These types of initiatives need high-level support, for example, David Craig's "CEO-sponsored" business unit and Mike Bracken's backing from Cabinet Secretary Francis Maude. And it's also smart to build allies in other business units, especially those you have to work with in the future. Again, Mike Bracken was very conscious of this, with his network of digital leaders across all the major government departments.

A practical tool to help you out is relationship mapping. Take some time out of your busy schedule and make a literal map (as an individual or a team) of your current relationships. Let the size of circles imply the importance of that person or team, and the thickness of the line how strong the relationship is. Then, create another map of the relationships you need in order to secure the resources and support required to move forward faster. Identify the gaps, prioritize, and start filling them.

Scaling

The third step in riding the S-curve is to scale up: to take your embryonic product or technology and let it loose on a grand scale. This may sound straightforward, but in our experience, it is actually here that most companies fail. Once again, look at some of the high-profile failures of recent years. Blockbuster trialed several ventures, including mail order and streaming, during the 2000s, but never made the big commitment away from its retail-based business model. The major music labels (Universal, Sony, Warner) made a half-hearted attempt to sell their music online before the launch of iTunes in 2003 took the digital retail market away from them. Apple, in turn, was slow in responding to the streaming-based solution of Spotify. When we discuss these steps with executive teams, they typically agree with this diagnosis. One senior executive at a large consumer products firm said, "We are very good at trying out new business ideas, and once we commit there is a lot of corporate support; but there is a gap there—we struggle to scale."

Why do firms struggle here? In many ways this is an old problem, captured in the title of Clay Christensen's book *The Innovator's Dilemma* that we mentioned earlier. Business A is in gradual decline, business B is growing at the expense of business A, but at an uncertain pace. At what point do you deliberately cannibalize business A with business B? It is easy to argue that you need to act now, but there are good reasons why this doesn't happen. The following quote from Rebecca Henderson at Harvard Business School[14] captures the tension nicely:

> I see. You're suggesting that we invest millions of dollars in a market that may or may not exist but that is certainly smaller than our existing market, to develop a product that customers may or may not want, using a business model that will almost certainly give us lower margins than our existing product lines. You're warning us that we'll run into serious organizational problems as we make this investment, and our current business is screaming for resources. Tell me again just why we should make this investment?

The key point is that Business B's growth is uncertain. It may look like a classic case of a disruptive threat, coming up from below, but that doesn't necessarily mean it will fully cannibalize Business A. Here is a case in point: a senior executive from Intercontinental Hotel Group (IHG), the largest chain in the world by number of beds, was speaking to one of our MBA classes. Inevitably, the discussion turned to AirBnB, the San Francisco–based room-lending service. Several of the students were convinced that IHG would be wiped out, Kodak-style, as AirBnB gradually overran its market. The executive's view—and one we share as well—is that AirBnB will have a big impact on its low-end segment, but very little impact on some of its high-end segments, such as conferences and big corporate accounts. There are many cases in which Business B ends up growing alongside Business A—as a complement not a substitute. And the uncertainty about how things will pan out in each individual case is enough to make the aggressive cannibalization decision very hard.

So how to get scaling right? Following are three possible approaches.

One option is making an aggressive scaling move. Recall from earlier that Reed Hastings had always seen Netflix as a streaming company; it was just a question of timing. Several companies, including Apple and Blockbuster, had experimented with video on demand from 2000 on, but were scuppered by a combination of poor-quality technology (especially slow download speeds) and protectionism by the movie studios. By 2007, the technology was sufficiently robust for video on demand to work, and illegal sites, from Pirate Bay to MegaUpload, sufficiently powerful that the movie studios realized they needed to get involved.

Netflix launched its streaming service that year, taking its philosophy of unlimited access, an extensive body of content, and high-quality user experience online. In 2010 it launched its first major piece of original content, the impressive *House of Cards* with Kevin Spacey and Robin Wright. Rather than drip-feeding it with one episode a week, like a regular TV network, the entire series was made available at once.

In July 2011, with the company riding high, Hastings made the fateful decision to separate out the old DVD-by-mail business (renamed Qwikster) from its online service, and charge a 60 percent premium for anyone who wanted to use both together. It was a big mistake. Netflix lost 805,000 subscribers over the next three months, and the share price dropped a whopping 50 percent. Hastings backtracked, reversing the decision and posting a *mea culpa* on the website ("members felt we lacked respect and humility. . . . I offer my sincere apology"[15]). The change of track worked, and Netflix resumed its scaling strategy, moving quickly into international markets, creating more exclusive content, and building out its movie library. At the time of writing, Netflix was the clear industry leader, with sixty-one million subscribers around the world.

Netflix is an unusual case, but it is not unique. There are now reasonable numbers of large firms that have successfully bridged the analogue-digital gap in their industry. Examples include Amazon leading the development of electronic books with the Kindle, Reed Elsevier making the transition from paper-based publishing to digital information services, and U.K. magazine *Autotrader* becoming the leading online site for second-hand car sales.

For an example of a more systematic approach to scaling, consider IBM. In the late 1990s, IBM was pushing for growth but found itself frequently missing out on emerging new markets, even though it often had the necessary technologies in place to be successful in those areas. To counter this problem, it set up a program called "Emerging Business Opportunities" (EBO). Essentially, this was a small team of very experienced executives reporting directly to the CEO, whose job was to provide expertise and oversight to help scale promising new business opportunities. These nascent businesses were operated through the line organization (so they could benefit from sharing key resources and customers with adjacent businesses), but they also reported to the EBO team to give them the visibility and careful attention they needed to grow. In 2000, there were seven EBOs, in such areas as life sciences, pervasive computing, digital media, and e-Markets, and between 2000 and 2005 they added $15.2 billion to IBM's top line.

The EBO program worked, in our view, because it took scaling seriously. It focused on the big opportunities that were "changing the dynamics in the marketplace," according to its head, Bruce Harreld. There was senior sponsorship—both from the relevant business unit and from the EBO team. The businesses were run by "very experienced people who [had] built big businesses" in the past. And great care was taken over *when* these growing businesses should "graduate" from the EBO structure and operate as stand-alone business units.[16]

Finally, there is judging when to integrate. Recall the initiative to develop Thomson Reuters' GRC. For the first four years it was run as an autonomous unit, with a separate physical location and its own salesforce, to give it the visibility and distinctiveness it needed to survive. But in 2013, David Craig, who was now responsible for the entire Finance & Risk division in Thomson Reuters, decided the timing was right to fold it back into the global operations. In his words, "To really scale our risk management offerings, we needed to move beyond the 2,000 customer relationships in the GRC unit and to access the 40,000 institutional relationships held by Thomson Reuters as a whole." As part of this change, GRC simply became the "risk" business, and by 2016 it had grown to more than $700 million in sales revenues—impressive growth for a business that had not existed five years earlier.

These different approaches underline how difficult it is to get the scaling decision right. We can draw out three broad lessons here.

Match the activity to the disruption. Most of the well-known stories, such as those described earlier, were firms that failed to make the necessary commitment until too late. But there are other cases when firms have moved too aggressively. Apple's Newton was ahead of its time. Motorola's satellite service, Iridium, was a disaster. Petrofac, the U.K.-based oil services firm, placed a big bet on "Integrated Energy Services" five years ago and has had to backtrack to avoid upsetting its big oil and gas customers. The point is, you can get it wrong in both directions. Being just-too-late or way-too-early is more common than being just in time, in life and in business. As we noted earlier, London Business School is dabbling in e-learning offerings, while some other business schools are aggressively pushing this new way of providing business education. Only time will tell which is the right model.

Also keep in mind that issues of timing vary across geography. This of course, potentially gives international firms a huge advantage as they can sequence the launch in line with the acceptance level of local markets—bet on the favorites rather than a random horse, so to speak. Toyota, for instance, first launched its upscale car Lexus in the United States in 1989. Only sixteen years later, when Lexus had become a status symbol in North America, did the firm introduce the brand on its home market, where wealthy consumers in the high-end segment traditionally favored German automobiles. "This has been a dream of ours for years," said Toyota's president Katsuaki Watanabe at the launch.[17] "The premium European brands have more than a hundred years of history behind them. Our history is much shorter," commented Takeshi Yoshida, managing officer of Lexus product development. Rather than launching prematurely, Toyota waited, not passively but with a focus on first building the reputation of a luxury brand where they had a stronger position and a greater chance of succeeding.

Act on your hunch. The key point here is that the data will never give you the answer: no amount of analysis will give you definitive evidence on how big a threat or opportunity this emerging market, technology, or trend represents. So this is when intuition becomes really important, and when courage pays dividends. Look back at the Netflix case, and the 2011 Qwikster fiasco. Observers have castigated Reed Hastings for that decision, but we view it differently—it was a bold move, in retrospect too aggressive, but one that the firm was able to recover from quite quickly. And it was a move highly consistent with Netflix's entire way of operating.

As a side note, it is interesting that most of the successful cases of aggressive scaling are from companies with extremely powerful CEOs (Reed Hastings, Jeff Bezos, Steve Jobs). This is no coincidence, we believe. The scaling discussion is always contentious for reasons we have discussed, so if the *modus operandi* in your boardroom is polite and consensus-oriented, you will likely take the risk-averse route and end up stuck in the innovators' dilemma. Sometimes you need a "benevolent dictator" to make things happen, a point we will return to later in the book.

Fast second isn't a bad outcome. Our colleague Costas Markides wrote a book called *Fast Second* a few years ago,[18] arguing that the smart strategy for established firms is to wait for others to create the new market and then to move quickly when the right way forward becomes clear. Sometimes this involves acquiring one of these new players— for example, Microsoft buying Mojang and Yammer, Unilever buying Ben & Jerry's, Roche buying Genentech. In other cases it means putting a lot of resources into playing catch-up—for example, Microsoft building X-Box to counter Sony's lead in the console market. Costas isn't wrong—often this works out well. But we view it as a second-best solution, perhaps even a backup plan, as it can be expensive, and sometimes the first-mover advantage ends up being unassailable (as Netflix's appears to be in video streaming).

The Fast/Forward Approach to Strategy

In this chapter we have described a fast/forward view of strategy that privileges decisive action—when doing something is more important than thinking about it or seeking approval from above. But we also recognize the need for balance. Action has to be balanced by reflection, and action has to be directed toward the most potentially worthwhile opportunities. The classic "cascade" logic, in which all action follows from the grand master plan, is inherently flawed, but the idea of encouraging everyone to act on their intuition is equally dangerous. Some sort of middle ground between these two extremes is where we need to end up.

Figure 4.2 is a simple graphic summary of the strategy-making process as we see it. The foundation stone is the overall purpose of the organization, and we will have a lot more to say about that in the next chapter. On the basis of that underlying purpose, a leadership team will identify a set of strategic priorities (where to play and how to play) and typically a set of financial targets. These define the overall scope of activity, but they should also leave some room for those closer to the front line to figure out exactly what they should be doing. The fast/forward strategy-making process is then a set of linked activities:

- *Experimenting*—working with customers and potential customers, trying out new ideas with them, seeking to make a connection, building simple prototypes.

- *Insight-gathering*—carefully collecting data from your experiments, for example seeing how customers and competitors react, so you can establish what works and what doesn't. Sometimes this is a heavy-duty analytical exercise, making use of the latest advances in big data methods; sometimes it is more qualitative and intuitive, depending on what sort of emotional connection you make with your customers.

- *Sense-making*—figuring out how your new insights about what is possible link back to your existing priorities. Does it make sense to pursue this possibility, or are there other opportunities that are actually a better fit or offer a higher level of profitability?

- *Revising*—Periodically, you need to think again about your overall

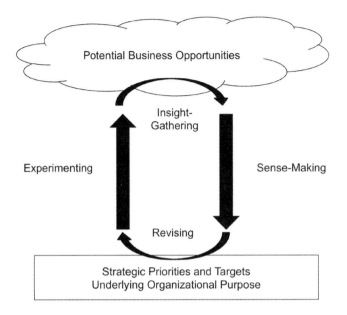

FIGURE 4.2 Strategy Making in Action

strategy, and whether it still provides the right set of stimuli for guiding action. You don't want to be changing your direction too often; otherwise people get confused. Equally, you shouldn't think of your strategy as being cast in concrete.

These four elements together form a loop, and the speed with which you move around this loop is obviously going to be linked to the dynamics of your marketplace. Many technology-based companies iterate their strategies on a monthly or even weekly basis, because of the pace of technological change. The U.K.'s Government Digital Services unit also went through the loop on a monthly basis because of the changes it was seeking to make in the various governmental departments it was working for. In many larger firms, or firms operating in slower-moving industries, the frequency of iterations can be much lower.

Chapter 5

LINKING STRATEGY BACK TO PURPOSE

MONTY PYTHON'S MOVIE *The Meaning of Life* was released in March 1983. The original tagline read, "It took God six days to create the Heavens and the Earth, and Monty Python just 90 minutes to screw it up." The movie sought to provide irreverent and humorous answers to the ancient questions of why we are here, what life is all about, and what the purpose of existence is. These are difficult questions to be sure, but they are worth grappling with because in answering them we gain a sense of direction, which helps us to make difficult choices and trade-offs.

These questions are equally important in the world of business. So take a moment to ask yourself: What is the meaning of business life? Why is your firm here? How would the business world be different if it did not exist?

In this chapter we make the link from strategy back to purpose.[1] Remember our core argument: that fast/forward firms link decisive action with emotional conviction. In the prior chapter, we talked a lot about action, from small-scale experiments through to bet-the-farm decisions. Now, we shift the emphasis to emotional conviction, and specifically to the things you can do to cultivate an organizational environment in which people feel inspired to serve a particular cause.

Overcoming Attention Deficit Disorder

We have argued that strategy making in an unpredictable world by necessity involves putting a lot more emphasis on action—experimentation and trial and error. This tends to start with a real opportunity to create value in the marketplace, rather than a comprehensive plan hatched in a windowless room at headquarters. But action alone is not enough. When you are playing a game of strategy that is focused on options for moving fast/forward, rather than one in which the aim is merely not to fall behind, you need a light that guides the search. And trust us, that light is never provided by the closest lamppost.

Most of the companies we admire have routines for "exploiting" existing strengths—the stuff that increases efficiency and boosts that extra dime of profits. What fast/forward firms are looking for, in addition to that, are the right principles for "exploration"—for guiding the creation of novelty. Action and purpose are complementary—yin and yang—and feed off each other. As the saying goes, Vision without action is a daydream. Action without vision is a nightmare.

The term *innovation routines* may sound like a contradiction in terms—sort of like Microsoft Works or sweet sorrow. Yet there is strong evidence suggesting that the most imaginative firms in the world are far from anarchical.[2] Instead, their success is usually derived from having a clear purpose that channels creativity and energizes employees. But delivering on this promise of peak performance is often easier said than done. In reality, managers who act purposefully, rather than disparately, are few and far between.

Our former colleagues Sumantra Ghoshal and Heike Bruch conducted a detailed study of how managers spent their time, and they estimated that 40 percent were "frenzied"—they had high levels of energy but no focus, and spent most of their time fighting fires, abandoning projects, shooting first and aiming later.[3] These were well-intentioned and motivated individuals, and yet the bulk of their time was spent on unproductive activities.

Why does this sort of activity occur in firms? In part, it is down to the problems identified earlier, namely that we are easily distracted by what we might call negative stimuli—e-mails, Facebook updates, and tweets that take us away from what we are supposed to be doing. The end result is a form of Managerial Attention Deficit Disorder. But alongside the 40 percent of workers who were frenzied, Ghoshal and Bruch also found 10 percent engaging in "purposeful action" with high energy and high focus. These extraordinary individuals weren't just good at ignoring distractions, they also received what we might think of as positive stimuli—clear messages from those above and around them about what they should be focusing on and why. Their organizations, in other words, had articulated a clear sense of purpose, and this more than anything else was what ensured that their action was both focused and energetic. A strong belief can indeed inspire ordinary people to do extraordinary things.

"There's a great future in plastics." Perhaps you remember this famous line from the 1967 movie *The Graduate*. A company that certainly has taken that idea to its heart is Tupperware Brands. Somewhat surprisingly perhaps, this is a great example of a firm with a clear sense of purpose. The company and its products need little introduction: they have been a staple of American consumerism since the World War II, and today Tupperware has revenues of some $2.3 billion across almost a hundred countries. Tupperware uses direct selling—like Avon, Mary Kay, Oriflame, and a host of other companies—typically through home parties, product catalogs, or on a one-to-one basis—and has almost three million people around the world involved in this process. Over the years, Tupperware has broadened its offerings from Earl Tupper's original plastic containers to a wide range of kitchen items, as well as beauty and personal care products.

Central to Tupperware's success is a focus on the identity and values of its predominantly female salesforce. As CEO Rick Goings says, "We invest a lot of effort in understanding what makes women tick. They are looking for conversations they can be part of; they love to talk; they want to be included in conversations that take place in a community. Then there's this overwhelming urge to give back. They want to feel fulfillment, and they want to be respected."[4] In turn, these insights drive the Tupperware vision—an "unwavering commitment to enlighten, educate and empower women and their families"—which then shapes the way the firm is run.

Tupperware has several distinctive features in terms of how it is organized. One is the blurred boundary between salespeople and customers. Like Apple or Harley Davidson, Tupperware believes its best customers are also its best advocates. But it goes further, by encouraging its customers to actually become salesforce members. The governance model, in other words, is deliberately inclusive of all the people who buy into the Tupperware vision.

Another important feature is that activities are coordinated around a shared set of values. The company has a clear business model—what Rick Goings calls the formula for success—that does not vary: unique and high-quality products, the direct-selling method, a career path for salespeople. It also has explicit values—empowerment, integrity, responsibility, innovation, collaboration, and celebration. But as long as they stay true to these elements, salespeople are encouraged to make their own choices. "One thing we talk about all the time is mind-set," observes Rick Goings, "having a mind-set of purpose, of adventure, where you really think about what I am trading my life for. And we also talk about 'response ability'—the ability to respond to whatever is thrown at you. This kind of stuff is the glue that holds our organization together."

The third key feature is that intrinsic drivers motivate people at Tupperware: the opportunity to affirm their self-identity and to reinforce their values. Of course, making money is still important, but to get a flavor for what makes Tupperware an unusual company you need to attend one of their sales conferences or recognition events, where Rick Goings will speak for two hours to an audience of five thousand salespeople. His style is closer to that of a self-help guru or religious preacher than a traditional CEO: "What is your life philosophy? What do you want to be?" He uses stories from his personal life, and he is frequently interrupted with hollers and applause from the audience. Goings spends 70 percent of his time traveling the world and giving these talks, because motivating his salespeople is perhaps the most important part of his job. "The essence of our competitive advantage is relationships. The glue that holds this company together is relationships based on purpose and responsibility. And the propellant is opportunity—I can change my life."

We use the Tupperware story here for a couple of reasons. First, selling plastic food containers is pretty mundane stuff. Many of the firms that make a strong emotional connection to their customers do so because their products are innately sexy—Apple, Harley Davidson, BMW—so arguably their job is much easier. Tupperware has created a clear sense of purpose despite, not because of, what it sells. If it can inspire the people who work for it, then so can you, whatever industry you are in.

Second, purpose is much more than just a slogan or a statement of intent. Even the most inspiring vision statement counts for nothing unless it is backed up with constant reinforcement and with a set of complementary structures that make it meaningful. As we will show, the real challenge most firms face is that their purpose is *fragile*—it is easily undermined or damaged when other priorities, typically profit-based, intervene, so executives have to put a lot of conscious effort into maintaining it.

What Is the Purpose of a Business?

The importance of having a clear sense of purpose is well established in the business world. As observed by Ratan Tata, the recently retired CEO of the Tata Group, purpose is "a spiritual and moral call to action; it is about what a person or company stands for."[5] When such a purpose exists, it provides employees with a clear sense of direction, it helps them prioritize, and it inspires them to go the extra mile, which is ultimately good for profitability as well. And there is a sizable body of empirical evidence to support this idea, described in such books as *Built to Last, Firms of Endearment,* and *Higher Ambition.*[6]

In the context of this book, a firm's purpose is the engine that produces emotional conviction. Successful firms generate decisive action infused with emotion, and typically this is achieved much more effectively when the purpose of the enterprise is clear, communicated, and consistent, rather than when a fact-based argument is presented.

How should you think about your firm's purpose? A number of approaches have been proposed over the years. For example, business consultant Nikos Mourkoigiannis talks about four forms of moral purpose (discovery, excellence, altruism, and heroism),[7] while consultants Jim Collins and Jerry Porras distinguish between a core ideology (mission) and a desired future state (vision).[8]

We prefer a simple starting point, namely a point of view about which stakeholders your firm exists to serve. A basic approach is to focus on shareholders. This leads down the well-traveled path to profit seeking as an end in itself, with all its associated benefits and risks—the most obvious risk being that it hardly contributes in making an organization unique (few competitors actively focus on destroying shareholder value—at least not on purpose).

The alternative is to focus on a different stakeholder group and to show how by serving their needs, the firm has a *raison d'etre* above and beyond money making. We typically think in terms of five such stakeholders: employees, customers, suppliers, local communities, and the planet. Following are examples of each one.

Employees. HCL Technologies was a second-tier player in the Indian IT services sector when Vineet Nayar became CEO in 2005. Nayar decided to differentiate HCL through the quality of its management—by putting his employees first, and by enabling them to create value in their relationships with customers. He embarked on a major transformation program with a series of specific initiatives designed to help employees serve their clients better. For example, he pushed all managers to place the results of their 360-degree appraisals online (to make them more accountable to their employees). Nayar also created a "service ticket" scheme, so that if an employee wasn't happy about something he or she could open a ticket to get the attention of the relevant manager. As these initiatives began to take hold, Nayar captured his philosophy with the slogan "employees first, customers second," which he announced—with some trepidation—at the annual global customer meeting. Six years on, HCL had recorded an industry-leading compound annual growth rate of 24 percent, and had lower turnover rates than those of competitor companies.[9]

Customers. Handelsbanken, established in Stockholm in 1871, was the only bank to steer a course through the Swedish financial crisis in the 1990s and the global crisis of the 2000s without getting into trouble. Its success is largely down to its customer focus. The firm is "strongly decentralized and operations are always based on the customer's requirements. This means that all business decisions regarding individual customers' relationships with the Bank are taken close to the customer." Managers of individual branches have much more discretion regarding loans and employee salaries than is customary in the industry. The company does not set budgets on a top-down basis; it expects branch managers to set their own targets. There is also no emphasis on maximizing shareholder returns; instead, the goals are to track a moving target by always having higher customer satisfaction and profitability than a weighted average of the competition. These goals are then linked to a combined profit-sharing and employee stock ownership scheme called Oktogonen, which all employees take part in, so that when the bank's after-tax return on equity is higher than the industry average, shares are issued to all employees. So successful has the firm been that Oktogonen, which was set up in 1973, now owns 10 percent of the bank.

Suppliers. The Danish-Swedish food company Arla is a cooperative—it is owned by dairy farmers, and its mission is to secure the highest value for its farmers' milk while creating opportunities for their growth. From the outside, Arla looks like any other consumer products company, with strong brands such as Lurpak and Castello, a strong private-label business selling milk to supermarkets, and a growing international footprint. But under the surface, the company has a highly unusual governance structure, with the CEO accountable to an elected board of farmer representatives, clear guidelines around reinvesting profits, and a scorecard that gives the price paid for milk to farmers equal weight to customary measures such as sales growth and profitability. Arla's strategic choices also reflect its mission: it seeks to achieve high market share in its core markets to gain some pricing power over the large supermarkets it sells to. It builds premium brands in milk-based products such as butter and cheese, and it sells treated and powdered milk products in emerging markets as a way of using up the excess milk that it cannot sell through other means. Arla is not the most profitable player in its sector, but it is a vibrant and well-run firm, with a much clearer sense of direction than most of its competitors.

Local communities. With revenues in excess of $100 billion, The Tata Group is one of India's most successful companies, with operations in IT services, steel, cars, chemicals, and hotels.[10] Tata's goal is "to improve the quality of life for the communities we serve." As stated on its website, "the community is not just another stakeholder in business, but is in fact the very purpose of its existence." This statement is then backed up with a number of distinctive structural features. For example, the charitable trusts that own 66 percent of Tata Sons spend their profits on causes such as clean water delivery, literacy, and health care. The Tata operating companies are then expected to put significant investments into the local communities they serve, typically more than $100 million per year. The group also makes a highly visible commitment to community development through its innovation activities, for example, in its launch of the Nano car and the low-cost Swach water purifier.

The planet. While many large firms talk about their responsibility to the natural environment, few have gone as far as Unilever in putting sustainability at the core of their operations. Under CEO Paul Polman, the company has committed to its "Sustainable Living Plan," which seeks to double the size of the business while reducing its environmental footprint and increasing its positive social impact. This includes specific initiatives on addressing sanitation, deforestation, and sustainable agriculture, and also a reprioritization of the company's innovation program, so that new products and services that support the plan get funded. Business managers are evaluated on how their activities are contributing to sustainable living, and training programs have been developed to give everyone the knowledge and the tools to contribute. It is too soon to know whether Unilever will achieve its ambitious targets, but we know from talking to executives in the company that its renewed sense of purpose is having a positive impact on how they are perceived in their operating environment.

Each of these examples has its unique flavor, but there are some common themes here, and perhaps the most important of all is that you don't need clever words or a unique angle to have a clear purpose. We are occasionally asked to facilitate meetings in which the objective is to come up with a new mission or vision statement for the company, and many participants fall into the trap of trying to find a "silver bullet"—a brilliant string of words that inspires and enlightens everyone. In reality, as the five examples suggest, the wording doesn't matter that much. Often, it is enough simply to have one clear set of stakeholders that you care about, and then a complementary set of structures and tools to back it up. By making up your mind you implicitly begin the process of prioritizing, and you send a clear message of what people are expected to do and not to do.

Think about a marriage. Why do people get hitched? Google "reasons for getting married" and you get some 12 million hits (Google "reasons for getting divorced" and you get 53 million hits; "reasons for not getting married" comes in at a whopping 123 million!). We guess people decide to tie the knot for a whole lot of different reasons. Some marry out of love and others out of convenience. We have even had a Russian executive at a conference proclaiming that he got wed because it made division of labor a lot more efficient. Any purpose for a marriage is fine—although we have our own preference—so long as the two people marrying agree. If you say "I do" out of love, but your partner walks down the aisle for reasons of convenience, at some point in time you are going to have a major discussion. The same is true in a corporate setting. Many different purposes can work well, but to be effective as a generator of coordinated action and emotional conviction the purpose unconditionally must be shared.

Why Is It So Hard to Sustain a Clear Sense of Purpose?

While there are quite a lot of purpose-led firms out there, there are many more examples in which the stated purpose has no discernable impact on the way people behave. Some companies have vision and values statements of empty rhetoric that no one relates to (Enron talked about "Respect, Integrity, Communication and Excellence"). Some *had* visions that were valid for a while but either lost their relevance (Microsoft's "A Personal Computer in Every Home"), or gradually atrophied (JP Morgan was built on the "Nobility of Banking"). And many others have visions that employees can buy into, at a superficial level, but don't influence how they behave on a consistent basis. IKEA, for example, has an almost altruistic vision to "create a better everyday life for the many people," but most observers nowadays see it as a highly effective but financially driven company.

Why do most firms struggle to align the behavior of their employees around a defined purpose? One obvious reason is that way too many organizations still hire people for skill and train for attitude. A few unusual firms such as Southwest Airlines do the reverse—hire for attitude and train for skill. They know that the half-life of knowledge is coming down dramatically, so that people will constantly have to be retrained, and they realize that it is a lot more difficult to change the norms and values of a person than his or her capabilities. As former Southwest Airlines CEO Herb Kelleher once pointed out, "We can change skill levels through training, but we can't change attitude."[11] Sherry Phelps, a veteran at Southwest's People Department, helped design many of its progressive hiring practices. She explains the philosophy like this. "The first thing we look for is the 'warrior spirit.' So much of our history was born out of battles—fighting for the right to be an airline, fighting off the big guys who wanted to squash us, now fighting off the low-cost airlines trying to emulate us. We are battle-born, battle-tried people. Anyone we add has to have some of that warrior spirit."[12]

Here is another useful way of tackling the question of aligning purpose and behavior, using a concept called "goal-framing theory." It starts from the idea that at any moment, people have a major area of concern that makes them focus on specific aspects of their work and neglect others. The framework has three components.

First, when people are concerned about feeling good and improving their situation, they will look for the fun parts of their job, for the one activity in their job that really excites them. They will neglect things that feel boring or a bit uncertain. This is called a *hedonic* goal and the focus is on the "now."

Second, when the major concern of employees is for improving the resources they have, such as income or promotion, they will focus on opportunities to earn extra money, or make a good impression that helps getting promoted, and neglect other aspects. This is called a *gain* goal.

Finally, when people are concerned about realizing a common goal, such as getting a product launched on a tight timeline or delivering on a fundraising campaign, they will attend mainly to that goal and downplay concerns for relaxation, making more money, or getting a better position. This is called a *normative* or *pro-social* goal. The essence of such a goal is that it motivates the employee to ask "What should I do to make *us* succeed?" rather than "What should *I* do to get ahead?" or "What will be the most enjoyable thing to do?" "We" trumps "I." Needless to say, this is the kind of goal that companies want their employees to have at the forefront of their minds.

What factors then influence the relative strength of these goals? Obviously there are innate differences between individuals that play their part, but a much stronger influence is typically the immediate stimuli employees receive from those around them in their working environment and from their superiors. If all the talk is about the size of the annual bonus, the gain goal will immediately dominate others. But, for their own benefit, many companies want their employees to help them realize common goals, rather than to prioritize personal gain or fun on the job. So the challenge becomes how to make such common goals more salient and meaningful to employees across the company. To a large extent this is a matter of trying to convey the purpose of the company to employees. When they can see how their efforts fit with those of other employees the overall purpose can be fulfilled. This works best of all if the purpose is normative because then there is a very direct link from the company goals to a pro-social orientation of the employees.

Unfortunately, and this is the key point, the motivation to pursue normative goals is inherently fragile. It takes a great deal of effort to establish and maintain such goals, and they are easily displaced by gain or hedonic goals.[13] There is no simple solution because the gain and hedonic goals cannot be abandoned entirely; having employees work toward company goals without being rewarded and without feeling good is not a stable long-term proposition. So there is a delicate balance needed here, and goal-framing theory provides some valuable insights into how it might be maintained.[14]

Here are a couple of guidelines to bear in mind. For one, it is typically a good idea to consistently prioritize pro-social goals ahead of financial goals. If a medical products company is seeking to "put patients first," then this goal should be center stage in all external and internal communications. Financial goals, in contrast, should be approached in an *oblique* or indirect way—they should be seen as the natural consequence of achieving the normative goals, rather than as an end in themselves. If financial goals are given too much prominence, they will typically displace the pro-social goals.[15]

Second, the fragility of normative goals also means they need supporting on a regular basis, through incentive and reward systems, through informal conversations and discussions, through symbolic management, and through formal structures.[16] For example, managers should seek to acknowledge and highlight behaviors that support the pro-social goals of the company, by building them into annual reviews and by publicly celebrating and rewarding employees that successfully strive to meet pro-social goals.[17] Without such reinforcement, employees see a disconnect between the demands of their immediate job and the espoused goals of the company. In effect, the normative goals end up being displaced in favor of gain or hedonic goals.

One reinforcing structure that is worth emphasizing is what we call a *counterweight*, by which we mean any institutional mechanism that exists to enforce a continued focus on a nonfinancial goal. In Handelsbanken, the Oktogonen profit-sharing system is the counterweight. At Arla, it is the elected board of farmer representatives that the CEO is accountable to. In Tata Group, it is the family-endowed trusts. At U.K. retailer John Lewis the counterweight is the Employee Council, which represents the employees as the ultimate owners of the company. At London Business School, it is the "appointments committee" that ensures faculty are promoted on the basis of academic excellence, not just because they are good at teaching or selling executive programs. At the *Guardian* newspaper, the counterweight is the editor, who is appointed by the ultimate owner of the newspaper (the Scott Trust) and is free to exercise editorial control over content, regardless of the company's commercial priorities. The counterweight has an analogous role to the independent press or judiciary in most democracies—it exists to hold the power of the executive office in check, and to ensure that the long-term interests of the organization are not sacrificed for short-term benefits. And the key point is that the counterweight has to have real influence—it has to be able to hold the leader to account.

Reshaping the Purpose of Your Own Team

The challenges in building and maintaining a clear purpose are substantial. And because of this, most people assume that the "purpose stuff" belongs to the chief executive officer. Indeed, most well-known examples, including those that we discussed earlier, were all led from the top.

But we think this is a cop-out. There are many difficult challenges in the business world that people are inclined to think of as "someone else's problem." But there is no reason why a division of a large firm, or even a small operating unit, cannot develop its own sense of purpose and drive profound changes in behavior as a result.

Consider the case of Jesper Ek, a mid-level manager at the highly successful Swiss pharmaceutical company Roche. He was asked by his boss to take charge of an underperforming twenty-person diabetes team in Sweden that had seen sales drop year by year since 2006. When he took on the assignment in April 2012, the employee engagement score for the team was 22 percent, and even more disturbing, the disengagement score was as high as 66 percent. "I realized that they had lost their sense of purpose," he recalled. So for the first three months, he focused solely on understanding the team: their fears, motivations, and concerns. "I had one-on-one meetings with everyone, typically two hours each, and lots of team meetings."

By June, he felt he had the measure of his team, and he switched from an internal to an external focus. He held a workshop to discuss their collective goals, and they agreed on a common purpose: "to enable people with diabetes to live their lives as unrestricted as possible." This normative purpose created real clarity for the team, enabling them to push two particular offerings that linked to solutions for the common purpose (an integrated mobile meter and a pump system with remote control that enabled unrestricted life with diabetes), and reduced their attention to the other fifteen products in their portfolio. This focus also made it possible for the team to gain access to clinics they had previously struggled to get into and, when there, for them to have more effective and purposeful meetings. Just a year later, the engagement score had risen to 75 percent and disengagement was down to 0 percent, with only two of the original twenty people having left during this period. There were market share gains of more than 3 percent, an impressive 250 percent growth with the integrated meter, and growth both in total sales and in operating profit.

"My approach," Jesper observed, "was to not think about profitability at all for the first six months. By getting my team on-board, we were able to come up with a purpose that provided clarity and got everyone motivated. It helped that I had a supportive boss who gave me a clear mandate to do what I felt was necessary and then got out of the way—but it turned out that the turnaround was sufficiently quick that he didn't have to cut me much slack."

Despite the presence of many competitors with very similar products, Jesper's focus on vision and purpose helped to differentiate the business's positioning in the marketplace. His approach was so successful, in fact, that he was promoted to run the whole Nordic region, and his statement of purpose was adopted across the worldwide diabetes care business for Roche.

Jesper's experience underlines nicely what purpose is all about. Recall the overarching framework we are putting forward in this book. In an increasingly uncertain business world, the firms that are able to pair decisive action with emotional conviction will outperform those that tend to fall back on formal processes and intellectual debate. By defining the *raison d'etre* of the diabetes care operation in Sweden, he gave the team great clarity about what sort of actions to take (that is, concentrate on selling the mobile meter and pump system), and he ensured they understood why those were the priorities, which in turn boosted engagement and conviction.

Indeed, this same logic applies at all levels of analysis. Think about the relationship you have with your direct subordinates. Most of us fall into the trap (at least occasionally) of giving our team members direct orders about what to do, but without explaining why, what will happen when they succeed, or the consequences if they don't deliver. In effect, they don't understand the assignment or why it matters, so they end up following the instructions to the letter, for fear of getting it wrong. At worst, and this typically happens if they are fairly young, these people are avid fans of WIIIFM—what is in it for me—and can't be bothered. Regardless, they default to a bureaucratic mode of operation, without a lot of enthusiasm or bereft of any energy. Now, imagine defining the job the other way round—with a clear explanation of why it matters, personal consequences linked to the success of the team, and a lot of openness on how exactly it could be done. This is an invitation for the team member to bring her creativity to the table—to make her own decisions and to do it in her own style. This approach typically takes a bit longer at the outset, but the quality of the outputs is likely to be much richer.

Purpose Enables Action

A clear, communicated, and shared purpose is an important feature of any business organization in general. But we see it as particularly important in the fast/forward world we are concerned with here. In a bureaucracy, work is undertaken according to fairly well-defined rules and procedures, so there is not a lot of scope for employees to misinterpret the firm's sense of direction. And in a meritocracy, with its emphasis on knowledge and debate, there are also checks and balances in place to avoid someone acting "inappropriately," or indeed acting at all.

The adhocracy, on the other hand, gives priority to action, which in turn means empowering individuals also on the front line to a much greater degree than would be likely in other organizing models. This is when a clear statement of purpose pays dividends—it helps employees make the right choices, and it also ensures that those choices are made with good emotional buy-in.

To conclude this chapter, it is useful to summarize the key points about building and maintaining a clear purpose for your operation, whether it is an entire corporation or a small business unit.

A statement of purpose doesn't have to be elaborate or novel. There are only a limited number of pro-social goals that a firm can meaningfully target. The five examples we gave at the beginning of this chapter are the major nonfinancial stakeholders in the firm, so a statement of purpose is typically going to revolve around one of them. There is no evidence that firms have thrived because they dreamt up a highly unique normative goal that nobody else had thought of. Rather, the evidence suggests the successful firms are the ones that were able to translate pedestrian-sounding pro-social goals into consistent and committed action.

Purpose needs supporting systems if it is to stick. We know that people take cues from those around them, but they are also fickle and easily confused, and the gain and hedonic goals can quickly drive out normative goals.[18] So a key insight is that firms must build a wealth of supporting systems to help them operationalize their pro-social goals at different levels, and thereby make them stick. At Handelsbanken, the supporting systems are relatively formal: the highly decentralized branch structure, the removal of budgets, and the equal profit-sharing system. At Tata the supporting systems are more informal, and reinforced through the visible initiatives and pronouncements of the top executives. At HCL Technologies, it is a combination of the CEO's personal promotion of the "employees first" agenda plus a set of innovative practices designed to reinforce it. And in the first two, in particular, there has been consistency in these systems over many years, which further reinforces their value. Such consistency matters because it signals that management is sincere.

One important form of supporting system is to *incorporate tangible manifestations of the company's purpose into the day-to-day work of employees.* For example, IBM sends future managers to work with NGOs on development projects in Nigeria, Ghana, Tanzania, and the Philippines to put substance to its Corporate Citizen's Core program.[19] We have also seen health care companies bring patients into their offices to talk about how the company's products have helped them. The world leader in insulin production, Novo Nordisk, requires that all new employees spend a day with a diabetes patient. For employees working on the front line of their company, such systems are unnecessary, but many back-office employees lose touch with what their company's *raison d'etre* is, so this is a good way of making it visible.

Another important supporting system is to *find ways of measuring progress on purpose and to report them publicly.* For companies that see customer focus as their goal, the Net Promoter Score has become a popular measure; for those that seek to put their employees first, engagement scores are often used; and for those that focus on safety, Lost Time Injuries are typically the preferred metric. Unfortunately, there aren't yet established measures for community or environmental pro-social goals, though several companies are experimenting with them, for example the *Guardian* newspaper's annual sustainability report. But regardless of the measure used, what matters is that it is shared in a transparent and consistent way with the relevant stakeholders. HCL's initiative to share feedback on how well managers are doing for all employees to see is a good example.

Purpose needs a "counterweight" to endure. Goal-framing theory shows how easy it is for normative goals to be driven out by gain or hedonic goals. Even with the types of supporting systems just described, it is quite common to see executives bowing to short-term financial pressures. So a key factor in creating enduring pro-social goals is a "counterweight" as we described earlier. Counterweights vary a lot in how they are implemented, but the common feature is that they give voice and influence to named individuals who represent the nonfinancial stakeholders in the enterprise.

Alignment works in an oblique not linear way. In most companies, there is an implicit belief that all activities should be aligned in a linear and logical way, from a clear endpoint back to the starting point. The language used—from cascading goals to key performance indicators—is all designed to reinforce this notion of alignment. But goal-framing theory suggests that the most successful companies are balancing multiple objectives (pro-social goals, gain goals, hedonic goals) that are not entirely compatible with one another, which makes a simple linear approach very hard to sustain.

So an important mental leap to make here is the notion that long-term profits are often best achieved obliquely, that is, in an indirect fashion.[20] As Ratan Tata, former CEO of the Tata Group, has observed, "Profits are like happiness in that they are a by-product of other things. Companies need sustainability strategies that recognize you can make money by doing good things rather than the other way around."[21] In the best-selling business book *Built to Last*, Jim Collins and Jerry Porras showed that their "visionary" companies with normative goals had better long-term profitability than their benchmark competitors that typically opted for narrower financial goals.

In practical terms, this means providing your employees with scope to choose their own oblique pathway. This means emphasizing the normative part of the story on a consistent basis. It also means thinking very differently about the processes and structures you use to guide people's actions on a day-to-day basis. This is the subject of the next chapter.

Chapter 6

OPPORTUNITY-FOCUSED COORDINATION

FRIDAY, APRIL 6TH, 1453, marked the beginning of the siege of Constantinople, capital of the East Roman (Byzantine) Empire, by the Ottoman Turks.

Under the leadership of twenty-one-year-old Sultan Mehmed II, the hundred-thousand-strong Ottoman army prevailed while four thousand of the defending army, commanded by Byzantine Emperor Constantine XI, lost their lives. The Fall of Constantinople, as it is commonly known, represented an important turning point in Western history. It marked the end of the Roman Empire, and it slowed the spread of Christianity. But it also helped to initiate the renaissance in Western Europe, as Greek scholars who fled the city brought with them priceless knowledge and rare manuscripts. The fact that this event also cut off European trade links with Asia led them to seek out new trade routes to the east by sea—hence the voyage of Columbus, who was really on his way to India but landed in North America by accident. One missed opportunity, it seems, can open up many others—given the right combination of action and conviction.

Originally, the odds were dead set against the invading army of Ottoman Turks. While they outnumbered the Byzantine soldiers ten to one and had more ships, the defending army had a huge tactical advantage—the highly secure walls surrounding Constantinople, allegedly the "best-defended city" in Europe at that time. The Ottoman army tried everything: attacking the walls to find weaknesses, digging tunnels, rolling ships across the Galata (a neighborhood opposite of the city) on greased logs. They basically tried every trick up their sleeves in a fifty-day experimentation frenzy.

The final assault came right before midnight on May 28. Attacking the city at multiple locations, the Ottomans had some early success breaking through the old and weakened Blachernae wall, but victory was still far from certain. Then the Byzantines made one critical blunder. They forgot to close the Kerkoporta gate in the Lycus Valley. To call this the organizational own-goal of that century is no overstatement. The Turks quickly seized the opportunity and poured into the city through the open gate, raised their flag, and took control of Constantinople. As a perk, Mehmed allowed his men to plunder its riches for three days.

History is littered with examples of organizational coordination gone wrong and someone else using it as an opportunity to prevail. Think of Napoleon, and later Hitler, trying to invade Russia without preparing for the harsh winters. Or consider White Star Line's "unsinkable" ship *Titanic* that failed to stock enough lifeboats for the passengers onboard. The point is, effective coordination is inherently difficult, and the more people and activities involved, and the more uncertain the circumstances, the harder it gets.

In this chapter, we take a fresh look at the challenge of coordination, and in particular how the appropriate mode of coordination varies according to the activities you are performing. We will end up with some very practical ideas about how you can coordinate around opportunities—along the lines suggested by the adhocracy—but before getting there let's first take a quick look at the different principles.

Bureaucracy Revisited

Whether a small start-up or a large multinational, organizations exist to do things that individuals can't do on their own. A firm enables people to bring their own skills and effort together and create a whole that is greater than the sum of the parts. It is a way of coordinating human activity to achieve useful and sometimes amazing outcomes.

But how is coordination achieved? What means do the individuals in the firm use to ensure that everyone is working on the right activities, and that everyone contributes and is rewarded for their efforts in a fair way? These are big questions, and over the years many bodies of academic thinking have emerged to answer them.[1] In your own personal experiences, you will have seen many different approaches. In a small firm, say less than twenty people, everyone knows everyone, and can see what each other is working on. So coordination mostly happens on an informal basis. Roles are flexible, the objectives are clear, and you just muck in together to do what has to be done.

But as the firm grows larger, this informal approach doesn't work—you no longer know everyone and you don't understand what happens in other parts of the firm. So effort has to go into keeping track of people, and making sure they are working on the right things, or there will be problems in the form of delays, duplication of effort, and data loss. The process of coordination becomes an activity in its own right, and the bigger the firm, the more complex the coordination job becomes. We remember, as kids, walking past large building sites with hundreds of men laying bricks, moving earth, and digging trenches, and wondering how on earth each one knew what he was supposed to be doing. It is the same in a large corporate office—we still wonder, to this day, how these people figure out what they are supposed to be doing each day, and indeed how their activities actually help the firm to deliver its objectives.

And yet somehow it all works. Despite all the self-evident challenges they face, large firms orchestrate the efforts of often tens of thousands of people in a reasonably effective way. People get paid. High-quality outputs are created. Profits are made. It is no coincidence that the largest and most successful economies on the planet are often those with the biggest and most professionally managed firms.[2]

But there is still a puzzle to be solved here. Despite all their benefits, large firms are slow moving and ridden with politics, and they suppress creativity and individual freedom—in a word, they are bureaucratic. And as we argued in earlier chapters, these are increasingly dangerous afflictions when facing the paradoxes of progress. Our colleague Gary Hamel, always the master of colorful rhetoric, set out the challenge thus:

> Bureaucracy must die. We must find a way to reap the blessings of bureaucracy—precision, consistency, and predictability—while at the same time killing it. Bureaucracy, both architecturally and ideologically, is incompatible with the demands of the 21st century.[3]

While we don't go as far as Gary on this point, we believe there are better ways of organizing than the bureaucratic model that most large firms default to. In particular, we see the opportunity-focused model of coordination in an adhocracy as highly promising. If bureaucracy was built on the principle of decomposition—breaking things up—adhocracy succeeds because it applies the principle of recomposition—putting things together in new, unexpected, and flexible ways.[4]

But before getting into this new model, we have to be clear about what came before. So let's briefly step back in time, to the early twentieth century when large industrial firms started to take shape. Of course, there had been many large organizations in existence before this period—for example the Ottoman army of 1453 had around a hundred thousand soldiers. But we prefer to focus on the industrial age because there is good documentary evidence for exactly *how* they worked, and how effective their methods were.

As we have discussed in the previous chapters, the problem of coordination was resolved through a way of working that came to be known as bureaucracy. In essence, bureaucracy means coordinating through standardized rules and procedures. The workplace innovations that made this highly efficient way of working possible emerged mostly from North America, thanks to the likes of Frederick Winslow Taylor, Henry Gantt, and Frank and Lillian Gilbreth. But it was a German sociologist, Max Weber, who developed the concept of bureaucracy that we still recognize today.[5] Weber saw bureaucracy as a highly rational mode of organizing in which authority was vested in the "system" rather than in an all-powerful leader. This meant having a clear hierarchy of authority, so that work could be broken down effectively into its constituent parts; a clear framework of rules to ensure compliance; and hiring and promoting people on the basis of merit and expertise.

These are all sensible principles, especially when contrasted with the informal, paternalistic, and corrupt ways of working they replaced. They enabled industrial-age firms to generate enormous economies of scale and scope, and they resulted in productivity improvements that fueled the economic growth of the twentieth century. Even today, many large and successful firms, from Walmart to McDonalds to Exxon, continue to operate in this way.

But as we observed in Chapter 3, bureaucracy comes with a price:

- It is internally focused—the people responsible for formal processes never see customers, and often these processes end up taking on a life of their own.

- It is slow moving—rules and procedures are made to be followed, and important decisions require multiple levels of sign-off.

- It kills creativity—bureaucrats are risk averse, and rules are designed to avoid mistakes.

- It is disempowering—most employees have narrowly defined jobs, and they rarely see the fruits of their efforts.

These downsides are all well documented, and indeed Max Weber himself was aware of most of them when he developed his ideas about a century ago. But the point is that as we moved from the industrial age to the information age, these disadvantages became increasingly acute.

Recall the argument we developed in the first chapter: in the information age, firms like Apple of the United States, Toyota of Japan, or Novo Nordisk of Denmark succeed because of their ability to create and capture value from information. This means attracting and retaining the smartest people; entrusting them to experiment and make mistakes; encouraging collaboration across functional, institutional, and geographical divides, and so on. These are not things you can do in a bureaucracy. Indeed, as the information age has matured, the term *bureaucratic* has gradually become a byword for all the bad aspects of working in a large firm (as a colleague once said, "Bureaucracy is the art of making the possible impossible").

Self-Organization

What is the alternative to bureaucracy? In earlier books, we have talked about the principle of emergence or self-organizing as a fundamentally different way of coordinating activity.[6] This language comes from the somewhat mysterious world of complexity theory. You may not have thought about it at the time, but you have most certainly come across examples of self-organizing in nature, such as beautiful formations of geese in flight or the sophisticated workings of ant colonies. Or think about our languages: there was no central planning team tasked with inventing English, Chinese, German, or any other tongue for that matter; words and idioms, tenses and grammatical rules, conjugations and declensions, they all took shape over many thousands of years, order emerging out of chaos.

Researchers have shown that geese and ants are, essentially, pre-programmed with a small number of rules, and by following these simple rules they interact in a way that results in coordinated activity. And something similar happens in the emergence of language. Think about German grammar—"the horror, the horror," to quote Marlon Brando's unforgettable Colonel Kurtz from *Apocalypse Now*. As complicated as these almost mathematical guidelines seem, there was no great congregation in Trier, the oldest city in Germany, back in the fourth century B.C. where people gathered to agree on the rules. In fact, back then, as you probably know, there wasn't even a country called Germany. The guidelines evolved and emerged. And still they make sense, at least to most Germans. In nature and elsewhere, what often looks like a carefully designed system is, in fact, nothing more than an artifact of thousands of individuals combining in an organic way.

Another classic example of self-organizing can be seen in the world of town planning. Most large cities from London to Los Angeles and Beijing to Buenos Aires are incredibly congested with lots of traffic lights, one-way systems, and the like. Whenever accidents occur, the city authorities typically respond by creating even more rigid rules to govern the flow of traffic.

But what if there is a different way? A little-known Dutch road traffic engineer, Hans Monderman, had the bright idea in the late 1990s that traffic systems in cities should be dramatically simplified. He persuaded a few municipal authorities in Dutch towns, such as Drachten, to take out the roundabouts and traffic lights and replace them with "shared space" paved areas where the cars, cyclists, and pedestrians were free to work their way through busy intersections as they saw fit.

By now, you are thinking anarchy, road kill, and possibly too many visits to the infamous coffee shops in Amsterdam, but give the Dutch a break. Let us look at the facts. Careful analysis was done before and after these shared space areas were created, and sure enough the simpler model worked better.[7] Car drivers were respectful of cyclists and pedestrians, people adjusted to each other's behavior, and the flow of traffic through these busy intersections actually improved.

This logic of self-organization has been applied with gusto in a business setting. Strategists have talked about how companies define "simple rules" to make decisions in a complex operating environment. Organization theorists have described how successful firms operate on the "edge of chaos" with neither too much structure nor too little. Leadership writers talk about a simpler, servant-based model of leading that empowers individuals to make their own choices.[8] The common theme across these theories can be summarized as "less is more"—fewer rules and structures provides people with the freedom to create, collaborate, and experiment as they see fit. And the more unpredictable and fast-changing the business world, the more effective these models become.

Of course, the paradox that we are all becoming increasingly ignorant further strengthens the argument and increases the importance of ensuring that the capacity to act and react is dispersed throughout the organization. In essence, bureaucracy operated with a core-periphery logic in which the right to take decisions was located at the center. Now, think about where signals of change usually first appear? Is it in the boardroom at corporate HQ? No, it is almost always in the periphery—at the edge, on the front line.

While the organization of the past operated with the business equivalent of the CIA—central intelligence agency—the modern firm needs a PIA—peripheral intelligence agency—with many ears to the ground and a variety of voices communicating. Again, think about language. Consider the ten newest words in your own tongue. Where did they come from? Who invented them? In all likelihood, the answer is either someone on the Internet or people in one of the suburbs where a majority of our immigrants live—in other words, the periphery. They were certainly not the product of any of the members of your local *Académie Francaise*. The phenomenon is not new. Historically, language evolved mainly in the harbors where people with diverse backgrounds and nationalities met. Creativity does equal diversity squared.

Self-organization, in other words, has a lot going for itself as a concept. But there are two important caveats.

To begin with, there are plenty of downsides to self-organizing. Giving people freedom within a simple structure works well if you have competent, well-intentioned, and highly motivated employees, but if those conditions are not in place there is lots of room for shirking and cheating, and for mistakes to be made. Self-organized workplaces can also appear highly chaotic, with people working on overlapping or duplicate projects because of the lack of a master plan, and with little or no thought given to career management or personal development.

An interesting recent example is Zappos, the online shoe company owned by Amazon, which recently adopted "holacracy," a self-organizing model developed by Brian Robertson, a thirty-five-year old former programmer. Holacracy gets rid of the traditional management hierarchy and shifts decision-making power to semi-autonomous "circles" of employees who coordinate with each other on a lateral basis. Many observers have applauded Zappos's innovative new way of working but it remains a work in progress. According to a *Wall Street Journal* article, 14 percent of workers have chosen to leave since it was introduced, with one observer commenting that it "has been confusing and time-consuming, especially at first, sometimes requiring five extra hours of meetings a week as workers unshackled from their former bosses organize themselves into circles."[9]

We shouldn't be surprised at these sorts of challenges. Every organizing model has its pros and cons, and particularly in the early stages of implementing a new way of working there will always be some pushback from those who aren't comfortable with change. We certainly hope Zappos is successful in making holacracy work for them, but we wouldn't be amazed if the company reverted back to a more traditional organizational model at some point in the future.

Another caveat is that self-organizing is a very broad concept. There are dozens of management theories out there paying homage to the science of complexity theory, and each has a slightly different take on what emergent behavior looks like in practice. Some people have emphasized the speed and responsiveness of emergent ways of working, some have focused on the opportunity for self-expression, others have emphasized the absence of formal rules. And of course it is hard for any organizing model to do all three of these things equally well.

Alternatives to Bureaucracy

If you have been reading this book all the way through, you will know that we don't see a unitary alternative to bureaucracy. Instead, we see two alternatives—meritocracy and adhocracy. And they offer significantly different views on how coordination should be achieved.

In a meritocracy, knowledge is privileged over formal position. Expertise and understanding are important, and the people with the smartest insights call the shots. In this system, coordination is achieved through *mutual adjustment*. Picture, for example, the large team of scientists at CERN in Switzerland, who found proof in 2014 of the Higgs Boson: how did they work together? They discussed their theories, they ran experiments, they adjusted their views as the work unfolded. Rather than coordinating their activities through depersonalized processes and formal hierarchies, they worked on the basis of mutual adjustment. While there was surely a lot of disagreement along the way, the overall tone was based on respect for the views of others and a desire to uncover the truth.

Or look at the university environment in which we spend our time. Apart from the few weeks a year of teaching (which is coordinated in a highly bureaucratic way), we are free to set our own agenda, collaborate with others as we see fit, and attend meetings when they seem worthwhile. We adapt to the needs of others not because they tell us to, but because we can see the mutual benefits in doing so.

In an *adhocracy*, action is privileged over position or knowledge. Getting something done—trying things out, testing, experimenting—is more important than debating it or following the rules. In this system, coordination is achieved through *opportunity-focused action*. In other words, the focal point is the opportunity, whether it a specific problem that needs solving (for example, keeping the patient alive in an emergency room) or a task that needs completing (such as getting a project finished before a deadline). Think of a small start-up company or a skunk-works unit in a large firm—the people in these operations don't worry about rules, and they aren't bothered about building the perfect plan; their emphasis is on achieving a clearly understood goal.

There are some obvious similarities between these two alternative models. Both are based on the assumption that employees are highly competent and well-intentioned, whereas the control systems in a bureaucracy start with the opposite assumptions—that most employees are competent only to work within their narrowly defined box, and that some are not that well intentioned. They also assume that there is some sort of overarching purpose or goal that everyone can relate to, as discussed in the previous chapter.

But these approaches to coordination are also different in two important ways. Opportunity-centered coordination (adhocracy) is best suited to fast-changing and uncertain environments in which there is a premium on responsiveness and learning by doing—environments in which the durability of knowledge is limited. Coordination through mutual adjustment (meritocracy) is best suited to a high-science world in which there is a premium on getting to the "right" answer through inquiry and debate—environments in which the depth of knowledge is central.

Opportunity-centered coordination is more externally oriented—it is about identifying unmet needs or challenges in the business world that you want to address. Coordination through mutual adjustment, in contrast, is at least partially internally oriented, because it is about adapting to the views and beliefs of your fellow employees.

Interestingly, despite these significant differences, there is no research we are aware of that really teases apart the meritocracy and adhocracy models. Most management writers have fallen into the trap of saying "bureaucracy bad, nonbureaucracy good" but without really clarifying what nonbureaucracy looks like. Our story here, as you should have gathered, is a lot more nuanced—we see the three organizing models as coexisting with each other, and each one having its own advantages and disadvantages. Understanding the relative merits of each, and how to combine them in an effective way, is absolutely critical for those aspiring to move forward faster than the competition.

In the rest of this chapter, we do a deep dive into the opportunity-focused approach to coordination that is central to the adhocracy. We begin by describing three company examples, each one illustrating a different aspect of the phenomenon. Then, we identify and describe the six design principles that are common to all these examples.

Costa Coffee—Developing a Third-Generation Coffee Machine

Costa Coffee is the second-largest coffee chain in the world after Starbucks. To deliver on its mission of "saving the world from mediocre coffee," Costa has expanded beyond its traditional coffee shops into forecourts, gas stations, supermarket chains, transportation hubs, and corporate offices—to places where the coffee is usually so sad that you think you have had a "depresso." But accessing these channels means moving away from barista-made coffee and into the arena of self-serve vending machines. Following a decade during which the skills of the barista were lauded, it isn't so easy to persuade customers that a machine-made cappuccino is, actually, just as good.

It was with this context in mind that Costa launched Project Marlow in early 2012.[10] This was a scheme to "fundamentally transform" the company's vending offering by creating an entirely new self-serve coffee system that would "engage all the five senses" of the prospective customer by giving her the sight, sound, smell, and feel of a café, as well as a consistently great-tasting product. Proposed and headed by Eric Achtmann, an independent entrepreneur and seasoned private equity investor, Project Marlow brought together an elite team with diverse backgrounds and skill sets. It included designers from Italy's Pininfarina, a sound technician for U2 and the Rolling Stones, an online designer for the Harry Potter movies, scent technology from Givaudan and Scentys, computing technology from Intel, advanced payment solutions from the Swiss stock exchange, and manufacturing capabilities from Thermoplan and Verwo, both leading Swiss firms.

Project Marlow was agreed to on a handshake in January 2012. The formal kick-off meeting with twenty people was held on April 19, and the 95 percent beta version was delivered, on time and budget, five months later. Operating on a tight budget, and using very few Costa employees, Marlow was a classic example of informed, decisive action, and coordination built around a specific opportunity. Recalled Achtmann, "This project was based on principles I had picked up from my time in McDonnell-Douglas's (now Boeing) "Phantom Works": the pace of work was uncomfortably high; the autonomous team was small and world-class without exception; the team worked 24x7 with 5-minute communication cycles, decisions were made on a 24-hour cycle; there was a relentless focus on total system cost, performance, quality, and delivery. This was not a model that had ever been tried before in the world of coffee retailing, or on many other non-defense related industries."

A couple of features of Project Marlow are worth highlighting here. The governance model was a "mission" with aggressive, clearly defined goals. It was a disposable vehicle for making something happen. The Marlow team was largely disbanded when the project finished. Its members are still in contact, but they are mostly working on other priorities now.

Coordination was achieved through alignment around a specific opportunity. For example, the deal with prime contractor Thermoplan was done on a handshake over dinner, with work starting the next day, months before a formal agreement was in place. Domenic Steiner, Thermoplan's founder, had invested a million Swiss francs before the contract was signed. Needless to say, an atmosphere of mutual trust, benefits, interests, and excitement was key.

Finally, decisions were first and foremost based on informed judgment and speed—as a function of what moved the project forward based on total system cost, performance, quality, and delivery. "Eric had a maniacal focus on vision and delivering the goods," recalled Rod O'Shea from Intel. "Give him credit: he was even able to track me down late one Saturday night to ask me a question." Those who lacked an entrepreneurial mind-set or required a legal agreement first were bypassed. In one case, the inadequacy of potential suppliers for a key subsystem threatened to delay things, so Achtmann created a parallel team to find a way around. The individual closest to the action was also the person who took the decisions. "In this project, I work for Eric," said Jim Slater, the managing director of Costa Enterprises—the exact opposite of what the formal org chart would have suggested. "Entrepreneurial spirit and leading by example are hallmarks of Marlow," recounted Achtmann.

Valve—A New Approach to Game Development

Valve, the Bellevue, Washington–based gaming company behind such best-sellers as *Half-Life* and *Counter Strike*, and whose economist Yanis Varoufakis became a controversial minister of finance in Greece, has developed an interesting version of adhocracy, even though it doesn't actually use the term. Founded by ex-Microsoft executive Gabe New-ell in 1996, Valve is deliberately structured in a highly informal way to get the most out of its employees. There are no managers, job descriptions, or formal reporting lines. Instead, employees are encouraged to initiate new projects and to choose what projects to work on themselves, on the basis of where they see the greatest opportunities to add value. As the new employee handbook says, "Deciding on what to work on can be the hardest part of your job at Valve. . . . You were not hired to fill a specific job description. You were hired to constantly be looking around for the most valuable work you could be doing." Employees will sometimes join existing teams, when the project looks interesting and important, and occasionally they will create entirely new projects, recruiting their own team in the process. To reinforce this logic, the desks in Valve's office are all on wheels, so employees can physically move their desks to where their project team is sitting.

This seemingly chaotic way of working means that teams emerge spontaneously, according to where the most exciting opportunities appear to be, rather than according to a strategic plan or product development roadmap. In many ways, the system is similar to the stock market, but at Valve people invest their competence and conviction—in the form of time and talent—instead of capital. As observed by employee Michael Abrash in his blog, this attraction approach, rather than the more traditional allocation-based one, is appropriate because "most of the value [in gaming] is now in the initial creative act . . . what matters is being first and bootstrapping your product into a positive feedback spiral. . . . Hierarchical management doesn't help with that."[11]

The company has established a number of important practices to help ensure that this organic model works. The recruitment process is critical—"more important than breathing, nothing else comes close," according to the employee handbook. This means that all employees spend large amounts of time interviewing prospective candidates. Compensation is based on a peer-review system, with the highest-ranked employees getting large bonuses, sometimes five times the basic wage. The ranking considers technical skills and productivity and also an individual's contribution to group goals. There are also informal "cabals" that grow up around specific projects, to build consensus on major decisions.

Valve has become a highly successful gaming company, and its ability to repeatedly come up with hit products seems closely linked to its unusual way of working—more specifically the absence of a top-down allocation of roles. As one employee has observed, "There is a boss—the customer," and by ensuring that all work is focused around customers and prospective customers, the company avoids the rigidities of a traditional structure.

There are some limitations to the Valve model, for sure. One is that employees spend a lot of time building consensus on the right way forward, because there is no boss to overrule their debates. Some people find the lack of clarity about what is expected of them to be unnerving. Others have commented on the emergence of an informal structure: "Like high school, there are popular kids that have acquired power, then there are the troublemakers who actually want to make a difference."[12] Linked to all these points, there is the issue of size. At almost four hundred employees, Valve is already stretching the limits of what is possible without some sort of formal structure.

ING Bank—Agile Working in a Traditional Industry

Banking is rarely the place to look for innovative new ways of working. Since the financial crisis of 2008, most banks have been trying to get their operations in order, restore profitability, and get the regulators and lawmakers off their backs. Bureaucracy is alive and well in the banking industry, and that is not altogether a bad thing for the stability of the global economy.

One exception to this rule is Amsterdam-based ING Bank. In the early 2000s it became very well known for its fast-growing subsidiary, ING Direct. More recently, ING has undertaken a dramatic transformation of its thirty-five-hundred-strong headquarters operation to create an "agile way of working" built around 350 semi-autonomous squads. This model, as we saw in Chapter 4, is now commonplace in the software development world, and it is often seen in high-tech start-ups more generally. But ING is a pioneer among large, well-established firms in rethinking its entire organization using agile principles.

What inspired this change? Bart Schlatmann, the Dutch COO, had led a series of internal change programs since the financial crisis to clean up and simplify the bank's internal processes. In 2014, with mobile banking becoming a major strategic opportunity, he and his team started looking for inspiration from tech companies to develop ING's "omnichannel" experience, and this led them to Spotify's head office in Stockholm. "We were blown away by their way of working," he recalls, "teams were fully empowered and responsible, free to set their own key performance indicators (KPIs), manage their budgets, choose their own working hours, everything." Schlatmann and his team made the bold decision to rethink their entire headquarters operation this way.[13]

Rather than a traditional hierarchical segmentation of activities, ING's new model was built up of "squads" of nine people whose *raison d'etre* was to address a particular user need. Some of these squads were oriented around external customer needs, for example, "improving the daily banking experience" for a specific customer group. Others provided internal services—for example, a cybercrime detection squad or a squad working on customer information management. The squads defined their own KPIs through discussion with peers and senior managers, and then set their own priorities for action. Work was done according to agile principles—broken down into a series of short "sprints," with daily updates on progress and frequent feedback from users.

ING's new model also involved changes to the supporting structures: squads were clustered together into "tribes" working on related user needs, and individuals were encouraged to join "chapters" of like-minded colleagues to enable personal development and learning. A group of agile coaches were also appointed, to support their squads in their work.

The new way of working has already paid dividends, with substantial improvements in customer service, cost efficiency, employee engagement, and innovation. But it has not been an easy ride. As Schlatmann observes, "We had to work very hard to persuade the regulators and the works council that we were on the right track. And it has required a massive change for us as senior leaders, because we don't have the same level of formal control that we used to."

Design Principles for Adhocracy

As the three examples in the previous section illustrate, adhocracy manifests itself in many ways. Sometimes it is created through a formal top-down change initiative (ING), sometimes it emerges in an informal way (Valve), sometimes it is a one-off project (Costa). Rather than copying any one of these approaches, you should instead focus on the basic principles and apply these to your specific circumstances. Following are six key points.

Principle 1: Organize around opportunity. An opportunity is some sort of hypothetical market space from which you can create value—a customer or client, or a problem, usually external but sometimes internal to the firm. Costa and Valve saw opportunities in the unmet and unarticulated needs of their coffee-drinking and gaming customers, respectively. ING saw opportunities to dramatically improve customer responsiveness and to develop new digital banking services. There are also many companies that are structured in a devolved way around their customers. Haier, the Chinese white goods manufacturer, has more than four thousand self-organized customer-facing teams called ZZJYT.[14] Worley Parsons, the Australia-headquartered engineering consultancy, has about 650 projects on the go at any given time, each focused on a specific piece of client work and with team members drawn from across the worldwide organization.

This all sounds pretty obvious, but take a look at your own organizational chart and ask yourself, do the major subdivisions of activity correspond to your current market environment, or are they an artifact of your historical way of working? As an example from our own world, take a look at how business schools divide up their faculty and you will see departments with curious names such as "Operations Research," "Business Policy," and "Industrial Relations." Meanwhile, executive education clients are increasingly asking for programs in such areas as leadership, social media, and service innovation. Of course, we find ways of meshing these old structures with the changing demands for our skills, but the old structures don't add any value. In fact, they are dangerous because they encourage faculty to relate back to a world that doesn't exist anymore. Periodic changes in structure, along with creative use of labels to reflect current market opportunities, are a vital part of staying action-oriented. To paraphrase Sir Winston Churchill, "First we shape our structures, and then our structures shape us." Fast/forward companies shape their future by being opportunity led.

Principle 2: Opportunities are transient. The corollary to organizing around opportunity is that once an opportunity has passed, the people focused on it should move on to another opportunity; think disposability, not eternity. This means you have to become much more decisive about closing down units or projects that are no longer adding value. Or as the native American Dakota tribal proverb goes, "When you discover that you are riding a dead horse, the best strategy is to dismount." The biggest problem with a dead horse is of course that exchanging riders, buying stronger whips, hiring outside contractors to ride it, or forming a committee to study it just won't do the trick.

Figuring out when to stop doing things may in fact be *the* acid test of an effective organization. We recall meeting a senior Xerox executive back in the mid-1990s, and he described how R&D projects often lived on for years, long after they had been officially killed. The inability to focus on the big opportunities was one reason for Xerox's problems in that era. Many large companies suffer from this affliction, and end up with significant numbers of "zombie" projects that don't have formal support but are not entirely dead either.

In contrast, the companies described earlier have very clear expectations on the transience of their core activities. ING's squads are formed to tackle a particular set of customer needs, with the expectation that they will evolve (or be abandoned) as those customer needs change. Costa's Marlow project was created with a clear endpoint in mind, and it was indeed wound up once the low-rate production of the machine had begun.

Fast/forward companies apply a stop-loss logic akin to that which you find in the world of finance. Consider the case of Mundi Pharma, a fast-growing mid-size player in the pharmaceuticals industry. Whereas traditional pharmaceutical companies make long-term commitments to specific therapy areas, Mundi's business units are based on specific drug opportunities. If a drug is successfully launched, the business unit continues; if it fails, the business unit is wound up and employees move over to other more promising business areas. As a result, the company is more market-focused than its competitors—its model is more like that of a VC, in that it only invests when there is a clear pathway toward a drug that is commercially viable.[15]

Principle 3: Speed is essential. One of the exciting-but-scary consequences of defining your structure around opportunities is that you know a given opportunity won't last forever: it comes with a best-before date. This puts an onus on speed—you want to move as quickly as possible to ensure that you don't miss the boat. Costa's Project Marlow is our best example of this. Of course, there was a competitive imperative for moving fast, because Costa wanted to steal a march on Starbucks by bringing a third-generation vending machine to market first. But there was also a behavioral imperative, namely the need to move quickly so that Eric Achtmann's small team could make an impression on the slower-moving bulk of Costa's organization. By setting wildly ambitious deadlines, Achtmann was also able to generate greater levels of effort, energy, and commitment from his team members than would have been possible in a more normal organizational environment.

Focusing on speed *for its own sake* requires a real change in mindset. Most senior executives in large firms enact control by giving out budgets and deadlines. But for complex and uncertain tasks, these are impossible to define accurately. As Jeff Sutherland, founder of the *Scrum* management methodology says, "I'll know what the date [of delivery] will be when I see how much the team improves. How fast they'll get."[16] Most teams, in fact, are capable of getting dramatically more done than anyone realizes, and a lot more quickly. The only way to release that potential energy is to shift their focus toward delivering on a specific opportunity or goal, rather than conforming to a predefined plan.

Principle 4: Activities are transparent. If you want coordination to occur naturally, that is, without being imposed from above, you need a high level of transparency. The reason Hans Monderman's traffic experiments in Holland worked is because the drivers could see exactly what the others were doing, and they adjusted their behavior accordingly. Feedback needs to be at full throttle. Equally, Valve encourages full sharing of information across the organization so that people can make informed choices about what projects to work on. Costa's Project Marlow was also run in a highly transparent way, to help team members prioritize their time effectively.

Transparency in the business world is very much in vogue. We see increasing levels of sharing of sensitive information including accounts, plans, and salary scales. CEOs are opening themselves up to weekly "ask me anything" discussions, online forums for debating company plans, board meetings being recorded and posted online, and so on. There are two small caveats though. Transparency doesn't create an action focus on its own—in fact, it is equally important in a meritocracy, in which there is a tendency toward people talking and discussing things *ad infinitum.* So don't think of transparency as an end in itself. Instead, see it as an enabler of these other principles.

The other caveat is that you can take transparency too far. We have seen firms experimenting with sharing salary information and posting videos of management meetings on the Intranet for all to see, and the consequences are not entirely positive. Lots of noise is created by those who have access to information without properly understanding how it fits into the bigger picture, which in turn creates additional challenges for those in positions of authority.[17] There is, as with all things, a need for striking a delicate balance in the level of transparency provided.

Principle 5. Management is light touch. By concentrating on your market opportunities, you automatically relegate your internally focused management activities to a subordinate level. As a case in point, Valve does not have a human resources department as such. People are so important that rather than making this a big thing for just a few, it's a natural thing for everyone. At Valve, hiring is everyone's responsibility. This means that people put the amount of energy into hiring that is needed, and no more. They don't write policy documents or detailed job descriptions, because they know such things are a distraction from the real work.

ING Bank, in similar fashion, sees all the work being done through the squads, with a minimal managerial overlay to provide oversight. And as Bart Schlatmann observes, this shift toward light-touch management is a very difficult transition for established firms to make. "As a manager, you have to be willing to give up a lot of your traditional sources of power, for this new model to be effective."

Another company with an opportunity-focused structure is Eden McCallum, a London-based strategy consultancy. Like other consultancies, it creates teams to deliver on client-focused projects. But none of these consultants works full time for the company; they are freelancers who devote between 10 and 80 percent of their working lives to Eden McCallum. When they do client work, they are paid a good day rate. When they don't work they are paid nothing. This model ensures that the small central team operates with a light touch. "Our consultants have no patience for internal meetings," observes Liann Eden, one of the founders, "so we keep the amount of bureaucracy to an absolute minimum."

Principle 6. Governance is flexible. The standard model of governance for large firms is the limited liability corporation (though clearly private equity has been growing in popularity in recent years). Like bureaucracy, this model is a relic of the industrial era. It still works pretty well, but it has significant flaws, most notably its short-term focus on shareholder value and its failure to address the needs of other stakeholders.

This institution was established when the financial capital needed to maximize the potential of the industrial revolution was the scarcest resource. The beauty of the limited liability corporation was that by minimizing individual risk (limiting it to the money invested), it maximized risk-taking on the societal level. In fact, since its invention, the limited liability company has, by and large, served us well.

But the changing basis of competition in the business world opens up a big question: What if, for many organizations, capital has been replaced by competence (or perhaps even something more ephemeral such as emotional conviction) as the scarcest resource for wealth creation?

As we move away from a bureaucratic approach to coordination, we should consider whether alternative governance models are needed. Among the examples described here, we see quite a few hybrids: Valve is a private company, so less susceptible to external scrutiny than a PLC; Project Marlow was undertaken under the umbrella of Costa Coffee (itself, a division of Whitbread PLC), but most of the players on the team actually worked for other firms or as freelancers.

And Eden McCallum, the strategy consultancy mentioned in the previous section, is a limited liability partnership, with the vast majority of its consultants working as freelancers on a project-by-project basis. In fact, the further you go down the opportunity-focused coordination route, the more unattractive the traditional salaried-employment model becomes.

Linking Adhocracy Back to Bureaucracy

As we have shown, coordinating activities in an adhocracy is based on a set of principles very different from those that most of us are familiar with. Getting this new way of working right is challenging enough on its own.

A big part of this challenge is that adhocracy is sometimes interpreted as a free for all—a license to take action for action's sake—00∞ rather than 007. But this can lead to all sorts of problems if those taking action haven't thought it through, or if they lack the basic competence to depart from the standard script. Remember, exploratory action is hypothesis-driven—it is designed to resolve specific uncertainties in the marketplace. Gaining clarity about what those uncertainties are and how they might be tested requires discipline and skill.

There is a secondary challenge as well, namely figuring out how the adhocracy-based parts of the organization are linked to those parts based on bureaucracy or meritocracy. Like oil and water, these different models don't mix well. In one seminar we were running, an executive described his company as consisting of "islands of adhocracy in a sea of bureaucracy." It requires a lot of careful effort from those at the top of the organization to bring the models together without losing the essence of either.

Costa's Project Marlow is an example of the challenge. While the project delivered on budget and on schedule, the rate of progress *after* the project work was finished slowed down considerably. It took approximately two years before the roll-out of the new machine began in earnest. The reasons for this delay were entirely understandable: Costa Coffee is a large firm with established sales and manufacturing teams, and they needed to be brought up to speed before fully embracing the product created by Eric Achtmann and his team. We have seen many similar examples of this phenomenon over the years.

So what can be done to avoid this problem? Or to state the question more specifically, what approaches should executives take to manage the inevitable tension between adhocracy and the more traditional bureaucracy and meritocracy models? Here are some practical suggestions—each has some merits, none is a panacea.

Use executive sponsorship to provide integration. The most obvious approach is for senior executives to act as the linking mechanism. This, in essence, is what their job is all about—seeing the big picture, dividing up work into suitably structured units, and then making sure those units link together in a joined-up fashion. But as we saw in Costa Coffee, it takes a long time for the gears to mesh.

IBM's Emerging Business Opportunities program, as discussed in Chapter 4, provides a good example of how to do this right. The group of senior executives led by Bruce Harreld provided guidance to the teams working on emerging opportunities. They helped them build contacts with people in established units, and they stepped aside once they were confident the necessary levels of integration had been achieved.[18]

Liberate the new opportunities. One option for Costa Coffee—at least on paper—was to let Project Marlow build its own sales organization and ultimately become a stand-alone business unit. By comparison, Nestlé did exactly this when it developed the Nespresso product line— rather than integrate it into an existing line of business, Nespresso was allowed to operate in a stand-alone manner, and this helped it to flourish. Another example is a defense electronics company in the United Kingdom called Racal, which was a pioneer in radio technology in the late 1980s. It opted to spin off its promising new technology into a separate company called Vodafone—which subsequently became the first mobile operator to reach a market capitalization of $100 billion. Sometimes, you shouldn't even attempt to integrate a high-growth opportunity into your existing bureaucratic structure.

Allow internal competition between businesses. In some industries, it is possible to allow fast-moving units to retain their adhocracy-based operating principles within an overarching structure. For example, the world's largest advertising and communication firm is WPP, a U.K. holding company that includes traditional agencies such as JWT and Ogilvy & Mather alongside more than a hundred digital agencies, social media outfits, PR firms, and market researchers. WPP encourages these operating units to retain their entrepreneurial, action-oriented way of working, often competing with each other directly. However, in places where economies of scale are important (for example in media buying), greater coordination across units is encouraged.

Create a two-speed organization. The most ambitious way of integrating adhocracy with bureaucracy is the notion of a two-speed organization, with people dividing their time between the slow-moving and fast-moving units. John Kotter has written about this model in his recent book *Accelerate*. He calls it a dual operating system, with "hierarchy on one side, network on the other" and with the two sides "seamlessly connected."[19] We think this is an exciting model in principle, but it is really hard to put into practice. Using the Costa Coffee example, it would be as if Eric Achtmann had taken 50 percent of the time of fifty Costa employees for eight months, so that they were working, say, one week on Project Marlow, then the next week back in their traditional roles. This approach would have been exciting for the Costa people on the project, and it would have enabled faster integration at the end, but chances are the machine would have arrived much later, and would not have been as good. Remember, Eric scoured the world for the "best" talent to create the Marlow machine.

From Coordination to Engagement

There is an ongoing search for better ways of working in the business world, and recent books from *Holacracy* by Brian Robertson to *Team of Teams* by General Stanley McChrystal describe some of these pioneering efforts to create alternatives to bureaucracy.[20] We applaud these types of initiatives, and we are especially impressed by the individuals who have had the courage to put their novel ideas into practice. But at the same time, we don't want to throw out the baby with the bathwater. Getting rid of bureaucracy *entirely* is the wrong goal—what we should be doing, instead, is finding new models for fast-moving or uncertain situations and having the wisdom to retain our tried-and-trusted ways of working in more traditional operating environments.

And the challenge here isn't just about rethinking our processes and activities. It is also about getting to grips with the emotional agenda—this means finding the right stimuli to get people motivated by their work and creating an internal culture that encourages experimentation and creativity. This is the set of issues we address in the next chapter.

Chapter 7

THE OVERACHIEVING ORGANIZATION

ON FEBRUARY 22, 1980, the U.S. Olympic hockey team shocked TV audiences around the world by beating the defending champion Soviet Union by a score of 4-3. Exceeding all expectations, team USA took a giant step toward the gold medal that was secured two days later by defeating Finland. The surprising win against the so-called "big red machine" later became known as the "Miracle on Ice." Not only that, so unexpected was the triumph that in 1999, *Sports Illustrated* named it the "Top Sports Moment of the 20th Century."

Beating the Soviets was a dream come true for the United States in general and the ice hockey team in particular. Think back some thirty-five years. It happened at the height of the Cold War. This was the year after the Soviet invasion of Afghanistan. A few months later, the United States and many other Western countries would boycott the summer games in Moscow. And there were certainly reasons for calling the victory a miracle. It was like Sly Stallone's Rocky Balboa character knocking out the evil Russian Ivan Drago, but for real.

The U.S. coach, Herb Brooks, had put together a group of amateurs to play against the world's best hockey teams. The Soviets entered the Lake Placid games as heavy favorites, having won the four previous ice hockey gold medals. After the 1960 Olympics, the Soviet teams had gone 27-1-1 (wins-losses-ties) and outscored the opposition by 175-44! Their current team was considered the best ever. Of the twenty U.S. players, only one had previous Olympic experience. Their average age was twenty-one.

Before the game, Herb Brooks, a guy that the U.S. players later described as "gruff," gave one of the most well-known, inspiring pep talks of all time—the American equivalent of Shakespeare's Saint Crispin's Day speech. The players were all sitting down. Herb entered, took in the room, and his opening phrase was, "Great moments are born from great opportunity." He went on to say that if they played their opponents ten times, the Soviet team might win nine out of ten, but not this game, not tonight! He and the team then went on to prove that at times conviction does indeed beat competence.

The U.S. gold medal in the 1980 Olympics is just one example of how ordinary people, under the right circumstances, can do extraordinary things. Now, let's make this a bit more personal. Think back to an occasion when you did your best work, when you were fully motivated and engaged, when you surprised everyone—including yourself. What were the key features of that piece of work?

When we ask our executive audiences this question, the majority of people don't recall a particular organization or job, or when they relied on a particular experience or a piece of knowledge they acquired at a university; they recall a specific *project*. They focus on how challenging it was, how they surmounted various obstacles and met a tough deadline, how they worked well with colleagues. The vast majority also focus on a *successful* endeavor, when something important was achieved and when they received due recognition for their efforts.

Recall the example of Costa Coffee's Project Marlow from the previous chapter. Under the guidance of Eric Achtmann, the Marlow team had thirty-eight core members spread over ten different partner organizations and six countries. The team was pulled together in less than two months, and within nine months they had created a 95 percent functioning Beta prototype, on time, and on budget. Despite the long hours, the weekend meetings, the conference calls late into the night, the team members all spoke fondly of the experience and praised Achtmann's "maniacal focus on delivering the goods."

How did Eric Achtmann recruit the team? Like Herb Brooks with the U.S. Olympic hockey team, he *inspired* them—he outlined his vision for the new coffee machine, how it was going to revolutionize vending, how exciting the work would be, and how he couldn't do it without them. He didn't offer enormous sums of money—in fact, up-front fees were lower than in a typical project, and the money only became attractive if the product subsequently sold well. But the "A team" players he approached all said yes. One was Steve Belgrave of eMixPro, sound technician for bands such as the Rolling Stones, U2, and Coldplay. "When the company I was previously working with turned down Project Marlow for organizational reasons, I decided to do it on my own. The concept, team, and approach were just too good to pass up," said Belgrave.

It isn't surprising at all that project work gets people's juices flowing and encourages them to go the extra mile. But it is a useful starting point for a discussion of what, exactly, drives behavior in the workplace. Our fundamental argument in this book is that firms need to foster decisive action coupled with emotional conviction to succeed in an uncertain business environment. To make this possible, we need to get to grips with the complex and slippery notion of employee motivation.

Motivation Revisited

Like pornography, motivation is a concept that is hard to define but we all know it when we see it. Think of it as the invisible engine that drives people's attitudes and behavior in the workplace—what we have previously referred to as organizational adrenaline. Some days, the engine is revving at high velocity, at other times it is firing on only two or three cylinders. One of the biggest responsibilities of leaders and coaches is to look for ways to tune up the motivational engines of employees, to help them do their best work.

There are many theories of motivation out there—for example, Maslow's hierarchy of needs, McGregor's Theory X and Theory Y, and Herzberg's dual-factor theory.[1] The reason for this somewhat confusing plethora of concepts is of course that human behavior is complicated.

We are motivated by many different things: U ≠ Me. And as we saw in Chapter 5, the goals and motivators that are salient to us vary over time.

Consider the rogue trader Jerome Kerviel, who lost €5 billion for Société Générale in 2008. Many people would surmise that he was "only motivated by money" because of the big bets he made, but in his own testimony he talked about his ambition, his desire for recognition among his peers, and his concern for his family.[2] We have several motivational dials in our heads, and depending on the stimuli we receive, some of those dials get cranked up, while others are wound down. Through a mix of his personality and his situation, Kerviel temporarily cranked up his financial-gain dial to a Spinal Tap level of 11, and paid the price. Now that he has recently been released from prison, it is a fair bet that his dials have been reset, with family and personal well-being now being much more important to him.

Even though motivation is a complex thing, we can still sketch out some useful generalizations.

In an industrial-age bureaucracy, motivation is primarily extrinsic—it comes from outside the individual, typically in the form of payment for services, or "money for minutes." Think of the assembly-line worker, the call-center employee, the building site laborer. In this world, work is tiresome and repetitive, but they do it to earn the money that allows them to seek pleasure elsewhere.

In information-age organizations, built on meritocracy and adhocracy, the employee deal is drastically different—less transactional and a lot more emotional. Motivation is primarily intrinsic—it comes from within. Work is sufficiently interesting, challenging, and enjoyable that for many of us it is an end in itself. We "live to work" rather than "work to live." Think of lawyers, scientists, or general managers. In this world, they don't worry so much about money because it is almost taken for granted; instead they are striving for the higher-order elements in Maslow's hierarchy of needs—belonging, esteem, and self-actualization.

But once again, we need to make a distinction between meritocracy and adhocracy, because the drivers of motivation are subtly different in each model.

In a meritocracy, knowledge is privileged over formal position or action, and motivation is based on the development and recognition of *personal competence*. Academics get a buzz from being more knowledgeable about a field of research than anyone else. Doctors want to make the smart diagnoses. Creative types in ad agencies love coming up with cool new ideas. These are all examples of what American author Dan Pink calls *mastery*—the desire to get better and better at doing something worthwhile.[3] The people who call the shots in a meritocracy are the "black belts"—the experts who have achieved the highest level of personal mastery in their chosen field.

In an adhocracy, action is privileged over formal position or knowledge, and motivation is based on *achievement*. People are turned on by the opportunity to take on tricky challenges, they like achieving results and beating the opposition, they relish the "thrill of the chase," and they value the recognition they receive afterward for a job well done. Picture a special-forces unit on an assignment in enemy territory, or a team in an investment bank pulling an all-nighter to clinch a deal, or Eric Achtmann's Project Marlow. In these cases, money making and personal mastery are far less important than getting the desired outcome.

There are, of course, some overlaps between these two approaches to motivation—a good lawyer, for example, wants to be highly knowledgeable about her area of professional practice, and she also wants to win her cases. But it is still useful to tease them apart, because we get slightly different outcomes depending on which approach we emphasize. For example, we have a couple of colleagues, let's call them Sam and Alex. They are both professors, and both very good at what they do. The difference is that Sam is a true scholar who loves the pursuit of knowledge for its own sake, while Alex likes nothing more than getting her ideas published in the top journals. Sam is driven by personal mastery, Alex by achievement. We don't have to choose between them—they are both valuable members of the community in which they work, and their skills and motivations are largely complementary. But the point is that different things drive them. So changes in conditions such as incentive systems are likely to have differential effects on their behavior. In fact, the university department where they work has recently put an explicit emphasis on top-journal publications. Alex is pleased by this turn of events; Sam is dispirited, and may leave.

So how can you structure work to play up the achievement orientation of your employees? Eric Achtmann's approach in Project Marlow was to spend a lot of time working on the team spirit, coupling grueling milestones and demanding standards with celebratory events every time a milestone was successfully achieved. He also created a plaque for all thirty-eight key team members, which would be permanently mounted in every production machine, with their names and the words "for exceptional and enduring contribution to the program, above and beyond the call of duty." The incentives were also geared to achievement, with all team members having a financial bonus linked to how many machines were sold.

Another example is Valve, the manager-free gaming company featured in Chapter 6. Challenge is the starting point: the handbook for new employees says, "Valve has an incredibly unique way of doing things that will make this the greatest professional experience of your life, but it can take some getting used to." Employees have very high levels of responsibility ("You have the power to green-light products, you have the power to ship products"), and as mentioned earlier, the company emphasizes that hiring great colleagues is "your most important role." There is also a significant extrinsic component to motivation that is linked to achievement: employees rate their peers, and a forced-ranking system gears discretionary pay toward those who contribute the most. Simply put, Valve is a competitive and challenging place to work, and its founders believe this makes it attractive to the most talented game developers.

Building the Context to Support Decisive Action

For Eric Achtmann at Costa, and for Gabe Newell at Valve, the structure they chose was drawn on a clean sheet of paper. But most of us don't have that luxury. Instead, we start with an existing organization that is rooted in bureaucratic or meritocratic thinking, and we have to use whatever limited tools are at our disposal to reconfigure things if we want to move in the direction of a more adhocratic model.

The rest of this chapter is all about the practical things you can do to make your organization, or indeed a single project team or unit within the larger organization, more achievement-oriented. In our experience, you can indeed make significant improvements without changing the people working for you.

The starting point is to recognize that high-achievement teams have two defining features that are, to some degree, in tension. On the one hand, they are inspired—typically by some sort of higher-order goal or purpose. They have a dream—not a five-year plan. This helps to build confidence, optimism, and hope. On the other hand, they have a strong support structure that provides them with the security and resources to do their job effectively. Resilience—the ability to bounce back after setbacks—also matters. An inspired team that doesn't have the necessary support is taking huge risks, and this creates a lot of stress for those involved. An uninspired but well-supported team will end up underperforming, though in a safe and comfortable way. See Figure 7.1. It is only when inspiration and support are operating in tandem that truly exceptional performance is achieved.[4]

We see this frequently in team sports. Think back to the Miracle on Ice in 1980, or to more recent cases of unlikely sporting victories— the Giants defeating the Patriots in the 2008 Super Bowl, Greece winning the 2004 European Soccer Championships, Leicester City winning the U.K.'s soccer Premiership in 2016, South Africa winning the Rugby World Cup in 2007. There is always a yin-yang element to these stories—a core of disciplined, hard work plus a sprinkling of inspiration from a coach or star player. Paradoxically, when players are allowed to fail, they often gain the freedom to succeed. In the academic world, this is called "psychological safety"—confidence that your team members will support your well-intentioned efforts regardless of how they work out.[5] Let's look more closely at these two dimensions in turn.

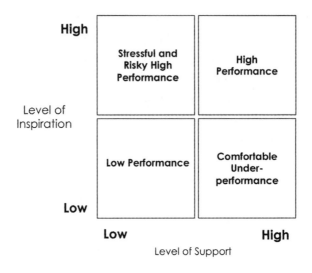

FIGURE 7.1 Two Dimensions of High Performance

Framing the Upside: Sources of Inspiration

To inspire someone, you have to get past their rational and calculating view of the world and tap into their emotional belief system. As we discussed in Chapter 2, most people don't form their views through careful, fact-based analysis. Instead, they reach a judgment based on intuition, personal experience, or influence from parents or peers, and then use facts and evidence selectively to justify the position they have taken.

We call these emotional beliefs, to distinguish them from purely rational beliefs. For example, our views on fairness, loyalty, authority, social justice, the importance of family, and so on are all emotional beliefs. And they are massively important in shaping how we look at the world and how we behave on a day-to-day basis. Research by Dan Kahan, a law and psychology professor at Yale, even suggests that at times most people are "fact resistant." Instead, he talks about "motivated reasoning"—our beliefs bend our thinking. For instance, it turns out that even those who are really good at math will unconsciously make systematic miscalculations if the result is against their own convictions.[6]

Politicians have understood how to use this to their advantage for centuries. Aristotle's notion of *pathos* was an appeal to emotion (whereas *logos* was an appeal to rational logic), and a political speech in ancient Greece, as much as today, made sure to tap into the emotions and passions of the populace to stir them up and get their support. Religious orders are also highly effective at firing up our intuitive or subconscious beliefs, and imposing a worldview on us that shapes our choices in life. For example, Kim Clark, a former dean of the Harvard Business School and a world-renowned operations management scholar, quit his job to become president of Brigham Young University in Idaho—a private university affiliated with the Mormon Church.[7]

The message should be clear: if you want to inspire your employees, don't give them a sales target to hit, focus on the bigger picture. Paint a compelling picture of a possible future—when an encumbrance has been resolved, when people are happier or healthier, when the planet is less threatened. And give your employees a reason to do something about it now, by playing up the challenge, the competitive threat from others, the kudos they will get from making it happen. When the upside opportunity is framed in an alluring way, people will bring more of their emotional energy with them, and they will often find creative solutions to any problems they encounter along the way. They will begin to think "must do" rather than "can or could do." Consider a few quick examples from the automotive industry that illustrate four different ways of inspiring people to move forward faster: by being bolder, better, more benevolent, or just bigger, respectively.

First, consider the most obvious example of a company that has pursued a strategy aimed at *boldness*. The entire essence of Tesla, founded in 2003 by super-entrepreneur Elon Musk, oozes of a desire to revolutionize an industry—to fundamentally challenge the hundred-year dominance of the internal combustion engine. For sure, most other contenders have a pinky-toe or two in the luxury electric car niche that Tesla now dominates, but unlike Tesla their main business lies elsewhere. However, despite Tesla's current niche-market focus, from the very beginning Musk has consistently maintained that the long-term goal of the company is to create affordable mass-market electric vehicles. Or as the company puts it, "Our goal when we created Tesla a decade ago was the same as it is today: to accelerate the advent of sustainable transport by bringing compelling mass market electric cars to market as soon as possible."[8] Back in 2006, in his first blog for the company, Elon Musk outlined his master-plan for the company. It looked like this:

- "Build sports car

- Use that money to build an affordable car

- Use that money to build an even more affordable car

- While doing above, also provide zero emission electric power generation options

- Don't tell anyone."[9]

Porsche follows a logic of action that appeals to a different set of people. The company is all about perfection. Everything should be *better* than the rest. More than sixty-five years ago Ferry Porsche formulated the Porsche principle: "In the beginning, I looked around and could not find the car I'd been dreaming of: a small, lightweight sports car that uses energy efficiently. So I decided to build it myself."[10] Since then, this dream of building the perfect sports car has been driving the company and its engineers. It is claimed that an amazing 60 percent of all Porsche cars ever built are still on the road.

Companies with an onus on *benevolence* have other drivers—appealing to those who prefer capitalism with a conscience. Consider the case of Hyundai, the world's greenest traditional automotive company according to the Union of Concerned Scientists. To reach this position, the company has championed smaller engines, electric hybrids, and other anti-pollution technologies. Their management philosophy is stated as, "Realize the dream of mankind by creating a new future through ingenious thinking and continuously challenging new frontiers."[11] The dream, in turn is broken down into three guiding principles: realization of possibilities plus unlimited sense of responsibility plus respect for mankind.

Finally, we have those firms that seek to dominate—to be the *biggest* on the block. While this vision appeals to many people, growth per se as an inspirational goal can also lead a company astray. Consider the case of Volkswagen, which in 2007 formulated a goal to become the world's largest automaker by 2018. Volkswagen achieved its goal three years ahead of plan. Yet, as we all know, they crossed a number of lines to get there, equipping their diesel cars with a "defeat device" that improved performance during tests but also allowed their cars to pollute up to forty times over the allowable limits. To our mind, being the biggest is not a viable purpose, unless there is something behind it. Domination must ensue as the positive outcome of doing something great for one or more of the constituents inside or outside the firm—talent, customers, the environment, and so on. Volkswagen once had such an inspirational vision. It was founded as the "people's car," but somewhere along the line, management lost its way and crashed the company.

The purpose of these brief examples is just to illustrate some of the ways you can inspire the people in your own business. Are there any big unresolved problems in your market that need addressing? Are there any assumptions, for example about quality-affordability trade-offs, that you can challenge? What are the real needs of your customers that you have been overlooking up to now? We often find ourselves working with executive teams on these types of questions, as a way of stimulating innovative business ideas.[12]

Managing the Downside: Support for Failure

If you take on a challenging task, there is a significant risk that you won't deliver—otherwise it wouldn't have been challenging in the first place. But this creates a big problem, at least if you work in a large organization, because most senior executives are allergic to failure. Your management processes (budgeting, resource allocation, risk control) are built on predictability and efficiency, and executives succeed by showing they are in control. The tolerance of failure is small, and often close to zero. Media mogul Sam Goldwyn said it best: "I don't want yes men, I want people who will tell me the truth, even if it costs them their job."

So how do you create a setting in which well-intentioned failure is not just tolerated, but actually seen as part and parcel of everyday working life? As noted earlier, academics use the phrase "psychological safety" to refer to a culture in which people feel supported when things don't work out, but we believe there are many additional dimensions to this problem—from the formal incentives through the implicit norms to the structured mechanisms for providing feedback. Our research suggests three specific areas in which you can intervene.[13]

Actively reflect on feedback. In the world of politics, governmental reviews are often absurdly long. They are designed to point fingers or seek scapegoats, and they are done only in response to a crisis. In the corporate world, reviews work best when they are the exact opposite: they are short and to the point. The purpose is to learn, not find someone to blame, and they take place on a regular schedule, through good times as well as bad times. Think of them as triple-F reviews: Fast, Frequent, and Future-oriented.

Consider the case of Kal Patel, who was parachuted in to lead consumer electronics retailer Best Buy's Asian operations in 2009. The company had acquired a Chinese retail chain, Five Star, a few years earlier, and it was performing well. But the stores under the Best Buy brand were struggling. After a quick assessment of the situation, Patel told the board, "We are going to treat these six stores as ventures, we are going to run a series of experiments in these ventures, and six months from now I am going to tell you if there is a viable business model here."

Over the following six months, Patel pushed the store managers to make a lot of changes—new layouts in the stores, new ways of working with suppliers, different pricing models—to see what might work, and he instituted weekly review meetings.

"On Friday mornings, we'd have a review of all the experiments. People would come in with their pitch. I would push them: What did you set out to learn? What did you learn? What is it costing you? Bang, five to ten minutes, move on to the next team."

This rapid-cycle review process quickly exposed the opportunities for growth and also the structural problems with the Best Buy branded stores. It also led to a dramatic change in the behavior of the hundred senior managers whom Patel had direct contact with. He showed that he wasn't interested in who had achieved what. "I don't care who has done it," he would say, "as a group, what did you learn?" He also encouraged his management team to adopt the same approach in their team meetings. "I set the expectations, this is how we behave. They all watched, then the next week they were doing the same."

At the end of six months, Patel recommended closing down the own-brand retail operation in China, but because he was also overseeing the Five Star chain, he was able to transfer a lot of specific insights across, and he was able to retain most of the employees as well.

The point is that learning from failure is a lot about consistency and discipline. Most venture capital firms, for example, are very diligent about following through on their review process even when things seem to be going well. Hussein Kanji, a partner at Hoxton Ventures, a $40 million European early stage venture capital firm, told us, "Every quarter we sit down for a half day, and go back through our original investment memos [for ventures we invested in]. We ask, did we get something fundamentally wrong here? Was there an error in our thinking? It's easy to be swayed by one big success or failure, so we push ourselves to do this systematically. This is how we fine tune and adapt our criteria."

Set a positive tone. A key part of your job as a leader is to shape the immediate working environment, so that your people know what types of attitudes and behaviors are acceptable. You are providing the cues and stimuli that motivate individuals close to you to take the initiative, and to help them internalize the message that failure is complementary to success. This is a highly personal thing—very different from the reflection process described earlier. Every person is driven by a slightly different set of factors, so you have to tailor your message accordingly. Consider a story recounted to us by the CEO of a newspaper business. A couple of years ago, he asked one of his brightest young editors to try out a new tabloid-size format, to see if that would help arrest the decline in sales. The young guy spent a month on the project, working up a prototype and market testing it with a group of customers. They didn't like it at all, and the project was killed. For the CEO, this was a good outcome—it confirmed his nagging worry that his readers wouldn't buy in to a tabloid-size offering. But the young editor was devastated—he felt he had personally failed, and he ended up taking a job elsewhere.

The lesson for the newspaper CEO was straightforward: if you want someone to take on a project that has a high chance of failure, you need to be very clear in advance about what you expect, and that a negative outcome can actually be the right result. "He thought he was developing a pilot, where success is about making it work. But for me it was an experiment, where success is about confirming or refuting a hypothesis. I should have been much more explicit with him, contracting with him in advance about what might happen."

The common theme here is that you need to tailor the message to the individual. Most people, in our experience, are inherently responsible, and typically more worried about failing than their bosses are. Kal Patel recalled visiting the struggling Best Buy stores in China and talking to eighteen- or nineteen-year-old employees "convinced that they themselves had failed," when in fact the problems were entirely outside their control. Simon Best, a life sciences investor, makes a similar point: "You have to establish a culture that says, we are taking calculated risks. Establish what evidence, what metrics we will use to make our decisions, simplify and standardize these as much as possible, and then follow them rigorously. And if I am giving someone a really challenging assignment, I will always give them a heads up that this is high risk, and then I will tailor the rewards accordingly—focusing more on process than outcome measures in cases where it is really high risk."

But there are also a few people who have a cavalier attitude to spending their company's money, and seem almost immune to criticism. These are difficult people to deal with, because they are often highly successful—dealmakers, super-salespeople, creative geniuses—and believe themselves to be above the rules. In such cases, you need to take a very different approach; you want to give them the freedom to do their jobs, but with great clarity around the boundaries as well. They need to be made aware of the risks they are taking, and the consequences of those risks if things go badly.

Be more open when things don't work out. The third part of supporting high-risk projects is to work on some of the intangible elements of your culture. Storytelling is one such element. GE executives are all familiar with Thomas Edison's famous statement, "I have not failed, I've just found 10,000 ways that won't work." At 3M, Art Fry's invention of Post-It notes has achieved legendary status, and a key part of the story is that it arose from failure—an adhesive that didn't stick very well. Former Coca-Cola executive Donald Keough spoke frequently about the New Coke story—to remind executives about where the company went wrong, and of course how it subsequently bounced back and recaptured market leadership from Pepsi.[14]

Visible symbols are also important. For example, Tata Sons, the holding company for the entire Tata Group of businesses, had an annual innovation award program called Innovista, with two categories: best new product or service, and best process improvement. In 2008, they launched a third category, the Dare to Try award, to recognize and reward the "most novel, daring and seriously attempted ideas that did not achieve the desired results." The first year they tried this, they had to work hard to get people to apply. By 2013 the number of Dare to Try submissions had risen to 240. "We want people to be bold and to not be afraid to fail," observes Sunil Sinha, head of Tata Quality Management Services.[15] Other companies have tried similar initiatives: Grey, the advertising firm, has an annual "Heroic Failure" award, while Google is known for hosting champagne parties for notable failed projects.

An even more visible approach to failure is provided by Engineers Without Borders International, a not-for-profit organization based in Canada that works with disadvantaged communities to improve their quality of life through education and implementation of sustainable engineering projects. Frustrated with the limited amount of learning that was going on between their various affiliates around the world, a group led by Nick Jimenez and Ashley Good decided to launch a "failure report" that would publicize, for all to see, the most significant failed projects each year. This first report was handed out at the annual meeting in January 2009 as a grassroots initiative that even the CEO didn't know about. As stated on their website, "It is painful . . . to acknowledge when we don't meet our goals and objectives. The paradox is that we do everything we can to avoid these pains even though we all know failure is the best teacher and we have to be open and talk about our failures in order to learn."[16]

Practical Steps: How to Build an Achievement-Oriented Organization

We have discussed a lot of the general principles for how to reorient your organization toward a focus on decisive action and emotional conviction. In this final section, we consider some of the practical next steps for making this happen.

Create the right vehicle. Most large organizations are so ill-equipped for decisive action-taking that they decide to create a special-purpose vehicle that operates with its own set of rules. But there are a range of options here.

Costa's Project Marlow was a classic example of an autonomous "skunk-works" team, operating outside the traditional power structure of the firm, with its own personnel and its own distinctive way of working. Many examples of this approach have been seen over the years, from the original Apple Mac project in the early 1980s to Google X, the unit created to spearhead Google's boldest ideas, such as driverless cars. They allow you to move very quickly and encourage decisiveness, and the people working in them are typically passionate about their work. Yet they suffer, almost inevitably, from isolation and skepticism vis-à-vis the mainstream business, and many, over the years, have failed for this reason. As we discussed in the previous chapter, there are a number of practical ways of keeping the skunk-works-type unit integrated with the rest of the organization.

A less visible alternative to the skunk-works is what we call a "sandbox" approach. In the world of software, the sandbox is the safe environment in which changes to the computer code are tested before going live. In a business setting, the equivalent logic is to find low-risk ways of testing out big ideas by breaking them into chunks. You can do this through *sequential de-risking*, when uncertainties are resolved in sequence. This is the standard model in the world of venture capital. As Hussein Kanji describes it, "We work through a set of questions: Can you prove there is a customer? Can you prove the product works? Do you have a viable business model? Funding is linked to each step." Many large companies would claim to use stage/gate processes for sequential de-risking, but they typically make it such a slow process, and so focused on evaluation rather than development, that its benefits are lost. The smartest companies, in our experience, are the ones that have figured out when to use their stage/gate process and when to fast track an idea through a leaner model.

You can also opt for *parallel de-risking*, in which there is a key area of uncertainty, perhaps around a technical issue, and there are two or more possible ways of resolving it. In such cases, the smart way forward is to pursue multiple pathways at the same time, for example, two different projects working on different technical standards. Again, this is a common model in the world of venture capital, in which one VC might make several bets in the same space. Hussein Kanji again: "We wouldn't let one of our companies pursue multiple paths, they need to focus; we would do this at the level of the portfolio."

Finally, a lighter-touch model is to provide people pursuing risky projects with peer support. At Saatchi & Saatchi, the global advertising agency, the "creatives" who come up with the agency's cutting-edge ad campaigns usually work in pairs. The duos often share a workspace, go out for coffee and lunch together, and work on lots of projects with each other over time. Their informal buddy system builds tacit knowledge and social capital and gives them a sounding board for trying out their craziest ideas before floating them to the rest of their team; they have each other's backs. At the World Bank, project teams must identify a couple of "friendly reviewers" from outside the team to provide expert input on the team's direction, such as the scope and specifics of a proposed development project, before it is finalized. This type of peer support has several benefits: helping the team members ensure they are not suffering from "groupthink" caused by talking only to each other, widening the community of those who understand their goals, and building buy-in for their project from outsiders.

Get out of the way. It almost goes without saying, but high-performing teams working on challenging projects hate to be micromanaged. As world-renowned jazz trumpeter Wynton Marsalis observed, "Don't be afraid of another person's creativity." As a manager, if you second-guess every move people make, you will cut them off before they can follow through on their ideas. Google X is deliberately located a long way from corporate headquarters, and its teams are given high degrees of freedom for developing their ideas however they see fit. Even when things don't work out there is no intervention from above. According to its head, Astro Teller, "You must reward people for failing. If not, they won't take risks and make breakthroughs. If you don't reward failure, people will hang on to a doomed idea for fear of the consequences. That wastes time and saps an organization's spirit."

The notion of unfettered delegation makes an absolute majority of all executives nervous. Most of the people we discuss this with prefer a model of light-touch oversight, which can be successful but still leaves many employees looking over their shoulder and covering their backsides. But there are a couple of exceptions. Henry Stewart, CEO of IT training company Happy Ltd, has a principle of "pre-approving" any proposal without even looking at the paperwork. A larger company example is Goldcorp Inc., a Canadian miner. When asked what happens when his employees make a mistake, chairman Ian Telfer replied, "You try not to let them wreck the place. But if you see them hiring the wrong person, let them. They'll figure it out. What happens is (that) people learn faster, they're more empowered and engaged, and they become better."[17]

Of course, getting out of the way doesn't mean that no over-sight or attention is needed. On the contrary, knowing what is going on and being prepared to pull the plug when things go too badly is a critical responsibility for senior managers. Still, thinking ahead about what that moment will look like if it comes, sharing those lim-its with the team, and sticking to the plan rather than jumping the gun will help.

Develop better metrics. Virtually everyone understands that there is a rhetoric-reality gap in large firms, with executives talking a lot about decisive action and radical innovation but still operating with pro-cesses that are biased toward conservatism and conformity. So what's the solution? One approach that we have already talked about in ear-lier chapters is to start small, engage with users early on, and build up momentum gradually. By reducing the downside risk, a company can manage a deep-seated aversion to failure.

While this approach has enormous benefits, it also has a signifi-cant flaw, namely that it treats experimental failure as something to be avoided at all costs. But this is short-sighted because failure is an inte-gral part of any innovation process, and failure also carries important information. As Pixar's CEO Ed Catmull observes, "Mistakes aren't a necessary evil. They aren't evil at all. They are an *inevitable* conse-quence of doing something new." So a more nuanced approach is to maximize the benefits of failing while also reducing its costs. Think of it as a management ratio, *return on failure,* analogous to the return on investment in an R&D project. If it is true that failure has some value, it would seem useful to start measuring what sort of return you get on it—so that the ratio can be improved.

What then are the components of return on failure—how do you calculate it? The denominator is simply the downside risk—the resources invested in an activity multiplied by the level of uncer-tainty around it. The lean-start-up perspective is all about de-risking projects—making the denominator as small as possible.

The numerator has several important elements. We like to think in terms of the "assets" that you might place on a hypothetical balance sheet. There are short-term assets created from failure, such as specific insights and opportunities to pursue, and there are long-term assets such as improvements in capabilities that encourage future initiative-taking. Some of these assets are specific to an individual person or team, while others are held at the level of a business unit.

$$\text{Return on Failure (ROF)} = \frac{\text{(insights, opportunities, capabilities to encourage future initiative)}}{\text{(size of investment, uncertainty)}}$$

The equation is shown here. Obviously, it is hard to make this into a quantitative analysis, but you can do a first approximation by measuring each one as low, medium, or high. The worksheet (see Figure 7.2) provides a list of specific questions to help you with this analysis.

Hold off on the performance review. While it is important to review how projects are going, as a way of gleaning insights and learnings that can be applied in other areas, you have to be very cautious before deciding whether your new organizing model is a success or not.

Let's imagine that your firm recently launched a major new scheme for funding high-risk innovation projects. The first two projects came back as failures. It would be completely natural to start questioning whether the funding scheme was ill-conceived, but it would also be entirely wrong to do so. Most high-risk innovation projects fail, so it is meaningless to even begin an analysis of the scheme until, say, ten projects have been completed. As renowned Silicon Valley investor Steve Jurvetson observes, "You have to strive for a process of decision making that over a large number of decisions gives good outcomes. . . . The folklore should be, we had a process whereby we did some brilliant things. Not 'are we making good decisions?' but 'do we have a process for making decisions that is statistically working?'"

Kal Patel was sensitive to this point when he took on the role of head of Best Buy Asia. By reframing the Best Buy–branded stores as "venture" operations, he bought some time and he kept the board at arm's length. This allowed him to do the necessary level of experimentation without constant interference. "I gave them a deadline, and they let me get on with it."

Unfortunately, it is human nature to extrapolate from a small number of data points. This is why people are so keen to get "early

Accounting for Failure—Individual Project Level

Consider a *recent failed project or activity* that you were involved with and describe it briefly:

Now answer the following questions about this project....

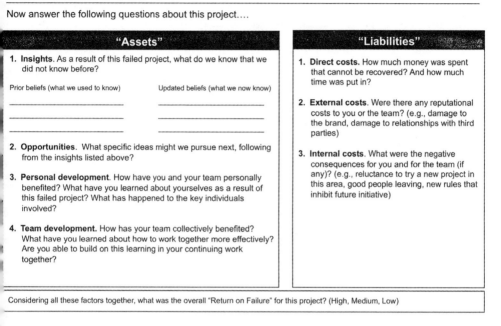

"Assets"	"Liabilities"
1. Insights. As a result of this failed project, what do we know that we did not know before? Prior beliefs (what we used to know) Updated beliefs (what we now know) _____ _____ _____ _____ _____ _____ **2. Opportunities.** What specific ideas might we pursue next, following from the insights listed above? **3. Personal development**. How have you and your team personally benefited? What have you learned about yourselves as a result of this failed project? What has happened to the key individuals involved? **4. Team development.** How has your team collectively benefited? What have you learned about how to work together more effectively? Are you able to build on this learning in your continuing work together?	**1. Direct costs**. How much money was spent that cannot be recovered? And how much time was put in? **2. External costs**. Were there any reputational costs to you or the team? (e.g. damage to the brand, damage to relationships with third parties) **3. Internal costs**. What were the negative consequences for you and for the team (if any)? (e.g., reluctance to try a new project in this area, good people leaving, new rules that inhibit future initiative)

Considering all these factors together, what was the overall "Return on Failure" for this project? (High, Medium, Low)

FIGURE 7.2 Evaluating Return on Failure

victories" whenever they try something new. Our advice, if you find yourself running such a process, is to get clarity at the outset that no review will take place for, say, the first eighteen months, and for that period of time keep the data to yourself as much as possible.

Linking Motivation to Individual Action

Since historical times, management thinkers have puzzled over how to get people do their "best work" and how to tap into the discretionary efforts of their employees. During the industrial age the tools of choices were, metaphorically speaking, the carrot and the stick, but gradually as we entered the information age a more human-centered way of thinking emerged that sought to harness the intrinsic motivation of people in the workplace.

Our approach in this chapter was to unpack the notion of intrinsic motivation into two elements—personal growth based on the development of knowledge, expertise, and mastery, and personal achievement based on pursuing a challenging goal, beating the competition, and winning a prize. The former works better in a meritocracy, the latter is more suited to an adhocracy.

We don't mean to imply that everyone should be achievement-oriented, but making the distinction between these two logics clear helps to put the right incentive systems in place to reinforce the chosen structure.

This completes our description of the type of strategy and structure firms need to succeed in a fast/forward world. We now switch our focus to you as an individual, first of all in terms of your role as a strategic leader.

Chapter 8

AMBIDEXTROUS LEADERSHIP FOR AN AGILE WORLD

JANUS IS THE ROMAN god of beginnings and transitions; he is the god of change. He is often depicted as having two faces—one looking to the past and one to the future. The duality of man is often featured in the worlds of literature, comic books, and movies. Who can forget the likes of Dr. Jekyll and Mr. Hyde; Two-Face, the righteous-turned-evil adversary of Batman; Darth Vader from *Star Wars*; or the Incredible Hulk. In such cases, and in most other walks of life, duality is portrayed as a negative—good versus bad, black versus white. We have been conditioned to view people with multiple and complex personalities as schizophrenic or bipolar, rather than multipurpose, flexible, and useful.

But not everywhere. Think about the realm of sports, in which the term *split vision* refers to one's ability to see out of opposite corners of both eyes at the same time. The best soccer players, from Maradonna and Messi to Mia Hamm, seem to live and envision the world in a fourth dimension—focusing and panning-out at once. The same is true if you look at the best quarterbacks, guys like Joe Montana or Tom Brady. In these cases, multidimensionality is celebrated and perhaps even sensationalized.

In this chapter, we argue that business is another realm that favors these types of protean capabilities. We believe it is actually necessary for today's leaders to become "shape shifters." If you or your kids are fans of TV shows such as *Supernatural* or *Haven*, or the Harry Potter books, you know that the characters therein are people or mythical creatures that are able to change identity at will, to assume different forms. As a leader, having all the right information at your fingertips is not enough. Shape shifting is a unique quality that allows you to deal with the variety of situations you encounter in a world of genuine uncertainty. Put simply, the best CEOs that we have ever encountered are more like Mr. and Mrs. Duality than Dr. Data.

What should we call these leaders? We favor the term *ambidextrous*, which is increasingly common in the management world[1] and has strong positive connotations. In simple terms, ambidexterity means being equally adept in the use of both left and right hands (or feet). Famous examples of people with such qualities include Albert Einstein, Benjamin Franklin, basketball player Kobe Bryant, and (former) tennis celebrity Maria Sharapova.

In business, ambidextrous leaders are adept at shifting their style of working according to the situation they are facing. When faced with a fast-changing business environment, there are times when you have to step in and take decisive action, and there are other times when you need to get out of the way and let those on the front line run the show. Of course, this isn't easy—not only do different situations require different skill-sets, there is also the challenge of knowing *when* to shift from one mode of operating to the other. But don't despair. Even if you cannot be fully ambidextrous, you can certainly make progress on developing this important but challenging capability. This chapter provides you with some perspective and some advice on how to do it.

The Many Faces of Fast/Forward Leadership

So what is the current state-of-the-art advice on what effective leadership looks like in the business world?

On the one hand, many contemporary books talk about the need for empowering, inspiring leaders who get things done through others. For example, best-selling author Jim Collins argued that "level five" leaders have the most enduring impact on their organizations by maintaining a combination of "humility and fierce resolve." The founder of the servant leadership movement, Robert Greenleaf, developed his ideas about "leading from behind" back in the 1970s. American writer and speaker Susan Cain has written about the power of introverts as leaders. Wharton professor Adam Grant has emphasized generosity to others as a key leadership trait, and so on.[2] You would think, from browsing on Amazon, that today's business leaders are a quiet, thoughtful, humble, and modest bunch.

On the other hand, we see the charismatic leaders who actually grace the covers of *Businessweek* and *Fortune* magazines: Jeff Bezos of Amazon, Larry Ellison of Oracle, Martin Sorrell of WPP, Bernard Arnaut of LVMH, and of course Donald Trump. These individuals have larger-than-life egos. They like to call the shots and rule their organizations through a combination of charisma, fear, and brute force. These extroverts are all highly successful—among the most powerful and wealthy businesspeople on the planet. And, of course, many former business legends, from Steve Jobs and Jack Welch to Italy's arch-seducer Silvio Berlusconi, were cut from the very same cloth.

How do we square these two perspectives? Why do academics and business thinkers espouse the virtues of introverted, softly-spoken leaders, when so many of the actual role models in the business world range from boisterous to bullies?

In part, there is an element of self-delusion at work here. We like to think that we want modest and unassuming people to lead us, but the reality is that the larger-than-life figures tend to be the ones we admire. As Stanford professor Jeffrey Pfeffer observes, "We secretly like the confident, overbearing people because they provide us with confidence—emotions are contagious—and also present themselves like winners. We all want to associate with success."[3]

Another part of the explanation is that we aren't seeing the whole picture. The leaders who appear on the cover of *Businessweek* and other glossies will be, by definition, successful and somewhat egotistical. Our fellow academics call this the "survivor bias."[4] In other words, we don't hear the stories about the leaders who stay out of the limelight, and we only rarely see stories about all the egotistical, domineering leaders that failed. It is quite possible that the Bezos's and Ellisons of this world are the exceptions that prove the general rule, but the truth is we don't know for sure, because these things are close to impossible to study in a systematic way.

Our notion of ambidextrous leadership offers a third perspective on the rhetoric-reality gap. The best leaders aren't one type or the other—they seek to be both. They choose the right style of working to suit the situation. As Daniel Craig's James Bond put it in the 2006 remake of *Casino Royale*, "So you want me to be half-monk, half-hitman."

We like to characterize this as a game of "performance poker": As a leader, you have been dealt a set of cards from the deck—position, knowledge, action, and emotion—and your challenge is to know when to play which card. Some situations might require the knowledge card (for example, using your expertise to solve a problem), others might favor the emotion card (such as showing empathy for a colleague whose project failed). Many leaders end up majoring in one card, because they are comfortable with it and it has served them well in the past. But operating in today's fast/forward world, you don't have that luxury. By better understanding the range of tools at your disposal, and with some additional self-awareness, you can become more ambidextrous in your style of leadership.

How to Get the Right Mix of Leadership Styles Across Your Organization

Let's return once again to the three different organizing models that are the red threads running through the book. What is the role of the leader in each of these models?

In a *bureaucracy*, the scarce resources are capital and labor, and success is built on operating efficiency. In such an organization, the role of the individual leader is to squeeze as much value out of the firm's existing resources as possible. Naturally enough, such leaders often use a controlling style of managing. Cost control is achieved through careful oversight, an eye for detail, and a disciplined approach to making cuts.

In a *meritocracy*, success is built on the firm's capacity to harness information in an effective way. Here, the leader plays a very different role. She acts as a conduit for information, making sure people are well informed about each other's work, and she is also expected to be a knowledgeable expert. In a meritocracy, most leaders rise through the ranks as professionals, and become first-among-equals as leaders. Their ability to influence others is a function of what they know, and how well respected they are by their peers, not their position on the org chart.

In an *adhocracy*, success is built on decisive action backed by emotional conviction. The role of the leader in this setting is first and foremost about making things happen—which sometimes means being decisive and forthright yourself and at other times means pushing others to experiment, to take action without deferring to others for approval. There is also a strong emotive component to this leadership role, which has two sides, both tapping into and arousing the emotions of others and bringing your own emotion and intuition to bear on ambiguous situations.

We need to remember that these are "pure" types. In the real world, every organization is actually a mix of these models. This puts the onus on the leader to develop a blended style of working. Here are a couple of well-known examples.

Jeff Bezos, the CEO of Amazon, is a colorful character, famous for his intense manner, his grating laugh, and a paradoxical style of operating, which makes him hard to pigeonhole. He runs Amazon in a frugal style—costs are kept to the bare minimum. Office desks are slabs of wood that could be used for doors. Employees pay for their own lunches.[5] He believes deeply in the power of data—his first career was as a quant on Wall Street—and pushes the use of analytical tools for decision making. Amazon has what it calls a culture of metrics in which it tracks its performance against something like five hundred measurable goals![6] And Jeff pushes people hard, very hard. There are frequent reports of burnout.

On the other hand, Bezos clearly relishes being a contrarian, acting quickly and decisively, and, in his terms, a "willingness to be misunderstood." As one commentator observed, "What really distinguishes Bezos is his harrowing leaps of faith. His best decisions can't be backed up by studies or spreadsheets. He makes nervy gambles on ideas that are just too big . . . to try out reliably in small-scale tests."[7] There is a dreamer side to Bezos. He loves the frontier. His hope as a young man was to become an astronaut. As noted in a recent *Forbes* article, "He spent summers as a teenager on his grandfather's 25,000-acre ranch in Texas, fixing machines, working with cattle and learning about self-reliance. The respect for that ethic explains why Amazon screens its job candidates for a strong bias to action and an ability to work through ambiguity."[8] He seeks to develop an entrepreneurial culture and has instituted the notion of a "two pizza team" whereby the maximum size of the team was one that could be fed with two pizzas—and he expects people to challenge and push each other.

Bezos has charisma and inspires great loyalty, but at the same time his style of operating is often pretty blunt. According to a recent book,[9] when he was unimpressed he would say things like, "Why are you wasting my life?" "I'm sorry, did I take my stupid pills today?" and "This document was clearly written by the B team. Can someone get me the A team document? I don't want to waste my time with the B team document."

Or consider *Carlos Brito*, the Brazilian-born CEO of Anheuser Busch Inbev (ABI), now the largest beer company in the world.[10] For Brito, a leader is someone "who must deliver results, with the team, in the right way." His style of operating, honed over a twenty-five-year career in brewing, is tough and focused. ABI uses "zero-based budgeting," which requires managers to justify all their line items of expenditure every year. People work in an open-plan, informal space, to encourage direct interaction. Targets are challenging. Everyone can see how each other is performing, and those who deliver are paid very generous bonuses.

Brito's *modus operandi*, in other words, is drawn in large part from the bureaucracy playbook, because making and selling beer requires careful attention to quality control and cost management. But that's not the whole story: he also believes strongly in meritocracy, in building an operating environment that attracts and retains the very best people. As he says, "If the best are not treated best, they will not want to stay in the company." Managers are given very high levels of responsibility and challenge; "the best way to develop your people is to get them out of their comfort zone." He seeks to develop "restaurant owners, not waiters" who see their personal future closely aligned to the success of the company. And he is not averse to bold moves—the acquisition of Anheuser Busch by InBev (where he was CEO before) in 2008 was viewed as highly risky at the time, though it was ultimately a big success. At the time of writing, Brito was finalizing his next big acquisition, SAB Miller.

These two brief portraits underline the complexities and challenges of leadership. Described with our terminology, ABI is primarily run as a bureaucracy with elements of meritocracy and a hint of adhocracy. Amazon, in contrast, has a logistics operation that is the epitome of bureaucracy, while in its customer-facing and business development activities Bezos seeks to get the right mix of adhocracy and meritocracy.

If there is one term that captures the style of leadership executives like Bezos and Brito, it is indeed ambidextrous. But remember, their job isn't just about being personally flexible; it is also about defining the operating styles across the whole firm.

Think back to the Costa Coffee story in Chapter 6. Jim Slater encouraged Eric Achtmann to create a fast-moving, autonomous team built on adhocracy principles, while retaining a more bureaucratic, efficiency-oriented way of working in the existing lines of business. But this separate arrangement could not go on forever. Slater had to take a view on *when* to integrate the two sets of activities, and on how best to do so, which required him to exhibit a high level of personal ambidexterity.

Taking a broader view, in fact, we can see that there are three basic ways of blending these different operating styles, each one involving different levels of separation across organizational space and time.[11]

Divide and conquer—Separate units into different types of activities. The first option is to keep the three different management models (bureaucracy, meritocracy, adhocracy) separate. This avoids confusion—it helps the people working in each unit to understand what their priorities are. But it creates challenges for those at the top whose job is to pull these diverse activities together.

For example, the Swiss food company Nestlé has typically emphasized this approach. It often creates separate units for its more experimental activities. Its Nutrition unit is responsible for developing novel nutritional offerings, Nestlé Health Science is an independent subsidiary focusing on medical patients' distinct needs, while Nespresso was set up as an autonomous division to grow the company's famous coffee machines. Such units are typically run on adhocracy, or occasionally meritocracy, principles, while the mainstream Nestlé organization continues to operate a highly efficient and more bureaucracy-based model built around strategic business units and geographical zones.

This approach creates several challenges. One is deciding when to set up these autonomous units and when to close them down; another is figuring out the right level of connectivity between the autonomous units and the mainstream operations. Then there is the question of who should run these autonomous units, which Nestlé has resolved by creating a separate career track for entrepreneurial leaders. The head of one exploratory unit explained, "Before we introduced the separate career track for entrepreneurs, people like me had a hard time to progress at Nestlé because we have our competences in areas that traditional businesses within Nestlé value less." The two career tracks are now part of Nestlé's long-term-oriented career development program.

Mix and match—Give operating units dual responsibilities. A second option is to push responsibility down, so that mid-level leaders learn to make the trade-offs between the three different management models themselves.

GlaxoSmithKline (GSK) provides an interesting example of this model. GSK has been at the forefront of the dramatic changes in the pharmaceutical industry for the last fifteen years, and in particular with its efforts to integrate biotech-like ways of working with its traditional "big pharma" model. Back in 2001, GSK created six "Centres of Excellence in Drug Discovery," teams of 300 to 350 scientists working in cross-functional ways and competing with each other for funding. In 2007, the model was pushed further with the creation of forty Drug Performance Units" (DPUs), each with a cross-functional team of thirty to forty people and focused on a single project. The intention of this model was to become more focused on discovering new drugs and putting them into development (that is, adhocracy), without losing the deep functional expertise (that is, meritocracy) that had been there before. According to one observer, it was a bet that "smaller focused, autonomous, and more accountable units would make more efficient decisions regarding portfolio advancement."[12]

While the jury is still out on how effective these DPUs have been for GSK, it exemplifies the benefits and the risks involved in blending different organizing models. For example, finding the right people to run these dual-focused units is really challenging, as they have to be top-notch scientists and also street-wise entrepreneurs. Indeed, during the mid-2000s, GSK realized it did not have enough of these people internally, and it had to hire in quite a few people, often from the biotech industry, to take on these ambidextrous responsibilities.

Equally, this model creates challenges for the leaders at the top of the company, because they have to create the right structure and culture to allow front-line leaders to do their jobs well. This type of context-shaping capability requires constant attention; otherwise there is a risk that people on the front line will end up prioritizing one set of objectives ahead of others.

Back and forth—Cycle between different models. The third option is to operate in pendulum-like fashion, switching back and forth over time between the different organizing models, from bureaucracy to meritocracy to adhocracy, and back to bureaucracy again.

BMW, the German premium car manufacturer, provides a good example of this approach. If you consider the last twenty years, BMW divested its loss-making Rover and Land Rover brands in 2000, and during this period it emphasized productivity and administrative efficiency, making BMW the world's most profitable full-range car manufacturer. The focus changed between 2002 and 2006, when CEO

Helmut Panke led one of the largest product expansions in BMW's history (the 1-Series model, the relaunch of the MINI, the Rolls-Royce Phantom, the X3, the revived 6-series Coupé), but when Norbert Reithofer took over as CEO in 2006, BMW changed again to emphasize profitable growth in its established segments. In 2010, Reithofer shifted direction toward "shaping the future," resulting in a wave of radical innovations (a range of electric vehicles including the i3 all-electric car and the i8 hybrid sports car, the i1 electric city vehicle and the i5 electric van, plus a range of mobility solutions, including the DriveNow premium car sharing business). These regular shifts of strategic priorities have enabled BMW to stay true to its overall vision, "to be profitable and to enhance long-term value in times of change."

This approach avoids the problems inherent in Nestlé and GSK's models, but of course it brings its own set of challenges. It requires ongoing discussions about the timing of these major shifts in direction, and it needs leaders to take a long-term view and to have a capacity for self-criticism that is often absent in successful firms. BMW is fortunate to have a long-term dominant shareholder (the Quandt family) that makes it less susceptible to stock market short-termism than many of its competitors. BMW is also famously self-critical: Reithofer has observed that one of the key attributes of BMW is that "they are never complacent about what they have achieved."

In sum, one important part of being an ambidextrous leader is assembling the right mix of management models. There is no one right way here. As the brief examples of Nestlé, GSK, and BMW indicate, there are pros and cons to each approach, and you need to choose the one that fits best with your corporate traditions and your personal style of leadership. You also have to be prepared to adapt your chosen model to circumstances, because of course in a fast/forward world these are ever changing and often not in predictable ways. The challenge of choosing the right personal style of leadership over time is what we discuss next.

What Is the Right Style of Leadership Over Time?

In 2013, the board of BlackBerry appointed John Chen, a "turn-around artist," as its new CEO, following his successful turnaround of software company Sybase. While BlackBerry's ultimate fate is still unclear, most observers have given Chen credit for stabilizing a very difficult situation. His appointment was an affirmation of the horses-for-courses logic of CEO selection: particularly in times of duress, specialists are often chosen to suit the particular conditions a company is facing.

The horses-for-courses leadership logic can be applied across the entire life cycle of a company; the whole S-curve of change. The skill-set you need to succeed in one part of the curve is very different from the one you need in another part. For example, when you are leading a company that is growing slowly and steadily, your job is a lot about empowering others, getting them to take responsibility and to help them to get the most out of their existing opportunities. But in periods of uncertainty, when the right way forward is unclear and the down-side of getting it wrong is huge, you need a much more hands-on, decisive style of operating. As we saw in Chapter 4, for example, with Netflix moving into video-on-demand, the "bet the farm" transitions only happen when leaders step in and make the big calls themselves.

So the challenge you face as a leader can be boiled down to two questions. First, when and how to "step in" and take charge? Second, when and how to "step back" and get work done through others? Let's look at each of these in turn.

When Do You Step In and Take Charge?

Public-sector organizations are notoriously slow moving and resistant to change. For example, consider the U.K. fire service: it was created to put out major urban blazes during World War II, but with the de-velopment of fire-retardant materials, sprinkler systems, and better social awareness, by the turn of the century it was no longer fit for purpose. A 2002 government review judged that "the Fire Service needs to be changed from top to bottom and every aspect of its work reformed to bring it into line with best practice at the start of the twenty-first century."[13]

For Steve McGuirk, head of the Greater Manchester force, the required transformation was enormous—a shift in mind-set from fighting fires to preventing them in the first place, with a significantly lower operating budget as well. Essentially, fire officers who had signed up to become heroes, like the one portrayed by Kurt Russell in the movie *Backdraft*, found themselves being asked to act as social-workers-cum-electricians, lecturing to suburban housewives on fire and smoke detectors. "There was huge resistance from the workforce, and many people thought the whole idea of firefighters going round knocking on front doors was crazy," he recalls.

But McGuirk was highly successful—over the decade following the government review, the number of firefighting jobs in his force dropped from twenty-one hundred down to fifteen hundred (mirroring a 38 percent cut to the grant from central government), and the number of fires in Greater Manchester went down from twenty-seven thousand to nine thousand, the best performance in the United Kingdom.

We asked him how he had achieved this level of transformation; what were the key things he did? The key role of a leader, he replied, is spotting and exploiting opportunity in changing circumstances. "There are times when you are going with the flow—helping the managers around you, and the union reps, to implement a chosen strategy—but there are other times when you know that won't be enough, and you have to make a bigger intervention."

For example, in the early 2000s, when they were first discussing ways of preventing fires, one of McGuirk's team said, "How about we knock on people's doors?" Everyone thought it was a crazy idea, but McGuirk followed up and commissioned a pilot study. Soon this approach, installing smoke detectors in people's homes, became a mainstay of their new way of working. McGuirk was also decisive in building a team of volunteer firefighters to guard against possible union strikes during the period of layoffs. And in 2014 he developed an ambitious new model, the Community Risk Intervention Team, for firefighters to work more closely with the ambulance service in the cases of accidents in people's homes. Despite initial resistance from the unions, he was able to get this launched successfully.

McGuirk's decisive approach to public-sector change parallels many of the business stories we have discussed throughout the book, from Amazon's push into e-books to Netflix's transition to video-on-demand. In all such cases, powerful inertial forces hold the organization on its existing trajectory, and it takes a very strong hand at the helm to push it in a new direction.

So how do you, as a leader, know when to step in? What are the warning signs that tell you it's time to start taking charge? We like the notion of *strategic dissonance*, as articulated by Stanford professor Robert Burgelman and the late Intel CEO Andy Grove.[14] Essentially, this means there is a growing disconnect between your intended strategy (where you are trying to go) and your *de facto* strategy (the actual activities the organization is performing). You don't do what you say, and you don't say what you do. If you are talking up your company's digital information strategy, but salespeople are continuing to sell paper-based subscriptions, then you have an acute case of strategic dissonance. When you realize that the head is detached from the body of the organization, you need to spend time on the front lines of your organization, finding out what people are actually doing and getting unfiltered, real-time information from them, to pick up on this type of dissonance. And you then need an inner circle of advisors to help you make sense of the often-contradictory views you are hearing: "Here is how I am interpreting this information, tell me why I might be wrong," is the type of question you should be asking.

But even this is not enough. You need to know when to step in, but you also need to have sufficient power to enact the changes you believe are needed. Consider, for example, the argument made by Pascal Cagni, the former head of Apple in Europe. At a conference in 2015, he made a case that companies in fast-moving industries are best served with a *benevolent, transparent dictatorship*.[15] As he observed, most large firms get stuck in decision-making processes that are consensus-oriented and ultimately very conservative, so when faced with tricky decisions you need leaders who are prepared to take a strong position and put their own credibility on the line. His own company, Apple, was of course led by such a dominant individual, and in their own ways you can see similarly autocratic behavior from Oracle's Larry Ellison, Mark Zuckerberg at Facebook, Google's Larry Page and Sergey Brin, and Rupert Murdoch at News Corp.

To be clear, we aren't advocating dictatorship as the new best practice in corporate leadership. Pascal Cagni rightly pointed to the need for benevolent and transparent behavior to temper the autocratic judgments of those at the top, and there is still the need for an overarching governance system to keep such individuals in check. But the observation that major, bet-the-farm type changes are only made when power is concentrated among a few people is well heeded. So if you are seeking to make decisive changes and you do *not* have this level of formal power, you need to work very hard on lobbying and building support before the decision gets made—otherwise the status quo will prevail.

When Do You Step Back?

An equally challenging leadership skill is knowing when to take a step back. There are many times when you should be seeking decisiveness through others, rather than through your own actions. Recall once again the basic principles of adhocracy—coordination is opportunity-focused, decisions are based on experimentation and learning on the front line, and motivation is based on individual responsibility and achievement. To make these things happen, leaders have to master the art of empowerment—they have to place responsibility in the hands of those on the front line and then ensure that it is grasped.

There is an important and subtle point here. It is very easy for a senior executive to "give" responsibility, but that doesn't mean the manager will always "take" it. Some managers are happy to do their narrowly defined job but not to take the initiative to do anything more. Others accept the responsibility handed down to them, but then fail to empower the layer of manager below them. The result is a vacuum in responsibility.

A case in point: we were running a corporate training program last year for a group of executives two levels below the CEO. They were unhappy with many aspects of how the company was working, and on the final day, in a Q&A session with the CEO, they expressed their frustration with their lack of power to make changes. The CEO could not believe what he was hearing: "I *want* you to take initiative. When did anyone ever stop you trying something new?"

This is a classic organizational paradox because you cannot mandate people to do something in a discretionary way. We were discussing this issue with a top leader in a large consumer products company, let's call him Niraj. While he was broadly okay with how his division was performing, he was frustrated by the lack of growth, and by the lack of initiative among many of his line managers. "I have been talking about empowerment for many years, but turning the words into action—three or four levels down—is where we struggle." It isn't hard to understand why the people who reported to Niraj (one or two levels below him) were struggling to delegate important work to those below them in the hierarchy. Put yourself in their shoes: we all believe we know best; we are worried about the costs of getting it wrong; we feel we don't have time to bring subordinates up to speed; and, in the backs of our minds, we know we are being evaluated more on the results we produce than on empowerment. All of these things stand in the way.

So what might Niraj do differently? What is your advice to him? He can try saying, "Everyone, please push more responsibility down on your team members," but that alone isn't going to have any real impact. He has to think carefully about the levers of influence he might work with to push his empowerment message deeper into the organization.

One such lever is to lead by example. Make sure you practice what you preach, by pushing responsibility down to those who report directly to you, and by providing the "psychological safety" that makes people comfortable with trying things that don't work out. Linked to this is the power of the good example. Celebrate situations when someone took the initiative or went out of their way to help a colleague. Recognize those people who are good at getting others to assume responsibility.

A second lever is to change the people in key positions. Over time, you can gradually promote those who exhibit the people-management skills you are looking for, while moving aside those who aren't playing along. And, of course, there is a personnel development angle to this as well. Being an effective line manager—in terms of getting the best out of those around you—does not come naturally to most people. You need to ensure that managers across the organization have the skill and will to do their jobs well.

What about rethinking performance reviews? Most reviews focus on the strengths and weaknesses of managers, but for real personal growth you also need to work on ambitions and needs. By influencing their ambitions and supporting their needs, you can mold your direct reports into the responsibility-seeking individuals you are looking for. Then, convince them to use the same logic with the managers below them so that the desired behavior trickles down the ranks.

Finally, there is sometimes scope for a major, specific initiative to put an important issue on the agenda. For example, Niraj was playing with the idea of getting managers to commit not just to specific financial targets but also to certain leadership behaviors. The challenge was to ask them to be clear about how they are adding value to those below them, not just how they are delivering their results.

This may not look like a hugely exciting inventory of things to do, but such is the nature of senior leadership in large companies. If Niraj becomes too heavy-handed, for example by mandating a particular way of working or a new formal process, he may get compliance but he won't get the discretionary, well-intentioned behavior he is looking for. And being entirely hands-off doesn't work either, because everyone will then just fall back into whatever way of working is most comfortable for them. Instead, Niraj has to influence others through an array of small initiatives and actions that provide a consistent message.

Decisive leadership is often about having the skill and courage to let go. We were talking to a senior manager at Uber, the San Francisco–based taxi-service provider. Because of its dramatic growth (sixty countries within four years), this manager had several hundred people reporting to him even though he had only been with Uber for two years. We asked him about his management style. "My biggest priority is hiring," he explained, "making sure we get people with the right values and skills into the key roles. But after that, my job is all about ensuring that people below me take decisions for themselves—we are moving too fast for everything to be referred back to me." At the end of each working day, he explained, he would make a few notes to himself about decisions he had been involved in, so that he could apportion his time more effectively in the future. In some cases, it was indeed necessary for him to be in the loop, but in most cases he resolved to push decisions back to those best placed to make them.

Making It Personal: The Role of Emotional Conviction

We have talked so far about knowing when to be decisive and when to inspire decisiveness and experimentation among others. But we also have to consider the role of emotional conviction in this equation. Again, there are two sides to the story of how to harness emotion in an effective way. We need leaders who can convey a point of view that resonates with others—to encourage and inspire employees to go the extra mile, to enthuse customers and gain loyalty for their vision. And we need leaders who are sensitive to the emotional convictions of others—who know how to tap into the intuitions and instincts of colleagues.

There are many good books on this subject: for example, Bill George's *Authentic Leadership*, Simon Sinek's *Start with Why*, and Rob Goffee and Gareth Jones's *Why Should Anyone Be Led by You?*[16] But we recommend a much simpler starting point. Think about leaders you have worked for—from your immediate line manager through to the corporate CEO. If we reflect on our own experiences here, we have had inspiring bosses whom we would do anything for, and we have had others that left us cold. What were the attributes of these inspiring leaders, the ones who were able to convey their emotional conviction to us in a compelling way? That is what we are seeking to grasp, and it is an elusive quality. There is no simple formula, but there are some guidelines that we can all take heed of.

Lead from the heart and the gut, not just the head. In 2014, Scotland held a referendum to decide whether to separate from the rest of the United Kingdom. The Yes campaign, led by the formidable campaigner Alex Salmond, emphasized patriotism, national pride, the opportunity to finally be free from foreign rule (think Mel Gibson in *Braveheart*). The No campaign, led by the cerebral former chancellor Alistair Darling, focused on the lack of clarity over the new currency, the risk of fiscal deficits, and the ambiguity over European Union membership. As the date of the referendum approached, with Yes in the ascendency, the No campaign finally figured out that voters wanted an emotional reason to say yes, as well as a logical argument. Former prime minister Gordon Brown gave an emotional and gripping speech ("Let us tell them what we have achieved together") that others then capitalized on, resulting in a 55 percent majority in favor of keeping the kingdom united.

This was Gordon Brown's finest hour. As prime minister, he had often appeared indecisive, perhaps listening too much to the opinion polls and his inner circle of advisors. But suddenly, when offered the opportunity to campaign for something he really believed in, he was transformed into an engaging and charismatic leader. Al Gore went through a similar transition, from wooden presidential candidate to inspiring campaigner once he found a cause he truly cared about. And this is the key point—if you want to lead from the heart, if you want people to be inspired by your words and deeds, you need to have a cause you actually believe in. We have all seen the video clips of Steve Jobs launching the iPhone ("Today, Apple is going to reinvent the phone") or Steve Ballmer yelling at a stadium full of Microsoft Employees ("I love this company"). Whether we love them or loathe them, we are left in no doubt that they are promoting a cause they believe in. That level of passion cannot be faked.

To be clear, we are not suggesting you throw out your logical, fact-based arguments. One of the hallmarks of ambidextrous leaders is that they are thoughtful about getting the right balance between logic (head), emotion (heart), and intuition (gut). This means adapting the style of decision making to the task at hand (recall the quote from Jeff Bezos of Amazon earlier in the chapter), and it also means tailoring the message to the interests of those listening—some audiences need to hear the evidence, others want to be inspired by stories. But as a crude generalization, we believe most leaders err on the side of analytical precision—they have spent their working lives building logical and defensible arguments, and they struggle to break free of this cerebral straitjacket.

Hone your self-awareness. There is a great deal of talk about *authenticity* in the world of leadership these days. The argument is that followers can sense when the leader is being disingenuous, so as a leader you are much better off being who you are—and true to yourself—than trying to be someone you are not. But don't be fooled into thinking this is an easy ride. As our colleagues from London Business School Rob Goffee and Gareth Jones have shown, the best leaders work very hard to accentuate their authentic traits, sometimes even exposing their flaws as a way of connecting with the audience. Goffee and Jones describe, for example, how Richard Branson communicates his vulnerability, appearing ill at ease and fumbling incessantly when interviewed in public.[17] In a similar vein, legendary investor Warren Buffett is a master of self-deprecation and humility, while U.K. politician Boris Johnson presents himself as a buffoon; they play these hands seemingly without damaging their credibility and authority as leaders.

There is another paradox lurking here: to be a good leader you need to be authentic, but you also need to skillfully accentuate certain traits. But showing some of yourself more boldly doesn't mean you're being false. You are accentuating the positive. You have to understand how people respond to you, which of your traits they find attractive, and how to amplify those.

This is tough! Academic studies have shown that we all have cognitive biases that hinder our ability to evaluate things accurately, and these biases typically become more acute the higher we rise in the hierarchy.[18] Senior leaders are typically overconfident, are highly optimistic, and have an exaggerated view of their own capabilities. Listen to Ray Dalio, the CEO of Bridgewater, a $169 billion behemoth in the asset management industry: "I believe that the biggest problem that humanity faces is an *ego* sensitivity to finding out whether one is right or wrong and identifying what one's strengths and weaknesses are."[19]

So what should you do to improve your self-awareness? Dalio's solution at Bridgewater is to create a culture of "radical transparency," in which individuals receive brutally honest and open feedback, and all meetings are recorded and archived. If you don't want to go to such extremes, we recommend using an executive coach, or creating some sort of peer network of like-minded people with whom you can discuss your own personal SWOT analysis (strengths, weaknesses, opportunities, and threats). And make sure to start this process before you get to the top—it's not so easy to build the capacity for constructive criticism when everyone around you is telling you how wonderful you are.

Here is a simple exercise you can try to improve your own self-awareness.[20] List ten facts about yourself, things you are willing to share with anyone. Giving away such facts makes people feel at home with you, and they come at a low cost to you because you are willing to share. Over time, you observe how people react to these facts, and you hone them to put a finer point on what you are willing to share and what these items communicate about you. While the facts aren't consequential, what they communicate about you can be. By reflecting on these facts (this is often best done in conversation with an executive coach), you can see things about yourself more clearly, thereby increasing your self-awareness.

Sharpen your two-way communication skills. It goes without saying that effective communication lies at the heart of great leadership, especially when the message has a strong emotional component. But what is sometimes lost is the two-way nature of communication.

There is a saying in the United Kingdom that "the Queen thinks the world smells of fresh paint." In other words, she lives in a bubble: whenever she visits a factory or hospital, the hosts make sure everything is clean and fresh prior to her arrival. She has no idea how ordinary people live, or what they think. And it's the same for leaders in large firms—they want to know what is really going on, but they rarely get a straight answer. People say what they think the boss wants to hear.

There are no simple solutions here either, but learning how to listen is a step in the right direction. Consider Richard Branson's advice: "We have two ears and one mouth, using them in proportion is not a bad idea! To be a good leader you have to be a great listener. Brilliant ideas can spring from the most unlikely places, so you should always keep your ears open for some shrewd advice. This can mean following online comments as closely as board meeting notes, or asking the front-line staff for their opinions as often as the CEOs. Get out there, listen to people, draw people out and learn from them . . . Great leaders are great listeners, who know their best asset is the people they work with."[21]

From a practical point of view, there are three things we can all do to hone our communication skills. First, understand that specificity beats ambiguity. "Ramble On" is a great song by Led Zeppelin, but not a trait of an effective leader. You need to be clear on your priorities and explain your intentions. Financial guru Suze Orman openly admits that very little of her advice is groundbreaking: "It's not the material that I know, but how I communicate the material I know that sets me apart."[22] Her success is based on the ability to deliver financial info with clarity and in direct language.

Second, practice makes perfect. Before a talk, John Chambers, former CEO of Cisco Systems, would review and rehearse his presentation. He memorized the slides and the flow of content. Extreme attention to detail is no exaggeration. It is reported that he even knew when and where he was going to walk into the audience, or put his hand on someone's shoulder.[23] Or consider the former New York City mayor Rudy Giuliani, who stated in his book, *Leadership*, that he began preparing for his annual State of the City address five months in advance so he would not have to read the presentation from notes.[24]

Third, make yourself accessible. As CEO of the online travel agency Travelocity, Michelle Peluso made a point of responding personally within twenty-four hours to every e-mail from her five thousand employees around the world, even if she was traveling or on vacation.[25] Many CEOs have weekly town halls or online Q&A discussions to open up a direct and immediate line of communication with their employees across the world. If you want to be a great listener, there just are no substitutes for time and presence.

Do You Want to Be an Ambidextrous Leader?

If all of the preceding makes it seem difficult to be an effective leader, then we have achieved at least one of our aims. In the words of ambidextrous academic Isaiah Berlin, good leaders are foxes, not hedgehogs—they know many things, rather than one big thing.[26] They don't walk around with a big hammer looking for nails to hit, they assemble an entire set of tools, and they think carefully before choosing which one to use.

But before finishing this chapter, we would like to offer one piece of general advice, namely a plea for leaders to exercise a bit more spontaneity. We understand that *spontaneous* is almost a pejorative term in some business circles, but hear us out.

Spontaneous is defined as *having an open, natural, and uninhibited manner.* As we have argued, most large firms end up being the exact opposite: the mind-set is *closed* (we know what we are doing, we don't need to listen to external points of view), the decision making is *unnatural* (based on computer algorithms and credit scores that yield precise numerical answers), the style of interaction is *inhibited* (rational, logical, and sterile). So if you are trying to make a difference as a leader—and move your firm away from its default destiny—you need to push in the other direction. Leave Plan Park, and take a stroll down Spontaneous Street. If you are surrounded by procedures, implicit norms of behaviors, and well-meaning colleagues who are pulling you back, you need to push the dial at least a few notches toward greater spontaneity.

How? In many ways, this entire book is our attempt to answer this question, so we don't want to fall into the trap of simplifying it down to a few bullet points. Instead, think of spontaneity as a set of operating principles—a more open-minded perspective, a greater emphasis on natural (human) intelligence, and a style of working that is free of inhibition. These are the hallmarks of effective leadership in a fast/forward world.

Chapter 9

BECOMING AN UNREASONABLE MANAGER

IN A FAST/FORWARD WORLD, it's not just the job of senior leaders that looks different—it is the work of every front-line manager who deals with sales targets, customer service, product supply, software releases, or accounts payable on a day-to-day basis. As we have said all along, these are the people who are often best placed to sense *and* respond to the opportunities facing the organization. Even self-professed all-seeing leaders such as Larry Ellison or Jeff Bezos need to find ways to use the insights of these types of individuals who have their ears to the ground.

So this chapter is about how *your* role is changing—what you need to do differently to help you and your organization succeed. Obviously the story varies significantly depending on your seniority, the type of firm you work in, and how enlightened your boss is. But we can still draw out some useful general ideas.

Taking the Leap

Sometimes, the deeper you go into a story, the more interesting it becomes. And that is certainly the case here. Take a look at the chart in Figure 9.1—it documents the changes in the men's high jump world record over a one-hundred-year period. As in other sports, high jumpers have become taller, stronger, and fitter, and they have improved

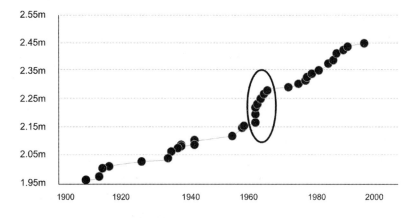

FIGURE 9.1 Men's High Jump World Record

their techniques. A century ago the record stood at just below 2 meters; now it is 2.45 meters, a height first jumped by Javier Sotomayor of Cuba back in July 1993, making it one of the longest-standing world records in male athletics.

We like to show this chart during our speeches, and we ask, "So what happened in the early 1960s, when the bar was raised no less than seven times? What caused this dramatic improvement in jumping prowess?"

Some wise guy always yells out "drug taking," which gets a laugh. But those people with an eye for sporting trivia say "The Fosbury Flop"—the technique for high jumping pioneered by the American jumper Dick Fosbury, in which one leaps over the bar backward, head first, rather than straddle it chest first. Most of us are acquainted with this story, and it seems to fit the facts. New, disruptive techniques lead to dramatic performance improvements, right?

Except that Fosbury is actually the wrong answer. The succession of world record jumps in the early 1960s were actually the work of two relatively forgotten jumpers, John Thomas from the USA and Valeriy Brumel from the USSR, both masters of the "old" style of jumping—the straddle jump. Dick Fosbury wasn't even competing at an elite level at this point. Indeed, Dick Fosbury *never* held the world high jump record.

When we first saw this data, we fell off our chairs, metaphorically speaking, because it seemed to invalidate our long-held beliefs about how innovation improves performance. But we dug a little deeper, and ultimately we made sense of what was going on. In fact, the implications of this story, for any aspiring innovator, are more interesting and surprising than you might expect.

In the early 1960s, at the height of the Cold War—think Khrushchev's shoe-banging incident at the UN, or the Cuban missile crisis—two brilliant young high jumpers arrived on the world athletics scene. John Thomas was an American who, aged seventeen while studying at Boston University, became the first person to clear 7 feet (2.13 meters) indoors. Valeriy Brumel was a Russian from eastern Siberia, a year younger than Thomas, who cleared 2 meters by the time he was sixteen. He moved to Moscow to get professional coaching help, and quickly made it onto the Russian Olympic team.

Thomas broke the world record three times (peaking at 2.22 meters) while still only twenty years old. Brumel subsequently broke the record a further four times (taking it up to 2.28 meters). Their head-to-head rivalry culminated at the 1964 Tokyo Olympics, where both cleared the same height, 2.18 meters, a new Olympic record, but Brumel won the gold medal because of fewer failed jumps. Both men, to repeat, were using the straddle jump—the established technique in which one leaps off the inner foot and crosses the bar, face down, with legs straddling it.

So what about Dick Fosbury? At the time of the Tokyo Olympics, he was a seventeen-year-old engineering student at Oregon State University, and a promising but by no means world-class athlete with a personal best of 2 meters (6 feet, 7 inches), some 28 centimeters below Brumel's record. Despite the "dire warnings" of every coach he worked with,[1] Fosbury persisted with a new style of jumping, taking off on the outside foot and immediately turning his back to the bar, leaping head-first and then kicking his legs up as his back cleared the bar. No one knows exactly what inspired him to try this new technique—it certainly wasn't his coaches, who tried to steer him back to the straddle jump. When describing it he used words and phrases such as "accident, intuitive, natural, experiments were permitted, anyone could have done it, kids are creative, there was no plan." One thing in his favor, though, was that his high school was one of the first to install large foam mats for landing on, making a head-first jump somewhat less dangerous.[2] In any case, he persevered, and despite all the criticism (he was likened to a "fish flopping in a boat"[3]), he continued to improve and by the mid-1960s was good enough to make the U.S. national team.

As a side note, it is worth mentioning Debbie Brill. She was a Canadian athlete, five years junior to Fosbury, and the first North American woman to clear 6 feet (1.83 meters), at the age of sixteen. Independently, she developed a similar technique that was called the "Brill Bend" about the same time as Fosbury was experimenting with his Flop. Unlike Fosbury, Brill went on to break the world record with her 1.99 meters (6 feet, 6 inches) indoor jump from 1982. (Regrettably Debbie doesn't get much credit—perhaps because back then it was man's world, as James Brown would have put it, or perhaps because Fosbury simply got there before her).

Meanwhile, in the world of male athletics, Valeriy Brumel had become the undisputed number one—he finished the 1965 season unbeaten. But then disaster struck: Brumel had a terrible motorbike accident, breaking his right foot and leg in multiple places, and was facing amputation. Following a lengthy series of operations he was able to walk again, but his professional jumping career was over.

It was this twist of fate that opened the door for Dick Fosbury. Brumel did not compete in the Mexico City Olympics in 1968, so Fosbury lined up against all the other athletes, every one of them using the established straddle jump, and beat them all with his crazy backward jumping technique. Suddenly, Fosbury was the star of the show— "Fearless Fosbury Flops to Glory" was the *New York Times* headline in October 1968.

But even with the Olympic gold medal in the bag, Fosbury's story isn't complete. His winning jump was still below world-record height, and indeed, as noted earlier, Fosbury never actually broke that record. He wasn't sure himself whether his technique was actually better than the straddle jump. Following his victory he said, "I think quite a few kids will begin trying it my way now; I don't guarantee results, and I don't recommend my style to anyone. All I say is if a kid can't straddle, he can try it my way."[4] Over the next decade, the world record was beaten several times by other athletes, some using the Fosbury Flop, others using the straddle jump. It wasn't until the 1980s that the Fosbury Flop finally became established as the technique of choice for serious jumpers—the "dominant design," as our academic colleagues would put it.

How Innovation *Really* Happens

Even though it has been told a hundred times before, we think it's useful to revisit the Fosbury Flop story to show just how "messy" the process of innovation and creative destruction is in real life. Everyone knows that truly disruptive innovations of this type need a maverick inventor—a game changer—someone who likes to flaunt conventional wisdom, think outside the box, and challenge the status quo. Fosbury and Brill were indeed such individuals. The context made one of them famous and the other one a footnote in history, just as everyone associates the light bulb with Edison while almost no one has ever heard of Henry Woodward and Mathew Evans (google them). But if we want to capture the real essence of the story, we have to roll a few other important points into the mix.

First, it took several years of unheralded effort from Fosbury—no one took him seriously at first, and all along the way people were advising him to switch back to the conventional way of jumping. Second, the timing of his innovation was good—thick landing mats had just become available, making a head-first jump safe for the first time. Third, he got a lucky break when Brumel had his motorbike accident, and he duly seized the opportunity (imagine if Brumel had won gold in Mexico City; would the Fosbury Flop have taken off? We will never know). Finally, Fosbury's breakthrough wasn't the end of the story at all—it took many years, even *after* the gold medal, before the merits of Fosbury's innovation became clear.

Put it all together, and you can see why game-changing innovation is so hard. It is tough for the innovators, the Fosburys, the Brills, the Musks, and the Jobs of the world. And it is doubly hard for the big organizations, which have to fight against their own corporate legacies as well as the entrenched norms of the marketplace.

And before we move away from the world of sports, let's not forget that plenty of innovative new techniques and theories fail to take off. For every Dick Fosbury with a "smart-stupid" idea that worked out well, there are plenty of long-forgotten individuals whose ideas were in the "stupid-stupid" category. Fosbury's coaches weren't just stuck-in-the-mud traditionalists; they were also drawing on their experience of seeing other athletes trying and failing with different techniques.

The Power of Unreason

It doesn't matter how perfect the conditions favoring innovation are, you still need *someone* to take the initiative, to grab the opportunity when it becomes possible. Dick Fosbury was the agent of change in the world of high jump. He was the quintessential unreasonable man, as portrayed in the famous George Bernard Shaw quote:

> The reasonable man adapts himself to the world, the unreasonable man persists in adapting the world to himself, therefore all progress depends on the unreasonable man.[5]

There are many examples of unreasonable people in the world of business. Steve Jobs was famous for operating in a "reality distortion field" that allowed him and Apple to conceive truly pathbreaking designs. Elon Musk is often credited with a similarly skewed worldview: "If you believe a task should take a year then Elon wants it done in a week, he won't hesitate to throw out six months of work because it's not pretty enough or it's not 'badass' enough. But in so doing he doesn't change the schedule."[6] And it's not just top executives or visionary founders who exhibit this type of unreasonable worldview.

Over the last twenty years, we have worked with many mid-level executives who have persisted with championing their bright ideas, often without any encouragement at all, and often taking a significant amount of career risk along the way.

Being unreasonable is not a function of your hierarchical position—it is a state of mind. As time has passed, we have come to realize that some people are just more unreasonable than others. Of course it isn't a binary thing—we all exhibit various shades of unreasonableness, with mavericks like Jobs and Musk on one end of the spectrum and the rule-following civil servant or boy scout on the other. But regardless of how much of that unreasonable gene you were born with, the ability to use it in a smart way comes down mainly to skill and experience.

So the rest of this chapter is all about how you can become smarter about being unreasonable. We aren't going to pretend it is easy. If you want an easy life, you can spend your time helping others to pursue their agendas, and you can conform to whatever norms and expectations your organization imposes on you. But this isn't going to help your organization get ahead in a fast/forward world. And it certainly isn't going to help you to get the most out of your job. If you took the trouble to buy this book, and to read it this far, then you are likely the sort of person who actually cares about doing things a bit differently. So this is our advice to help you in that quest.

The Fast/Forward Mind-Set

Let us put this discussion about unreasonable behavior into the context of the book. In a fast-changing world, in which organizations experience the full impact of the paradoxes of progress, decisive action and emotional conviction—not big data—are the order of the day. When faced with uncertain or ambiguous challenges, it is better for firms to emphasize action over formal authority or deeper analysis. How does this apply at an individual level? Consider Figure 9.2, which is based on the earlier Figure 3.1.

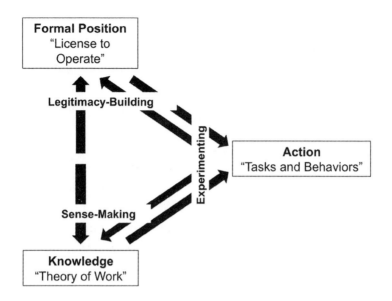

FIGURE 9.2 Elements of a Fast/Forward Mind-Set

The three boxes refer to your position, knowledge, and action within an organizational setting. Action is what you do on a day-to-day basis: the tasks you undertake and the behaviors you exhibit. Knowledge is your own understanding of how things work—how your activities contribute to the firm's success, what others think of you, or the customer needs your products satisfy. It is your own implicit "theory" of work. Position here isn't just your job title and the relationships implied by it; think of it as your license to operate within a corporate setting. Everyone has certain degrees of freedom in their job, as a function of their formal role, their informal influence, their track record, who they know, and so on. As you become more successful, and you build greater access to resources and networks beyond your formal control, your license to operate expands.

The arrows on the figure are about the processes you follow—think of them as the linkages between the three facets of your job. Experimenting is how you translate your license to operate (your formal role) and your pet theories about how things work (your knowledge) into action. Some people act only on clear instructions; others are more unreasonable and act on intuitive hunches. The term *experimenting* is used here because—as we have said throughout the book—it is better to try something quickly and in a small way rather than delay, fall behind, and end up being "just too late."

Sense-making is how you interpret what you do, and how you are perceived by others. If you try out a new product idea (action) and it doesn't work out, you reflect on and make sense of what happened. If your boss gives you positive feedback about your job performance (position), you incorporate this information into your worldview.

Finally, legitimacy-building is how your actions and your interpretation of the world shape your own license to operate. This process sometimes leads to a promotion—a new and bigger job. Sometimes, though, its impact is a lot more subtle, perhaps an informal recognition from your peers that you are doing a good job, and that you can flex your muscles a little more.

All three of these processes have a strong emotional component; as we said earlier in the book, emotion sits in the middle of this triangle. For example, experimenting is often a form of action that is taken without full knowledge, and is usually based on an emotionally held conviction. Effective sense-making and legitimacy-building rely on a high level of emotional intelligence (EQ)—you need to have sufficient self-awareness to build a credible view of your own strengths and weaknesses, and you need to have strong influencing skills to shape the views of others.

How does this framework apply in practice? Let us consider a couple of examples—someone who managed this dynamic well and another one who got it a bit wrong.

Jordan Cohen was director of organizational effectiveness at Pfizer back in 2005. By all standards, he was a successful mid-level manager, but with a growing sense of frustration about how much time his colleagues were wasting on run-of-the-mill work, such as building spreadsheets, booking travel, and doing background research. "I recall one of my team, an MIT graduate, spending time after hours doing tasks that were not just below his pay-grade but not core to his role either. I knew there had to be a way to unburden him from this low-value work."[7]

Jordan was an avid reader of business books, and the best-seller of that year was Tom Friedman's *The World Is Flat.*[8] As he attempted to make sense of what he saw as wasted effort within Pfizer, Jordan's eyes were opened to the possibility of taking advantage of the global marketplace for services at a micro level. He started to theorize about a new offering which he tried out on a couple of colleagues: "I think I can help by delivering that piece of work to your inbox within twenty-four hours so you don't have to do it . . . it may cost a little bit of money but it will be just as good as if you did it." People liked the idea, so he pushed it further. Jordan collected data to show that colleagues were spending 20 to 40 percent of their time on noncore work. He immersed himself in the practical realities of outsourcing. Working evenings and weekends, Jordan designed a prototype program within a few months: an online tool (accessible through the company intranet) that colleagues could access at the click of a button to secure one-stop support for such things as business research, data analysis, and creating documents.

That was stage one: on the basis of his existing license to operate (as a director of organizational effectiveness), he made sense of the evidence (wasted effort) before his eyes, and he designed and put into action a simple experiment.

But of course he was just getting started. His colleagues begun using the service, and he found himself on a steep learning curve, building the functionality and ironing out bugs. After a year, the service, now called "Pfizerworks," was working in pilot form. But before launching it, he needed to get formal approval—which meant a process of legitimacy-building, first with his boss and other potential supporters, and ultimately from the Pfizer CEO himself. Jordan was very smart here. He wrote a note about the Pfizerworks concept into his personal objectives, "So that if I was successful, my boss would get credit for it." And he linked his idea to a CEO-led initiative called "Adapting to Scale": "This was an effort to actually look at the way we we're doing things, to see if we were using the scale that Pfizer has, in purchasing power, knowledge sharing, and so on. By positioning Pfizerworks as an Adapting to Scale initiative, I was able to get the air cover I needed to move forward."

Formal approval for Pfizerworks meant Jordan's license to operate grew significantly. Thereafter, he was able to scale up reasonably quickly, by building a network of partners inside and outside Pfizer, and generate visibility for the initiative so that it was used on a consistent basis. For example, to persuade skeptics, he realized he needed to provide hard evidence of its value: "You have to put it in the language of business. I started calculating how much time people were spending doing the tasks they were subcontracting to our team of virtual assistants. This allowed me to create impact metrics—so I could report, on a monthly basis, how many hours and how many dollars had been saved, and what the level of service was like."

Tom Allison was the U.K. marketing director for Pharma AG, a Switzerland-based pharmaceutical company, with expertise in oncology, hormone replacement drugs, and fertility.[9] The U.K. operation had several hundred employees, including fifty working in clinical trials and product registration, but very limited autonomy—HQ approval was needed for all expenditures above £10,000.

In 2001, the parent company had worked on a project with 3M corporation to develop a transdermal (through the skin) formulation of Zanta, their main drug for hormone replacement. After several months of effort they had made very little progress, so they decided to scale back this project and focus instead on other priority areas.

Two years later, Tom Allison began to look into the transdermal technology issue. Working with a small British company called Morton Ltd, he made a presentation to management in Zurich, suggesting that they work with Morton to develop a transdermal formulation, but he was told it was a no go. He decided to continue working with Morton anyway, using a method different from the one the Swiss R&D group and 3M were working on. The work began to show promise, so Allison sought further involvement from HQ: "Pharma central laboratories saw Morton as a small, high-risk company. And the in-house experts in Pharma were not impressed, even when I took the Morton people to Zurich. I still haven't managed to persuade those people who were skeptical to come over to the U.K. to see Morton working. In the early part of the project, what they did was to send one of their juniors over to have a look at the project. He came over with a fixed brief, and tried to change the project guides, the thrust of the project, which would have added at least a year had he had his way. But we kept trying. . . ."

In early 2004, Allison became convinced that they had solved all the technical problems. Tests indicated that the transdermal patch administered the hormone in the correct dosages, and with no side effects. But to go to the next steps of clinical testing, Allison realized he really needed buy-in. He flew to Zurich and proposed a 20 million Swiss franc investment to develop this formulation for a pan-European launch. To his disbelief, the review committee turned down the proposal. They said the technology was still unproven, so it could be expensive to invest more money in the product if it turned out that there were unforeseen technical problems. The committee also pointed out that the U.K. subsidiary had been working with a different version of Zanta than the one being marketed in the rest of Europe, which could potentially create confusion for doctors.

What went wrong here? Tom was a talented manager, with considerable expertise and insight into U.K. market needs, and while he handled the experimenting efforts with Morton with skill, he didn't do a good job of making sense of his weak position in the firm, and he essentially failed in the legitimacy-building process. From the outside, it is perhaps obvious why the review panel turned down his proposal, but at the time he struggled to understand it: "I really can't believe this. I think they are just bitter because we managed to succeed where they failed. Part of me wants to keep on pushing, to look for other people higher up in the organization to overrule the decision of these R&D guys. And part of me just wants to quit."

Jordan and Tom's contrasting fortunes are simply a way of illustrating the value of this framework to you as a would-be corporate entrepreneur. Action is the most important element here—because without action we have nothing—but misguided or ill-thought-through action can get you into trouble. Tom pushed too hard too quickly, and without building the necessary support from the key people in Zurich. His sense-making was awry, and his legitimacy-building was poor. Jordan, in contrast, played his hand astutely and built the necessary support along the way.

How to Be Unreasonable—in a Reasonable Way

So what does all this mean for you? In our experience, the vast majority of front-line managers in large organizations have ideas for how to improve things. When we discuss the Jordan Cohen and Tom Allison cases with executive groups, and we ask, "How many of you have ever found yourself in their shoes?" about half the people in the room raise a hand. And this is the people who have had the guts to act on their ideas—there are also many others, we suspect, who decided that discretion was the better part of valor and kept their bright ideas to themselves.

To tap into this potential—this reservoir of bright ideas—and move forward faster, we need a better playbook. Of course, there will never be a recipe-book list of things to do because the specific circumstances facing each person are different. But it is useful to provide a set of operating principles that act as a checklist that you go back to from time to time, to ensure you are on the right track. So here it is—a set of principles that build on the framework in Figure 9.2 and on the experiences of Dick Fosbury and others, to help you become a bit more unreasonable, but in a reasonable way.

Think different. The starting point in being unreasonable is to have a slightly contrarian perspective—a point of view that differs from the established orthodoxy in your organization. Dick Fosbury had a nagging belief that there was a better way of jumping; Jordan Cohen couldn't believe how much time people were wasting on trivial tasks; Tom Allison found a clever new way of administering drugs through the skin.

Remember, though, that contrarian ideas rarely arrive fully formed. Usually what happens is that ideas take shape over weeks or months, through conversations with others and through low-risk experiments. This associative sense-making process, as shown in Figure 9.2, is an important and underappreciated quality among entrepreneurs. So if you are frustrated that you don't seem to have any really cool ideas to pursue, you should get out more—go to a conference, talk to colleagues in other departments, read more widely. As pointed out by Woody Allen, "Eighty percent of success is showing up." People who think different spend more time trying to do so. Success requires inspiration *and* perspiration.

Experiment early. The notion of small-scale experimentation has been a constant theme throughout this book, so we don't want to be too repetitive here. The key idea—which we introduced way back in the first chapter—is that especially in these days many of us are seduced by the power of information and end up, as a result, in analysis paralysis. This cycle can best be broken through baby steps, small-scale action, by experimenting early and gaining feedback that helps focus our information-gathering activities. Jordan Cohen was masterful in his experimental approach, making almost daily changes to the online tool in the early days, as he gained feedback from users.

There is still some built-in resistance to the concept of experimentation in large organizations, perhaps because it sounds as if it lacks conviction. This is starting to change though—if you were to do a quick scan through the last five years of *Harvard Business Review*, you would find more than a dozen articles banging the drum for more experimentation.[10] Gradually, the term is finding its way into the management lexicon, and this can only be a good thing. And people are starting to figure out what experimentation looks like in practice as well. In one large firm, we have now helped more than a hundred teams (under the auspices of an executive education program) to design and run management experiments across a wide variety of formats and activities.

Locate the safety mat. For Dick Fosbury, the deep foam safety mat made it possible for him to experiment without fear. But of course the term *safety mat* has a nice metaphorical meaning as well. Jordan Cohen's safety mat was a network of "friendlies"—colleagues on whom he could try out his online tool, safe in the knowledge that if it didn't work out, they wouldn't hold it against him. "I personally bought a lot of drinks for people, I apologized, that's what you do." Tom Allison, in contrast, never located his safety mat—so when he made his leap, there was no one there to support him.

To extend the metaphor further, you sometimes have to wait for the safety mat to be built, as with Dick Fosbury and his Flop. For example, the technological innovations of the last decade have made a host of new tools and techniques available for testing ideas in a low-cost way and while mitigating risks. You can run an A/B test for a new website in a matter of hours, you can use a crowdfunding website to gain financial support for a pilot project, you can use a crowdsourcing site to get initial market feedback on a new product idea.

The alternative is to build your own safety mat, typically a body of informal supporters across the organization who have bought into your idea and will provide "air cover" while you are still in the early experimental stages. These individuals provide you with feedback to help you correct your course, and they often provide resources as well.

Seize the moment. Valeriy Brumel's unlucky accident was Dick Fosbury's window of opportunity—the chance to showcase his new jumping style on a world stage. In the business world, the big opportunity is rarely as clear-cut as this, but timing is still vitally important. Jordan Cohen at Pfizer had a very clear strategy in this regard: "You try to keep it under the radar for a long time. All the while, you are learning, gaining confidence, you are spending money and starting to resource it. At some point, though, you have no choice but to get above the radar, but you have to be very deliberate about that."

Another example of careful timing comes from Jesper Ek at Roche, whom we met in Chapter 5. If you recall, he was asked to turn around Roche's struggling diabetes care business in Sweden. For the first couple of months he moved cautiously, meeting individually with every employee to get their input, to understand where they thought the opportunities were. Then, in May 2012 he organized a workshop for the entire operating unit, to build agreement for their new vision. It was a calculated risk on Jesper's part: he had no way of knowing in advance if they would reach agreement, or whether the vision they came up with would work, but he knew the people well enough by this stage to trust their judgment. And it worked out well: the wording they came up with ("to enable people with diabetes to live their lives as unrestricted as possible") became the foundation stone for the turnaround, and it helped shape a series of follow-on choices about what products and services to offer.

This also means that when you have ideas that fail in your initial experiments don't kill them—deep-freeze them so that you can defrost them when the circumstances change. For example, a few years on, you may have built more legitimacy or improved your sense-making abilities, or things beyond your control may have changed, perhaps new technologies or the state of the economy. These days there are even apps, such as ListMe, that help you save ideas for later use.

Learn to reflect. Our final principle is somewhat more philosophical than the other four. It isn't linked to the Dick Fosbury story (as we never met him personally). Rather, it comes from our conversations with Jordan Cohen, Jesper Ek, Tom Allison, and dozens of other unreasonable corporate employees who sought to make their organizations work better.

Our advice is to make time for reflection: to carve out a space in your day to make sense of the actions you have taken, the feedback you have received, the problems that need addressing, and to seek advice from colleagues, friends, or a therapist who understand your world sufficiently well that they can help you avoid getting into trouble.

We realize you have likely heard this advice before, but the point is that the more unreasonable you are—in terms of the changes you are trying to make to the system—the more self-aware you need to become. Unreasonable people are prone to being fired, for reasons we discuss in the following section, and while this isn't always a bad outcome it isn't something we recommend either. You are much better off staying one step ahead of your detractors, anticipating their concerns and building up the evidence or political support you need to keep your initiative on track.

Final Words: Condemned to Freedom

What are the consequences for you, and for your career, if you follow our advice? There is both good news and bad news here, and a final paradox to contend with.

Back in the late 1990s, we would often finish our talks to executives with the famous words of the French existential philosopher Jean-Paul Sartre: man is *condemned to be free*. In our interpretation, this meant that in a world of increasing choice, transparency, and accountability, individuals would have to accept greater accountability for their actions—there would be nowhere to hide and no one else to shoulder your responsibility. However, the word *condemned* also suggested that this increased responsibility would not be to everyone's liking.

Twenty years on, in a world of ubiquitous information and even greater transparency, our view on this point has changed somewhat. We now view being condemned to freedom as a personal choice. You can choose to remain inside the "iron cage" of bureaucracy, or the "knowledge is power" world of meritocracy. Both are comfortable in their own ways—in a bureaucracy you simply follow the rules, in a meritocracy you immerse yourself in thought and argument. Alternatively, you can seek freedom by opting to work in—or even to create—an adhocracy. This means opening up to whatever uncertainties the outside world throws at you, and it means taking on personal responsibility and seeking achievement as an end in itself.

But beware—this is a tough road to follow. Jordan Cohen left Pfizer soon after Pfizerworks was up and running. And there are others with similar stories. Leif Edvinsson at Skandia; Larry Huston at Procter & Gamble; Ross Smith at Microsoft; Art Schneiderman at Analog Devices; these are all entrepreneurially minded executives we have met over the years who didn't get the rewards from their parent companies that they deserved. There seem to be two reasons for this. One is that by taking the "unreasonable" path of trying something different, their horizons are expanded—they see and get access to a world of opportunities outside their old home. The other is that not everyone in the parent company appreciates their efforts—they are viewed as mavericks, and they often lose out in the race for promotion to the more traditional types who follow the established norms of the organization.

So think of this as a fifth paradox of progress, a very personal one: *The greater the change you achieve inside your organization, the more likely you are to leave that organization.* To be clear, this does not apply so much for the top executive who is already responsible for a whole business, and who has earned the right to shake things up. Rather, it is a paradox that affects those seeking to change the system from within.

Needless to say, we encourage you to take this unreasonable path anyway. Long-term tenure in a single organization is overrated, and indeed the whole notion that you would have your career managed for you by your employer is old-school, bureaucratic thinking. By adopting the fast/forward principles of adhocracy at a personal level, you are putting action and experimentation ahead of analytical rigor or deference to formal authority, and you are sufficiently self-confident to know that you can live with the consequences of this approach. That is what condemned to freedom really means.

NOTES

Chapter 1

1. See E. Brynjolfsson and A. McAfee, *The second machine age: Work, progress, and prosperity in a time of brilliant technologies* (New York: W.W. Norton, 2014); J. Manyika, M.Chui, B. Brown, J. Bughin, R. Dobbs, C. Roxburgh, and A. H. Byers, "Big data: The next frontier for innovation, competition, and productivity," *McKinsey Global Institute Report* (May 2011); J. Barney, "Firm resources and sustained competitive advantage," *Journal of Management* 17, no. 1 (1991): 99–120; B. Wernerfelt, "A resource-based view of the firm," *Strategic Management Journal* 5, no. 2 (1984): 171–180.

2. This quote is taken from A. Deutschmann, "Inside the mind of Jeff Bezos," *Fast Company*, August 1, 2004. See also A. Lashinsky, "Amazon's Jeff Bezos: The ultimate disrupter," *Fortune*, November 16, 2012.

3. Quotes in this paragraph are from R. C. Morais, "Kiss and punch," *Forbes*, April 21, 2008; see also J. L. Schenker, "WPP's digital push," *BusinessWeek Online*, July 1, 2007.

4. These insights into Oracle's strategy are taken from speeches by Larry Ellison and Thomas Kurian at the Oracle Open World Conference, San Francisco, October 2015. These speeches can be viewed at https://www.oracle.com/open-world/on-demand/index.html.

5. Quote from C. Copley and B. Hirschler, "For Roche CEO, celebrating failure is key to success," *Reuters News*, September 17, 2014.

6. This information is taken from the Air Liquide website, at https://www.airliquide.com/connected-innovation/innovation-showcase.

7. These quotes are taken from E. Dunkley, "Horta-Osório unveils his digital vision for Lloyds Banking Group," *Financial Times*, October 28, 2014; and P. Rodeia, "Refocusing and transforming a UK leader: An interview with the group chief executive of Lloyds Banking Group," *McKinsey Quarterly*, March 2015.

8. Deutschmann, "Inside the mind.".

9. N. Carr, *The shallows: How the Internet is changing the way we think, read and remember* (London: Atlantic Books, 2010).

10. See M. Mol and J. M. Birkinshaw, *Giant steps in management* (London: Pearson, 2008).

11. J. Rehman, "Accuracy of medical information on the Internet," *Scientific American*, August 2, 2012.

12. H. A. Simon, "Designing organizations for an information-rich world," in *Computers, communication, and the public interest*, ed. M. Greenberger, 40–41 (Baltimore: Johns Hopkins Press, 1971).

13. R. Friedman, "The cost of continuously checking email," *Harvard Business Review* online, July 4, 2014.

14. C. King, "Single-author papers: A waning share of output, but still providing the tools for progress," ThomsonReuters Science Watch, September 2013.

15. S. Chatrchyan, V. Khachatryan, A. M.Sirunyan, A. Tumasyan, W. Adam, E. Aguilo, T. Bergauer, and others, "Observation of a new boson at a mass of 125 GeV with the CMS experiment at the LHC," *Physics Letters B*, 716, no. 1 (2012): 30–61.

16. This "resource based" view of the firm has become enormous over the past two decades and is arguably the dominant way of thinking about strategy among academic scholars. See articles by Wernerfelt (1984) and Barney (1991); there is also a so-called "knowledge based" view of the firm; see, for example, R. M. Grant, "Toward a knowledge-based theory of the firm," *Strategic Management Journal* 17, no. S2 (1996): 109–122.

17. H. Gardner, *Frames of mind: The theory of multiple intelligences* (New York: Basic Books, 2011).

18. K. Roberts, *Lovemarks: The future beyond brands* (New York: powerHouse Books, 2005).

Chapter 2

1. There are many accessible accounts of Mansa Musa's life; for an introduction we recommend Wikipedia at https://en.wikipedia.org/wiki/Musa_I_of_Mali. For a lengthier account, see M. De Villiers and S. Hirtle, *Timbuktu: Sahara's fabled city of gold* (New York: Walker and Company, 2007).

2. See the Wikipedia entry for Dow Jones Industrial Average at https://en.wikipedia.org/wiki/Dow_Jones_Industrial_Average.

3. Of the original thirty, the ones still recognizable today as independent companies are Coats, GKN, Rolls Royce, BAT, and Tate & Lyle.

4. J. Yarrow, "Here's what Steve Ballmer thought about the iPhone five years ago," *Business Insider*, June 29, 2012.

5. Quote from Nokia's chief strategist, *MacDaily News*, November 30, 2009.

6. R. H. Hayes and W. J. Abernathy, "Managing our way to economic decline," *Harvard Business Review* 58, no. 4 (1980): 67–77.

7. For example, the term *Imagination Age* was coined by Rita J. King in her November 2007 essay for the British Council, *The Emergence of a New Global Culture in the Imagination Age*; the term *Age of Enlightment* was proposed by Dan Pink in his book *A whole new mind: Why right-brainers will rule the world* (New York: Penguin, 2006).

8. E. Brynjolffson and A. McAfee, *The second machine age: Work, progress, and prosperity in a time of brilliant technologies* (New York: W.W. Norton, 2014).

9. J. R. Flynn, "The mean IQ of Americans: Massive gains 1932 to 1978," *Psychological Bulletin* 95 (1984): 29–51.

10. See Kevin Kelley's blog at http://kk.org/thetechnium/the-expansion-o.

11. This observation from Derek de Solla Price is discussed in an article by Eric Gastfriend for the Future of Life Institute, November 2015; available at www.futureoflife.org.

12. The notion of T-shaped skill profiles has been around for many years. For example, see M. T. Hansen and B. Von Oetinger, "Introducing T-shaped managers. Knowledge management's next generation," *Harvard Business Review* 79, no. 3 (2001): 106–116.

13. Author interview with Mike Wing in 2008.

14. This quote comes from an interview between Gary Hamel and Eric Schmidt at the *Future of Management* conference, Half Moon Bay, California, May 29, 2008.

15. https://www.census.gov/foreign-trade/balance/c5700.html#2015.

16 The Economist Online, September 13, 2001.

17. http://www.un.org/sustainabledevelopment/blog/2016/01/244-million-international-migrants-living-abroad-worldwide-new-un-statistics-reveal.

18 https://www.statista.com/statistics/324786/global-business-travel-spending-growth-forecast.

19 https://travel.state.gov/content/passports/en/passports/statistics.html.

20. N. N. Taleb, *The black swan: The impact of the highly improbable.* (New York: Random House, 2001).

21 Over the years, this quote has been made famous by Tom Peters and many, many others.

22. Y. L. Doz and M. Kosonen, *Fast strategy: How strategic agility will help you stay ahead of the game* (London: Pearson Education, 2008).

23. For a recent discussion of the changes in military doctrine, see S. McChrystal, D. Silverman, T. Collins, and C. Fussell, *Team of teams: New rules of engagement for a complex world* (New York: Penguin Random House, 2015). On strategic thinking, see D. Sull and K. M. Eisenhardt, "Simple rules for a complex world," *Harvard Business Review,* 90, no. 9 (2012): 68–75.

24 The report is available at https://www.nirs.org/fukushima/naiic_report.pdf.

25. There are different views on this point. For example, some have argued that the significant number of suicides in the region since 2011 can be directly linked to

the Fukushima nuclear spill, such as I. Farlie, "Fukushima: Thousands have died, thousands more will die," *The Ecologist*, August 17, 2015.

26. Quote taken from the Greenpeace webpage at http://www.greenpeace.org/international/en/campaigns/nuclear/safety/accidents/Fukushima-nuclear-disaster.

27. G. Monbiot, "Why Fukushima stopped me worrying and made me love nuclear power," *The Guardian*, March 21, 2011.

28. J. Haidt, *The righteous mind: Why good people are divided by politics and religion* (New York: Vintage Books, 2012).

29. This was stated by Michael Gove, who at the time of writing was attempting to be chosen as David Cameron's successor.

30. M. Shermer, *The believing brain: From ghosts and gods to politics and conspiracies—How we construct beliefs and reinforce them as truths* (New York: Macmillan, 2011).

31. The term was coined by German neurologist and psychiatrist Klaus Conrad in the 1950s.

32. L. Wolpert, *Six impossible things before breakfast: The evolutionary origins of belief* (New York: W.W. Norton, 2006).

33. L. Tiger, *The pursuit of pleasure* (Piscataway, NJ: Transaction, 1992).

34. R. Dawkins, *The god delusion* (New York: Random House, 2009); R. Sheldrake, *The science delusion*. London: Coronet, 2012.

Chapter 3

1. Aristotle's "Rhetoric" has been translated and applied in many different contexts. A recent reference is J. Allen, "Aristotle on the disciplines of argument: Rhetoric, dialectic, analytic," *Rhetorica* 25 (2007): 87–108.

2. C. Handy, *Gods of management: The changing work of organization* (London: Souvenir Press, 1978).

3. R. M. Belbin, *Team roles at work* (London: Routledge, 2012).

4. We should acknowledge the contribution of our former mentor, Gunnar Hedlund, who pioneered this multidimensional way of thinking about organizations. See, for example, G. Hedlund and D. Rolander, "Action in heterarchies: New approaches to managing the MNC," in *Managing the global firm*, eds. C. A. Bartlett, Y. L. Doz, and G. Hedlund, 15–46 (London: Routledge, 1990) 15–46.

5. A. P. Sloan, *My years with General Motors* (New York: Crown, 1964).

6. M. Weber, "Bureaucracy," in *From Max Weber: Essays in sociology*, ed. H. H. Girth (New York: Oxford University Press, 1946): 196–244.

7. A. D. Chandler, *Strategy and structure: Chapters in the history of the American enterprise* (Cambridge, MA: MIT press, 1962).

8. P. Ekman and W. V. Friesen, *Unmasking the face: A guide to recognizing emotions from facial clues* (Englewood Cliffs, NJ: Prentice Hall, 1975).

9. D. Rock, *Your brain at work* (New York: HarperBusiness, 2009).

10. E. H. Edersheim, *McKinsey's Marvin Bower: Vision, leadership, and the creation of management consulting* (Hoboken, NJ: John Wiley & Sons, 2004).

11. See, for example, D. Miller, *The Icarus paradox: How excellent companies can bring about their own downfall* (New York: HarperBusiness, 1990).

12. W. G. Bennis and P. E. Slater, *The temporary society* (New York: Harper & Row, 1968); A. Toffler, *Future shock* (New York: Bantam,1990); H. Mintzberg, *Structure in fives: Designing effective organizations* (Upper Saddle River, NJ; Prentice Hall, 1993); R. H. Waterman, *Adhocracy: The power to change* (New York: W.W. Norton, 1995).

13. Henry Mintzberg in *Structure in Fives* (1993) offered a more nuanced view than this, seeing adhocracy as one of five generic structures.

14. When we started work on this book, we had in mind a fourth management model, the *emocracy*, which logically enough was one that privileged emotion over position, knowledge, or action. Conceptually, this makes sense. Indeed, most religious organizations or cults, and many cooperatives or not-for-profits, are of this type—what people believe, their ideals, and how stern they are in their faith is more important than what they do or know, or what their formal position is. But as we thought about it and discussed it with others, we bumped up against a couple of problems. First, we couldn't find any examples of high-performing firms where the emotional beliefs came first. We found many instances in which people's emotions, beliefs, and values were important, but these qualities were typically a means of enabling action, of getting something done, rather than the destination. For example, Disney is known to have a very strong culture, and its "cast members" clearly have a deep emotional connection to the firm and its mission. But Disney is still a for-profit enterprise, and its long-term survival depends on what its employees *achieve* on a collective basis, not what they *believe* per se. Even in well-known and successful not-for-profits like the Red Cross or Médecins Sans Frontières, emotions rarely trump all other dimensions.

15. Our terminology is a deliberate echo of Philip Selznick's notion that leadership is about "infusing" an organization with value beyond its technical requirements. We also build on Robert Franks's thinking on the role of emotion in organizations. P. Selznick, *Leadership in administration: A sociological interpretation* (Berkeley: University of California Press,1957); R. H. Frank, *Passions within reason: The Strategic role of emotions* (New York: W.W. Norton,1991).

Chapter 4

1. Blog posting on www.Mmorpg.com from blogger "mewhywhy" in 2013.

2. C. Christensen, *The innovator's dilemma: When new technologies cause great firms to fail* (Boston: Harvard Business Review Press, 2013).

3. *The Economist*, "Playing out the last hand," April 26, 2014.

4. A. G. Lafley and R. L. Martin. *Playing to win: How strategy really works* (Boston: Harvard Business Press, 2013).

5. Here are references to some of these alternative views of the strategy process: H. Mintzberg and J. A. Waters, "Of strategies, deliberate and emergent," *Strategic Management Journal* 6 (1985): 257–272; R. A. Burgelman, "A model of the interaction of strategic behavior, corporate context, and the concept of strategy," *Academy of Management Review* 8, no. 1 (1983): 61–70; D. N. Sull, "Strategy and execution," *MIT Sloan Management Review* (2007); M. D. Cohen, J. G. March, and J. P. Olsen. "A garbage can model of organizational choice," *Administrative Science Quarterly* 17, no. 1 (1972): 1–25.

6. *The Independent*, October 23, 2011.

7. R. G. McGrath and I. C. McMillan, *Discovery-driven growth: A breakthrough process to reduce risk and seize opportunity* (Boston: Harvard Business Review Press, 2009); S. Blank, "Why the lean start-up changes everything," *Harvard Business Review* 91, no. 5 (2013): 63–72; E. Ries, *The lean start-up: How today's entrepreneurs use continuous innovation to create radically successful businesses* (New York: Random House, 2011); T. Brown, *Change by design: How design thinking transforms organizations and inspires innovation* (Boston: Harvard Business Review Press, 2006); R. L. Martin, *The design of business: Why design thinking is the next competitive advantage* (Boston: Harvard Business Review Press, 2009).

8. A good discussion of the challenge of managing these inflection points is found in R. A. Burgelman and A. S. Grove, "Strategic dissonance," *California Management Review* 38, no. 2 (1996): 8–28.

9. Both these quotes are taken from W. Shih, S. Kaufman, and D. Spinola, *Netflix*, Harvard Business School teaching case 9-607-138, April 2009.

10. This quote and all other information on Thomson Reuters in this chapter come from personal interviews by the authors. See J. Birkinshaw and S. Turconi, *Thomson Reuters: The GRC Opportunity*, London Business School case study CS-11-035.

11. This information was taken from: G. R. Gavetti, R. Henderson, and S. Giorgo, *Kodak (A)*, Harvard Business School case study 705-448, April 2003.

12. The GDS materials are based on interviews undertaken by the authors. See also J. Birkinshaw and S. Duncan, *The Government Digital Service*, London Business School case study, 2014.

13. During 2015 there were changes in the leadership of GDS, with Mike Bracken stepping aside to join the Co-operative Group as chief digital officer, and Stephen Foreshew-Cain taking over as head of GDS.

14. This quote has been widely cited; see, for example, J. Naughton, "Could Kodak's demise have been averted?" *The Guardian*, January 22, 2012.

15. blog.netflix.com/2011/09/explanation-and-some-reflections.html.

16. C. O'Reilly, M. Tushman, and B. Harreld, "Organizational ambidexterity:

IBM and emerging business opportunities," *California Management Review* 51, no. 4 (2009): 79–91.

17. J. Sapsford, Toyota introduces new luxury brand in Japan: Lexus. *Wall Street Journal*, August 3, 2005.

18. C. Markides and P. Geroski, *Fast second* (San Francisco: Jossey Bass, 2005).

Chapter 5

1. This chapter draws extensively from J. M. Birkinshaw, N. J. Foss, and S. Lindenberg, "Purpose with profits," *MIT Sloan Management Review* 55, no. 3 (2014): 49–56.

2. See, for example, S. Brown and K. M. Eisenhardt, *Competing on the edge: Strategy as structured chaos* (Boston: Harvard Business Review Press, 1998).

3. H. Bruch and S. Ghoshal, *A bias for action* (Boston: Harvard Business Review Press, 2004).

4. The Tupperware quotes are from remarks by Rick Goings at the Drucker Forum 2013 and conversations with the authors.

5. R. Tata, A. Hart, and C. Sarkar, "Why making money is not enough," *MIT Sloan Management Review* 54, no. 4 (2013): 95–96.

6. J. C. Collins and J. I. Porras, *Built to last: Successful habits of visionary companies* (New York: Random House, 1993); J. N. Sheth, R. S. Sisodia, and D. B. Wolfe, *Firms of endearment: How world-class companies profit from passion and purpose* (Upper Saddle River, NJ: Pearson/Prentice Hall, 2003); M. Beer, and others, *Higher ambition: How great leaders create economic and social value* (Boston: Harvard Business Review Press, 2011).

7. N. Mourkogiannis, *Purpose: The starting point of great companies* (New York: Macmillan, 2006).

8. J. C. Collins and J. L. Porras, Building your company's vision, *Harvard Business Review*, 74, no. 5 (1996): 65–75.

9. V. Nayar, *Employees first, customers second: Turning conventional management upside down* (Boston: Harvard Business Review Press, 2010).

10. The Tata Group case study is based on data collected through interviews with company executives, and also A. Graham, "Too good to fail," *Strategy & Business* 58 (2010).

11. http://www.forbes.com/sites/danschawbel/2012/01/23/89-of-new-hires-fail-because-of-their-attitude.

12. https://hbr.org/2011/02/hire-for-attitude-train-for-skill.

13. A. Fuster and S. Meier, "Another hidden cost of incentives: The detrimental effect on norm enforcement," *Management Science*, 56 (2010): 57–70.

14. See S. Lindenberg and N. J. Foss, "Managing motivation for joint produc-

tion: The role of goal framing and governance mechanisms," *Academy of Management Reviewfa* 36 (2011): 500–525.

15. N. J. Foss and S. Lindenberg, "Microfoundations for strategy: A goal-framing perspective on value creation," *Academy of Management Perspectives* 27, no. 2 (2013): 85–102.

16. Lindenberg and Foss, "Managing motivation."

17. B. Frey, "Giving and receiving awards," *Perspectives on Psychological Science* 1 (2009): 377–388.

18. K. Keizer, S. Lindenberg, and L. Steg, "The spreading of disorder," *Science* 322 (2008): 1681–1685.

19. "IBM's Sam Palmisano: 'Always Put the Enterprise Ahead of the Individual'," Knowledge@Wharton, January 18, 2012, available at http://knowledge.wharton.upenn.edu/article.cfm?articleid=2927.

20. The concept of obliquity is developed more fully in John Kay's 2010 book *Obliquity—Why our goals are best achieved indirectly* (London: Profile Books). See also J. Birkinshaw, *Reinventing Management* (Jossey-Bass, 2012), chapter 5.

21. Tata and Sarkar, "Why making money is not enough."

Chapter 6

1. There are many relevant bodies of academic thinking here, including the traditional views of Max Weber and Talcott Parsons, through the Transaction Cost Economics perspective of Oliver Williamson, to more recent contributions from scholars such as Paul Adler. See, for example, P. S. Adler and B. Borys, "Two types of bureaucracy: Enabling and coercive," *Administrative Science Quarterly* 41, no. 1 (1996): 61–89; T. Parsons, *The system of modern societies* (Englewood Cliffs, NJ: Prentice Hall, 1971); M. Weber, *The theory of social and economic organization* (New York: Simon & Schuster, 2009); O. E. Williamson, *Markets and hierarchies* (New York: Free Press, 1975).

2. S. Ghoshal, M. Hahn, and P. Moran, "Management competence, firm growth and economic progress," *Contributions to Political Economy* 18, no. 1 (1999): 121–150.

3. Gary Hamel blog post, "Bureaucracy must die," on the *Harvard Business Review* website, November 4, 2014.

4. This contrast was first proposed by our former colleague and mentor, Gunnar Hedlund.

5. For an overview of the ideas of Taylor and his scientific management contemporaries, see D. A. Wren and R. G. Greenwood, *Management Innovators* (New York: Oxford University Press, 1998).

6. See J. M. Birkinshaw, *Reinventing management: Smart choices for getting work done*

(Wiley: London, 2012); J. Ridderstråle and M. Wilcox, *Re-energizing the corporation: How leaders make change happen* (Hoboken, NJ: John Wiley & Sons, 2009).

7. While shared space works well for most people, concerns have been raised about its consequences for visually impaired and disabled people. See the Holmes Report on shared space 2015, www.chrisholmes.co.uk.

8. D. Sull and K. M. Eisenhardt, "Simple rules for a complex world," *Harvard Business Review* 90, no. 9 (2012): 68–76; S. L. Brown and K. M. Eisenhardt, *Competing on the edge: Strategy as structured chaos* (Boston: Harvard Business Review Press: 1998); R. K. Greenleaf and L. C. Spears, *Servant leadership: A journey into the nature of legitimate power and greatness* (Mahwah, NJ: Paulist Press, 2002).

9. See B. J. Robertson, *Holacracy: The new management system for a rapidly changing world* (New York: Henry Holt, 2015); also the critical commentary in the *Wall Street Journal*: R. E. Silverman, "At Zappos, banishing the bosses brings confusion," *Wall Street Journal*, May 20, 2015.

10. The Costa Coffee story is recounted in a teaching case: J. M. Birkinshaw and K. Mark, *Costa Coffee: Project Marlow*, London Business School case study CS-13-013, 2013.

11. This quote is taken from a blog: https://blog.inf.ed.ac.uk/sapm/2014/03/14/management-at-valve-an-analysis-of-management-practices-at-valve-software. Other sources for the Valve story are E. Bernstein, F. Gino, and B. Staats, "Opening the valve: From software to hardware," Harvard Business School Case study 415-015; J. Newbry, "Innovations in company design: Lessons from Valve software," *Journal of Macrotrends in Technology and Innovation* 1, no. 1 (2013): 21–31.

12. P. Warr, "Valve's flat management structure like high school," *Wired UK*, July 9, 2013.

13. To be clear, the regulatory-and-compliance-based activities of the bank were *not* managed in this agile way—they retained their traditional bureaucratic way of working.

14. The Haier story is discussed in W. Fischer, U. Lago, and F. Liu, *Reinventing giants* (Hoboken, NJ: John Wiley & Sons, 2013). Interestingly, Haier's organizing model continues to evolve; see, for example, Andrew Hill's *Financial Times* column on management, November 2015. The GSK, Eden McCallum, Mundi, and Costa Coffee examples are based on personal interviews.

15. To be clear, there is no suggestion here that this commercially driven model could or should replace the science-driven approach of Merck, GSK, or Roche. Rather, the two approaches are complementary, and rely on different organizing models, with companies like Merck being meritocracies and companies like Mundi (such as Valeant, Actavis, and Endo) being adhocracies.

16. J. Sutherland, *Scrum: A revolutionary approach to building teams, beating deadlines and boosting productivity* (New York: Random House Business Books, 2014), p. 13.

17. See D. Cable and J. M. Birkinshaw, "The dark side of transparency," London Business School working paper, 2015.

18. C. O'Reilly, M. Tushman, and B. Harreld, "Organizational ambidexterity: IBM and emerging business opportunities," *California Management Review* 51, no. 4 (2009): 79–91.

19. J. Kotter, *Accelerate* (Boston: Harvard Business Review Press, 2012), pp. 21–22.

20. Robertson (2015); S. McChrystal, D. Silverman, T. Collins, and C. Fussell, *Team of teams: New rules of engagement for a complex world* (New York: Penguin Random House, 2015); F. Laloux, *Reinventing organizations: A guide to creating organizations inspired by the next stage of human consciousness* (Millis, MA: Nelson Parker, 2014).

Chapter 7

1. D. McGregor, *The human side of enterprise*, 25th Anniversary Printing, (New York: Irwin/McGraw-Hill, 1985); F. Herzberg, *The motivation to work* (New York: John Wiley & Sons, 1959); A. H. Maslow, "A theory of human motivation," *Psychological Review* 50, no. 44 (1943): 370; E. L. Deci and R. M. Ryan, "The what and why of goal pursuits: Human needs and the self-determination of behaviour," *Psychological Inquiry* 11, no. 4 (2000): 227–268.

2. C. Matlack, "Jerome Kerviel—In his own words," *Bloomberg Business*, January 30, 2008.

3. D. H. Pink, *Drive: The surprising truth about what motivates us* (New York: Penguin, 2011).

4. This tension has been studied in a number of different contexts; see, for example, J. Birkinshaw and C. Gibson, "Building ambidexterity into an organization," *MIT Sloan Management Review* 45 (2004): 47–55; S. Ghoshal and C. A. Bartlett, "Rebuilding behavioural context: A blueprint for corporate renewal," *Sloan Management Review* 37 (1996): 2–15; R. R. Blake and J. S. Mouton, *The new managerial grid* (Houston, TX: Gulf Publishing, 1964).

5. A. Edmondson, "Psychological safety and learning behavior in work teams," *Administrative Science Quarterly* 44, no. 2 (1999): 350–383.

6. See, for instance, D. Kahan, "Ideology, motivated reasoning, and cognitive reflection," *Judgment & Decision Making* 407 (2013).

7. J. Miller, "Hinckley over Harvard: When the LDS prophet phoned, Kim Clark headed to BYU-Idaho," *Salt Lake Tribune*, August 6, 2005.

8. www.teslamotors.com/blog/mission-tesla.

9. www.teslamotors.com/blog/secret-tesla-motors-master-plan-just-between-you-and-me.

10. www.porsche.com/usa/aboutporsche/principleporsche.

11. www.hyundaimotorgroup.com/About-Us/Philosophy.hub.

12. For some useful frameworks to help stimulate these discussions, see P. Miller

and T. Wedell-Wedellsborg, *Innovation as usual: How to help your people bring great ideas to life* (Boston: Harvard Business Review Press, 2013); P. Skarzynski and R. Gibson, *Innovation to the core: A blueprint for transforming the way your company innovates* (Boston: Harvard Business Review Press, 2013).

13. The second half of this chapter draws on ideas published in J. M. Birkinshaw and M. R. Haas, "Increase your return on failure," *Harvard Business Review* 94, no. 5, May 2016.

14. D. R. Keough, *The ten commandments for business failure* (New York: Penguin, 2008).

15. J. Scanlon, "Tata Group's innovation competition," *Bloomberg Business*, June 17, 2009.

16. This story is taken from the Management Innovation eXchange: A. Good, "Story: Fail forward," n.d., http://www.mixprize.org/story/fail-forward.

17. Telfer was interviewed by Gordon Pitts of the *Globe and Mail* newspaper and reported on July 23, 2007.

Chapter 8

1. M. L. Tushman and C. O'Reilly, *Lead and disrupt* (Stanford, CA: Stanford University Press, 2016).

2. J. C. Collins, *Good to great: Why some companies make the leap . . . and others don't* (New York: Random House, 2001); R. K. Greenleaf and L. C. Spears. *Servant leadership: A journey into the nature of legitimate power and greatness* (Mahwah, NJ: Paulist Press, 2002); S. Cain, *Quiet: The power of introverts in a world that can't stop talking* (New York: Broadway Books, 2013); A. Grant, *Give and take: A revolutionary approach to success* (London: Hachette UK, 2013).

3. J. Pfeffer, *Leadership BS: Fixing workplaces and careers one truth at a time* (New York: HarperCollins, 2015).

4. Survivor bias is a form of cognitive flaw whereby we emphasize those that have survived and neglect those with similar traits that might have fallen by the wayside. See, for example, M. Mangel and F. J. Samaniego, "Abraham Wald's work on aircraft survivability," *Journal of the American Statistical Association* 79, no. 386 (1984): 259–267.

5. A. Lashinsky, "Amazon's Jeff Bezos: The ultimate disrupter," *Fortune*, November 16, 2012.

6. "Inside Amazon's 'culture of metrics' by executive leadership," *Business Management Daily*, April 18, 2013.

7. A. Deutschman, "Inside the mind of Jeff Bezos," *Fast Company*, August 2004.

8. G. Anders, "Jeff Bezos reveals his no. 1 leadership secret," *Forbes*, April 4, 2012.

9. B. Stone, *The everything store: Jeff Bezos and the age of Amazon* (New York: Little, Brown, 2013).

10. The materials on Carlos Brito are taken from D. Sull, "Brahma versus Antarctica: Reversal of fortune in Brazil's beer market," London Business School case study CS04–015–001, and also a Youtube video of Brito speaking at Stanford Business School, "View from the Top," December 2, 2013, available at https://www.youtube.com/watch?v=xhFxw4mBre0.

11. These arguments and examples are taken from J. M. Birkinshaw, A. Zimmerman, and S. Raisch, "How do firms adapt to discontinuous change? Bridging the dynamic capabilities and ambidexterity perspectives," *California Management Review* (2016). It also builds on earlier work by G. Hedlund and J. Ridderstråle, "Toward a theory of the self-renewing MNC," in *International business: An emerging vision*, B. Toyne and D. Nigh, eds. (Columbia, SC: University of South Carolina Press, 1997).

12. G. P. Pisano, "Creating an R&D strategy," Harvard Business School working paper, January 2012.

13. This story of Steve McGuirk is based on author interviews and S. Caulkin and J. M. Birkinshaw, "Blazing a trail," *London Business School Review*, January 2016.

14. R. A. Burgelman and A. S. Grove, "Strategic dissonance," *California Management Review* 38, no. 2 (1996): 8–28.

15 Pascal Cagni was speaking at the London Business School Global Leadership Summit event in 2015. See https://gls.london.edu.

16. W. George, *Authentic leadership: Rediscovering the secrets to creating lasting value* (Hoboken, NJ: John Wiley & Sons, 2003); S. Sinek, *Start with why: How great leaders inspire everyone to take action* (London: Penguin, 2009); R. Goffee and G. Jones, "Why should anyone be led by you?" (Boston: Harvard Business Review Press, 2000).

17. Goffee and Jones, "Why should anyone be led by you?" p. 83.

18. Examples of studies of executive overconfidence include T. Astebro, "Assessing the commercial viability of new ventures," *Canadian Investment Review* (Spring 2003): 18–25; U. Malmendier and G. Tate, "European financial management. Does overconfidence affect corporate investment? CEO overconfidence measures revisited," *Journal of Finance* 11, no. 5 (2005): 649–659; N. Nicholson, "Personality and entrepreneurial leadership: A study of the heads of the UK's most successful independent companies," *European Management Journal* 16 (2008): 529–539.

19. The Dalio quote is taken from J. Cassidy, "Mastering the machine," *The New Yorker*, July 25, 2011. Dalio's principles can be found at http://www.bwater.com/Uploads/FileManager/Principles/Bridgewater-Associates-Ray-Dalio-Principles.pdf.

20. This exercise was suggested to us by our editor, Margo Beth Fleming.

21. These quotes are taken from www.virgin.com/richard-branson/great-leaders-are-great-listeners and M. Simoes, "Good leaders are great listeners," *Business Insider*, January 29, 2013.

22. M. E. Guffey and D. Loewy, *Business communication: Process & product* (Stamford, CT: South Western Cengage Learning, 2008).

23. C. Gallo, *10 simple sectrets of the world's greatest business communicators* (Naperville, IL: Sourcebooks, 2005).

24. R. Giuliani with K. Kurson, *Leadership* (New York: Little, Brown, 2002).

25. More information about Peluso's approach to leadership can be found at http://knowledge.wharton.upenn.edu/article/travelocitys-michelle-peluso-changed-the-business-model-and-the-company-took-off.

26. I. Berlin, *The hedgehog and the fox: And essays on Tolstoy's view of history* (London: Weidenfeld & Nicolson, 1967).

Chapter 9

1. J. Durso, "Fearless Fosbury flops to glory," *New York Times*, October 20, 1968.

2. Quote from Richard Hoffer, *Something in the air* (Lincoln, NE: University of Nebraska Press, 1968), page 76. He writes, "During Fosbury's sophomore year, the landing pit was only a pile of wood chips and sawdust. It was safe but not comfortable. By his junior year, though, his school had installed a foam pit and the idea of a head plant, while still daunting, was a bit more agreeable."

3. Taken from James Clear, blog, "Olympic medalist Dick Fosbury and the surprising power of being unconventional," n.d., available at http://jamesclear.com/dick-fosbury,

4. Durso, "Fearless Fosbury."

5. George Bernard Shaw, *Man and superman* (Westminster, UK: Archibald Constable, 1903).

6. D. Baer, "What it's like inside Elon Musk's 'reality distortion field,'" *Business Insider*, December 31, 2014.

7. The materials on Jordan Cohen are taken from personal interviews with him by the authors. There is also a case study published by IESE business school on this same story: P. Miller and T. Wedell-Wedellsberg, "Jordan Cohen at PfizerWorks: Building the office of the future," IESE DPI-187-E, 2009.

8. T. L. Friedman, *The world is flat: A brief history of the twenty-first century* (New York: Macmillan, 2006).

9. The materials on Tom Allison and Pharma AG are based on personal interviews with the authors (names are fictionalized). See also J. Birkinshaw, "Pharma AG," London Business School case study.

10. See, for example, T. H. Davenport, "How to design smart business experiments: Why make gut-feel decisions when you can put new ideas to the test?" *Harvard Business Review* 87, no. 2 (2009): 68; S. Thomke, "Enlightened experimentation: The new imperative for innovation," *Harvard Business Review* 79, no. 2 (2001): 66–75; D. Ariely, "Why businesses don't experiment," *Harvard Business Review* 88 (2010): 69.

INDEX

Page numbers followed by italic *f* or *t* indicate a figure or table.